The
PEOPLE'S
REPUBLIC
of
CHINA
COOKBOOK

RANDOM HOUSE

NEW YORK

The
PEOPLE'S
REPUBLIC
of
CHINA
COOKBOOK

Nobuko Sakamoto

Illustrations by Pat Stewart

Appreciation and thanks to my
husband and children,
who were so patient and supportive

Special thanks to my
teacher and friend Chih-hua Hsia

Library of Congress Cataloging in Publication Data

Sakamoto, Nobuko.
The People's Republic of China cookbook.

Consists of recipes selected and adapted from 3 cook-
books originally published by the Government of the
People's Republic of China.
Includes index.
1. Cookery, Chinese.   2. China (People's Republic of
China, 1949–   )   I. Title.
TX724.5.C5S24   641.5′951   7655063
ISBN 0-394-40286-3
ISBN 0-394-73380-0 pbk.

DESIGNED BY LILLY LANGOTSKY

Manufactured in the United States of America

2 4 6 8 9 7 5 3

First Edition

CONTENTS

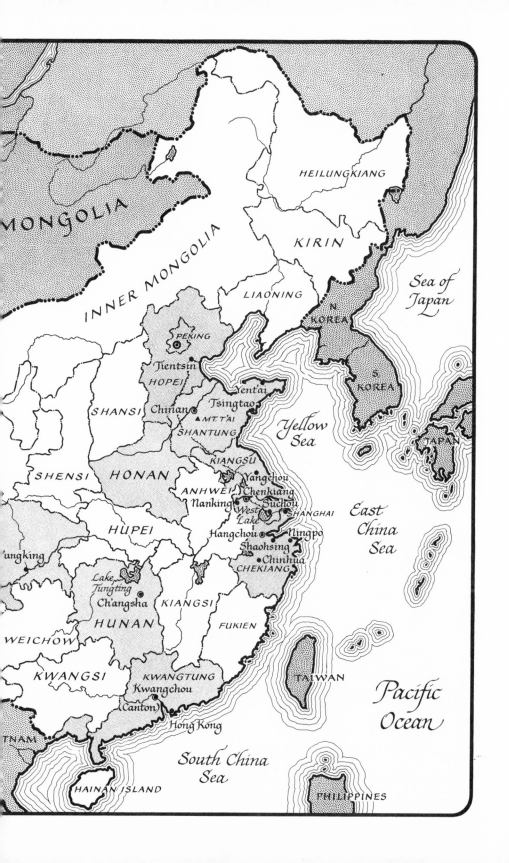

INTRODUCTION

China, with a total land area slightly larger than the United States, has one of the oldest continuous cultures in the world, dating from at least 1766 B.C. Because her arts, including the art of cooking, have developed independently of the West, they represent a unique genre.

China's culinary art remained largely unknown to the Western world until the mid-1800s, when Chinese cooking was introduced to the United States by immigrants (mainly from the province of Kuangtung in southeastern China) who came to the United States to work in the gold mines and in the building of the railroads. Before many decades had passed, acceptance of Chinese food had grown to such an extent that virtually every fair-sized community in the United States had at least one Chinese restaurant. The 1950s and 1960s saw a phenomenal interest in "eating Chinese" and a whole industry developed producing packaged and frozen foods. During the 1970s more and more people have enjoyed preparing Chinese dishes at home, and as a result there has been a great increase in the number of Chinese cookbooks published and sold.

Why, then, another Chinese cookbook? Because there has been no single comprehensive book based on officially published recipes from the People's Republic itself. In a search for more authentic and extensive information about cooking in China today, the author has been able to secure and translate three important sources.

The first is a set of eleven cookbooks, *Treatise on Famous Chinese Dishes*, compiled by the government of the People's Republic of China, 1958–1965, to provide textbooks for cooking classes in which chefs and helpers could be trained for the people's dining halls, restaurants and commune kitchens. The compilation was made by asking chefs from restaurants throughout the country to submit recipes of their specialties. Many of the restaurants that participated are centuries old and their recipes have been passed on by generation after generation of chefs. Thus, for the first time, recipes that heretofore had been reserved only for the privileged few have been assembled and made available to the people. This set of cookbooks contains traditional Chinese dishes, as well as palace dishes, an esoteric and distinct category served only at the imperial court. There is also a regional representation, since the books are categorized in this manner.

The second source is *The Cookbook of Famous Dishes from the Peking Hotel Restaurant,* published in 1960 by the government. This restaurant and hotel, which has been host to many Westerners and foreign dignitaries, is world-renowned.

The third source is *The Masses Cookbook,* published in 1966 also by the government. This book introduces the "new cuisine" of China which places special emphasis on nutrition, economy, and ease of preparation. It requires a minimum of ingredients (with emphasis on fresh vegetables) and uses the simplest cooking methods, largely stir-frying.

In using these three sources, an evolutionary aspect of Chinese cookery emerges which, supported by comment on the cooking of each region, helps to give a better appreciation and understanding of China's culinary art from the earliest times to the present.

China's four major culinary regions generally include the North (Hopei, Shantung and Honan), East (Kiangsu and Chekiang), Southeast (Kuangtung) and Southwest (Szech'uan and Hunan). There are subgroups within these designations based on ethnic origins, e.g., Moslem and Mongolian; social groups, e.g., palace and Buddhist; and individual cities, e.g., Peking, Chinan and Hangchou. Recipes were carefully selected from these categories and only those considered to be the finest were included.

There were some difficulties in translating the recipes from Chinese into English as well as in testing them. Measurements and directions were often intended for restaurant kitchens and therefore had to be reduced to home-kitchen proportions. Also, only Chinese measurements were given, so a fairly elaborate conversion table had to be devised. Directions were often incomplete. This required repeated testing of recipes so that the final version would have clear directions on how to achieve the desired results. On rare occasions, slight modifications were made because of the need to substitute ingredients or equipment.

The
PEOPLE'S
REPUBLIC
of
CHINA
COOKBOOK

EQUIPMENT AND TECHNIQUES

Agreat culinary tradition—such as that of the French or the Chinese—is embodied in both a menu of classic dishes and a complex of cooking techniques. The reader who is serious about learning Chinese cooking must acquire the basic techniques as well as the knowledge of how specific dishes should appear and taste. This section is designed to provide that knowledge. The utensils used in Chinese cooking are first discussed, after which cutting and methods of cooking are taken up. Finally, a method of programming the preparation of several dishes is discussed and illustrated.

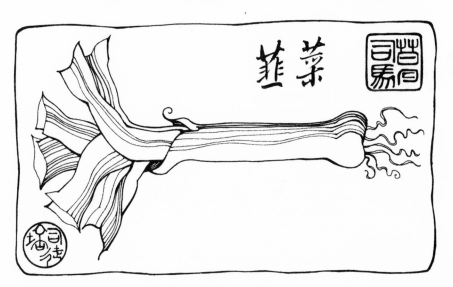

Utensils

The hardware necessary for Chinese cooking should not be difficult to acquire. Many of the important items will be found in an American kitchen, and the others should be available from Chinese stores in major cities. The following list provides information on the use of utensils in Chinese cooking and can be used to check off what you may need to buy.

STOVE

Gas stoves are best for Chinese cooking because they can be adjusted very quickly to varying temperatures. This is important especially in stir-frying and braising. If you are using an electric stove the wok should rest directly on the electric element rather than cradled on the metal ring supplied with the pan. Care must then be exercised to keep the pan steady. An overhead hood or fan is desirable for Chinese cooking.

WOK

The rounded bottom of this Chinese cooking pan (called *kuo* in Mandarin Chinese) makes it ideal for stir-frying. It disperses heat well and makes it easy to push foods around and mix them with oil and liquids in the bottom. A large frying pan can be substituted, but if you plan to cook Chinese food with any regularity you should acquire a wok, preferably one made of iron—and be sure to get a big one (a 14-inch one is ideal), which will let you cook small as well as large portions.

To season a new wok, add 3 inches or so of unsalted oil or fat and place over low heat until the entire surface of the wok is hot. Remove and cool. Discard the oil and wash.

Cleaning a wok between making different dishes or when you have finished cooking is easily done, as follows. Using pot holders, and without turning off the fire, take the wok from the stove to the sink. Run warm water into the wok, tilt it to one side and scrape it vigorously with a stiff-bristled kitchen brush (Chinese restaurants use a small broomlike scraper made of bamboo). When all sediment has been removed, rinse well, drain and put the wok back over the fire. The heat will quickly dry it, and rust stains will be avoided. Never store a wok that has not been completely dried.

SPATULA AND DIPPER

These are very handy utensils. The Chinese spatula is about the same size as the one found in American kitchens but is heavier and has an inflexible blade. Also, its leading edge is slightly convex so that it fits the rounded surface of the wok. As an aid when frying, the spatula is used to press food down as well as to stir it around and turn it over. Here the use of two spatulas is helpful. The dipper is used to ladle out oil, stock, water or sauce. It holds just about 1/2 cup (6 tablespoons) and in restaurants serves as the cook's "measuring spoon" for liquids. Thus, addition of 1 cup of soup stock means 2 dippers of stock, 3 tablespoons of oil is 1/2 dipper of oil and so on.

CHINESE KNIVES

These are cleavers. There are two types. One is thin and lightweight and is used for slicing vegetables and things easy to cut. The other is heavier and its sharp edge is used for cutting through bone; its flat side is used to smash such ingredients as garlic cloves, which then become easy to peel, and to serve as a handy surface on which to transport what has been cut to the stove; its blunt back edge is used to mash meats. A sharpening stone should be on hand so that you can keep your cleavers' cutting edge very sharp.

CHOPPING BLOCK

This, of course, accompanies the cleaver. The Chinese prefer a thick (4 to 6 inches) slice of a hardwood tree, particularly the wood of the soap tree—and preferably aged.

STEAMER

The Chinese bamboo steamer is an attractive handcrafted article but not as useful as a metal steamer. A large steamer is advantageous because it will hold more water and larger bowls of food. It should have at least two tiers.

MORTAR AND PESTLE

Most Japanese shops carry a very good type of mortar made of hard, high-fired ceramic. The inside of the mortar is grooved to provide an abrasive surface.

DEEP-FRYER

An electric fryer is ideal, as it maintains an even temperature, but a large heavy pot can be substituted, with a candy or deep-fat thermometer to check the heat. A useful adjunct is a Chinese wire scoop with a bamboo handle. The material to be deep-fried (which may range from won tons to a whole chicken) is placed on the wire scoop and put into the hot oil. The scoop can be used at any time to lift the food to see how the cooking is progressing. When done, the food is simply lifted up on the scoop and the oil quickly drains back into the pan.

ELECTRIC RICE COOKER

An electric rice cooker cooks rice automatically. The only judgment necessary is the amount of water to add to a given amount of rice. Usually the surface of the water should be 3/4 inch to 1 inch above the surface of the rice. However, since the "correct" amount depends both on how dry you want the cooked rice to be and how dried out the uncooked rice is, you will have to develop your own measurements. Use the 3/4 inch- to 1-inch rule as a starter.

Incidentally, rice should always be well washed before cooking to remove the talc which coats it. Wash rice in its cooking pan. Run about 1/2 cup of water into it and with one hand swish the rice around in a circular motion for a minute. Alternatively, you can rub batches of rice together between your hands. Then pour out the water and repeat the procedure. After four or five washings the water poured out should be clear, indicating that the rice is well cleaned.

If you do not have an electric rice cooker, use a heavy pot with a secure cover. Start the rice in cold water over high heat. When the water boils, remove the pan from the stove for a minute and reduce the heat to its lowest point. Return the pan to the stove and steam for 20 minutes. Remove from heat and let the pot stand covered for 15 minutes.

Cutting Methods

In Chinese cooking, the aim of precise cutting methods is to reduce ingredients to the same size or shape so that they will cook in the same amount of time. When skillfully done, the way in which food is cut also adds to the appearance of a dish. There are a few simple guidelines for cutting meats and vegetables.

Meats are either minced, sliced, cubed or cut into matchstick-sized shreds.

Mincing:	Slice the meat, then cut the slices lengthwise into shreds and, finally, chop finely across the shreds. Meat that is to be used in meatballs should be very finely minced.
Slicing:	Meat should be sliced across the grain to make it more tender, usually in slices about 1/8 inch thick. If this is difficult to do, try partially freezing the meat. Some meats, such as chicken breasts, are best sliced horizontally. Make a shallow cut downward as deep as the finished slice is to be thick. Then slice across to the cut.
Cubing:	The dimensions of the cubes depend on the dish.
Matchstick:	Cut long, thin pieces of meat, usually against the grain, about 1 1/2 inches by 1/8 by 1/8 inch.

Vegetables are usually cut into pieces about the same size as the other main ingredients of a dish. Before cutting, trim off undesirable parts, wash well and allow to drain dry.

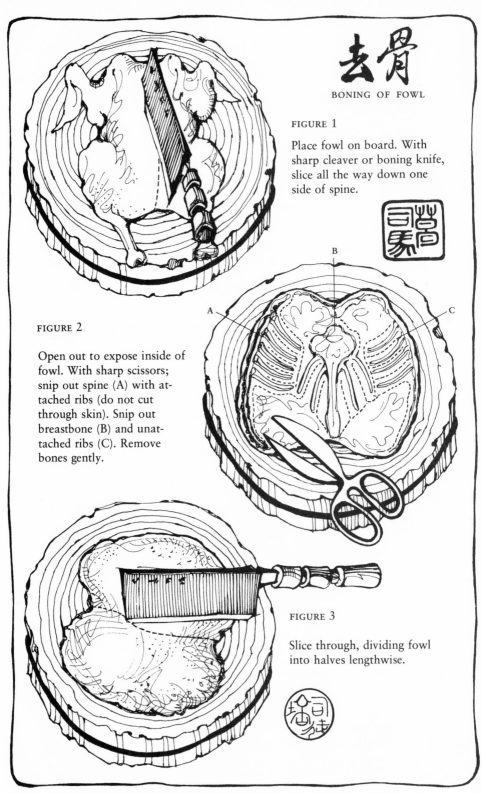

去骨

BONING OF FOWL

FIGURE 1

Place fowl on board. With sharp cleaver or boning knife, slice all the way down one side of spine.

FIGURE 2

Open out to expose inside of fowl. With sharp scissors; snip out spine (A) with attached ribs (do not cut through skin). Snip out breastbone (B) and unattached ribs (C). Remove bones gently.

FIGURE 3

Slice through, dividing fowl into halves lengthwise.

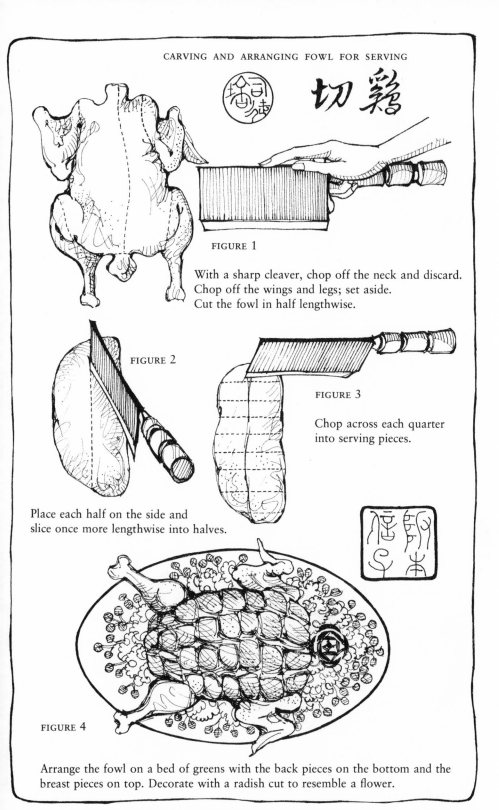

切鷄

FIGURE 1

With a sharp cleaver, chop off the neck and discard.
Chop off the wings and legs; set aside.
Cut the fowl in half lengthwise.

FIGURE 2

FIGURE 3

Chop across each quarter
into serving pieces.

Place each half on the side and
slice once more lengthwise into halves.

FIGURE 4

Arrange the fowl on a bed of greens with the back pieces on the bottom and the
breast pieces on top. Decorate with a radish cut to resemble a flower.

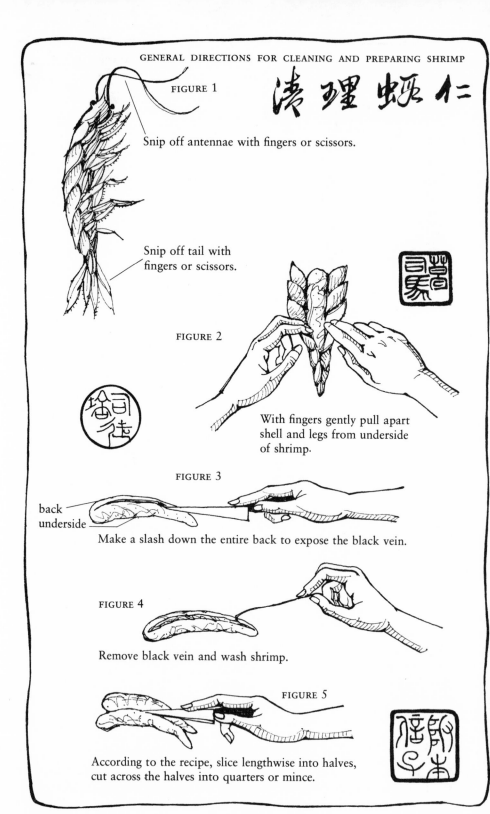

FIGURE 1

清理蝦仁

Snip off antennae with fingers or scissors.

Snip off tail with
fingers or scissors.

FIGURE 2

With fingers gently pull apart
shell and legs from underside
of shrimp.

FIGURE 3

back
underside

Make a slash down the entire back to expose the black vein.

FIGURE 4

Remove black vein and wash shrimp.

FIGURE 5

According to the recipe, slice lengthwise into halves,
cut across the halves into quarters or mince.

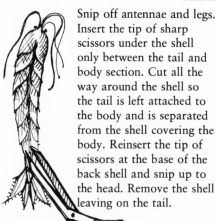

Snip off antennae and legs. Insert the tip of sharp scissors under the shell only between the tail and body section. Cut all the way around the shell so the tail is left attached to the body and is separated from the shell covering the body. Reinsert the tip of scissors at the base of the back shell and snip up to the head. Remove the shell leaving on the tail.

FIGURE 1

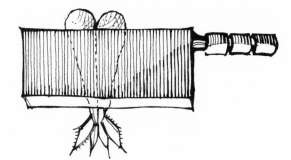

FIGURE 2

With a sharp paring knife, slice down the back and remove the black vein. Then cut down, *not through,* to the underside of the shrimp so that it can be opened out flat on a board. Gently flatten the inner side with the side of a cleaver to break up connective tissue.

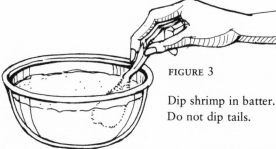

FIGURE 3

Dip shrimp in batter. Do not dip tails.

(Continued on next page)

Heat oil to proper temperature, and holding the tails, slide two shrimp at a time into a pan. Hold shrimp against the side of the pan for about 1 minute so that they will set in that position with tails up and bodies flat. Release shrimp into the hot oil and cook for about 2 seconds, or until the tails turn red. Remove immediately and drain.

PREPARATION OF FRIED SHRIMP WITH SHELLS

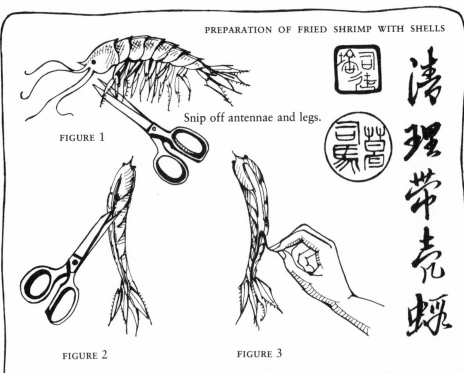

Snip off antennae and legs.

FIGURE 1

FIGURE 2

FIGURE 3

Insert the tip of sharp scissors into the tail end of the back and snip only the shell along the length of the back up to the head.

With a sharp paring knife, slice lightly through the length of the back flesh, exposing the black vein. Pull it out, then wash the shrimp and dry them with paper towels. Let them air-dry for 15 minutes to prevent splattering when deep-fried.

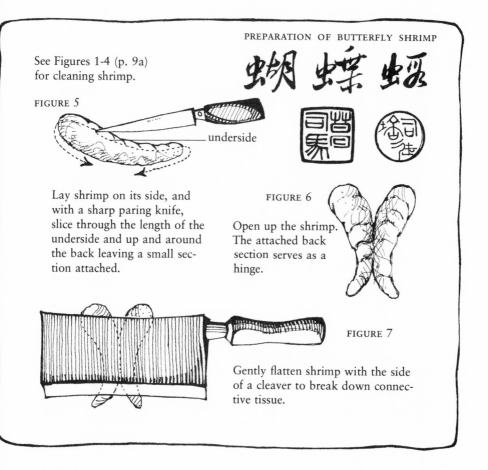

PREPARATION OF BUTTERFLY SHRIMP

See Figures 1-4 (p. 9a) for cleaning shrimp.

FIGURE 5

underside

Lay shrimp on its side, and with a sharp paring knife, slice through the length of the underside and up and around the back leaving a small section attached.

FIGURE 6

Open up the shrimp. The attached back section serves as a hinge.

FIGURE 7

Gently flatten shrimp with the side of a cleaver to break down connective tissue.

Cooking Methods

STIR-FRYING

This method of cooking aims at the maximum use of heat over a short period of cooking to seal flavors and juices in the ingredients. When cooked, vegetables should be crisp and meats succulent. The resultant pan juices are often thickened.

Guidelines for stir-frying are quite simple, but the timing can go wrong and detract from the desired result. The following sequence of steps describes the stir-fry preparation of a typical meat-and-vegetable dish.

1. The main ingredients are cut into relatively small pieces. Thin slicing, matchstick slicing, diagonal cutting, and mincing are chiefly used. All main ingredients should be about the same size. The object is to minimize cooking time.

2. Ingredients must be prepared and placed near the wok in order of use before the actual cooking is begun.

3. Use high heat throughout. First, the wok is heated until it is smoking hot and will sizzle a drop of water. Then oil is added, followed by salt and garlic, if used. (The oil is poured—using a circular movement—around the sides of the wok at the outer edge so that it coats the sides as it runs down to the bottom.) The garlic is pressed against the bottom of the wok with the spatula and quickly discarded so that it won't burn and impart a bitter taste to the dish. Sometimes, however, immediate addition of a main ingredient will lower the oil's temperature, so that the garlic need not be removed.

4. The main ingredients are added next—usually the meat first. Much

sizzling should occur. After stir-frying for a minute or two the meat would be about 80 percent cooked, and is then removed. Then the vegetables are added. When several vegetables are used, those requiring longer cooking are put in first. Then the meat is returned to the wok.

5. Seasonings (premixed) are added next, given a few stirs, then followed by soup stock, if used.

6. After a 1/2 minute to a minute the liquid in the wok will be well heated; cornstarch mixed with water, if used, is added and the mixture stirred for about 30 seconds until the cornstarch sets, at which point the cooking is completed.

This is the basic sequence regardless of variations such as marination of the meat, parboiling vegetables, the use of two seasoning mixtures, or covering the pan for a short time during the cooking. Several points require elaboration. Because of the high heat, ample oil must be used and the ingredients in the wok more or less continuously stirred and turned over. (The "less" in "more or less" refers to the cooking of meat, which can be briefly pressed with a spatula against the bottom of the wok so that it will cook faster.) If the ingredients appear to be in danger of burning, additional oil can be added. If vegetables begin to scorch, take the wok off the burner and then reduce the heat, and keep stirring. If soup stock is used it should be *hot* when added. The proportion of the cornstarch mixture to the amount of liquid in the wok is important. Too little thickening produces a watery sauce; too much results in an unpalatable gelatinous mass. When in doubt, the cornstarch mixture can be added a small amount at a time—until the sauce is sufficiently thickened. When adding cornstarch paste, always have in mind how thick you want the sauce to be. Then add more if necessary.

DRY-FRYING

A method of cooking (similar to stir-frying) in which no stock is used.

STEAMING

Steaming aims at cooking food with a minimum loss of its juices and flavor. The ingredients' own flavors will predominate. Fish is especially delicious when steamed, but must be checked for doneness. It should not be under- or over-cooked. Tea cakes, even those with pasta skins, and sponge cakes are steamed—a method of cooking pastry and pasta which may seem inappropriate to Westerners until the results are tasted. With the addition of one or more tiers to the steamer, one stacked on top of another, many dishes—including complete meals—can be simultaneously steamed.

In Chinese cooking, steaming is frequently combined with other cooking methods to produce results that neither method could achieve alone. Since steaming usually softens and tenderizes food, it is often used as a first cooking step, after which deep-frying produces a contrasting textural effect, as, for example, in Ta Tung Crispy Skin Chicken (p. 175).

The guidelines for steaming are simple: Have the water in the steamer boiling vigorously before putting in the food, and if you are using a platter or pan prewarm it; keep the fire high throughout the steaming. If possible, put enough water in the steamer to last the entire steaming period (but don't put in so much that the water will boil over the food). When steaming for long periods, as is necessary with some pork dishes, add boiling water every 30 minutes to the steamer.

Food can sometimes be put directly on the steamer tray, as with many types of tea cakes, in which case the tray should be oiled to prevent sticking. Restaurants often put such food on large bamboo leaves or on towels. Lettuce can also be used, but not cabbage leaves because they would cook and flavor the food. When a bowl is used to hold the food being steamed, some of the steam will condense in the dish, leaving the food standing in a water-juice mixture. In order to keep such water from accumulating, and to preserve the strength of any marinade mixture, cover the bowl with aluminum foil, with a half-dozen small holes punched in the top to let some steam enter.

Finally, care must be taken when uncovering a steamer. Always open the lid away from you to avoid a blast of steam. Also be careful when opening the cover to prevent rivulets of water on the inside of the cover from running down into the food.

DEEP-FRYING

This cooking method is used both for ingredients that are relatively small (such as pork or fish slices) or large (such as a whole chicken or duck). Larger items are usually cooked first by steaming or boiling before being deep-fried to produce a crisp outer surface. It is important to use oil that is not too old, and, of course, fresh oil is best. Any vegetable oil will do, but for deep-frying corn oil is preferred because of its higher smoking point. Oil that has been used a number of times has fine impurities in it that lower its smoking point. When reusing oil always strain it to remove particles, and use half and half with fresh oil. Oil that has been used to fry fish may have a fishy flavor, and is not recommended for reuse.

About 3 cups of oil should be enough for deep-frying most dishes, since it is best to fry only moderate amounts of food together.

Temperature is important in deep-frying and a candy thermometer should be used. If the temperature of the oil is too low, the food to be cooked will turn out to be soggy rather than crisp. A piece of bread dropped in the oil will sizzle and foam at about 370°. Some dishes, particularly those precooked by other methods, require deep-frying at about 375° in order to produce a very crisp surface. Generally speaking, temperatures from 330° to 375° are used for deep-frying. Some ingredients, such as fish and shrimp, in which the deep-frying must both cook the inside and crisp the outside, require a temperature of 350°. As a general rule, it is best if ingredients to be deep-fried are brought to room temperature before frying. Since immersion of food into hot oil lowers the temperature of the oil, judgment must be used as to how high the fire should be and when it should be turned up or down.

Some dishes call for deep-frying in two (or even three) stages. This technique usually involves putting in the ingredients for a brief period of time at a temperature of 350°, taking them out (so they cool and the oil heats up), and then again putting them in the oil to finish cooking. The object of this double frying is to achieve a very crisp texture.

BRAISING

This method of cooking aims at producing flavors shared by the ingredients and the resultant sauce. It requires enough liquid to cover the main ingredients, and a relatively long cooking period over moderate or low heat. Seasonings are put into the braising liquid, which is used as a sauce (usually without thickening). The main ingredients may or may not be fried before braising. Fish are usually braised whole, whereas meat and fowl are cut into pieces. Because of the long cooking time, the pieces can be relatively large. When soy sauce is added to the braising liquid, the process is referred to as "red cooking." Star anise and rock sugar are also often used in red cooking. The typical sequence of steps in braising is as follows:

(1) Put the wok over high heat.
(2) When the pan is hot, add oil, and then the meat, fish or fowl.
(3) Stir-fry, and when partially cooked, add seasonings and soup stock or water.
(4) When the liquid boils, reduce heat.
(5) Cook until well done (which may take from 30 minutes to 4 hours).
(6) Taste the liquid and correct the seasoning with regard to salt and sweeteners.
(7) Serve with the sauce.

If the braising liquid must be reduced in volume, do not cover the pan; otherwise, keep it covered.

Organization

For anyone interested in cooking, the kitchens of Chinese restaurants are fascinating places to visit. During the slack hour between meals a crew of helpers work steadily at the preparatory chores, which are more time-consuming than the actual cooking. Bushels of vegetables are washed, trimmed and sliced. Meats, chicken and shrimp are cleaned and sliced, and some are precooked, often in water which can later be used for stock. Barbecued pork is prepared and ducks are roasted. Fish are cleaned and doused with soy and wine. Seasoning, thickening and coating mixtures are made up, garlic crushed and ginger minced. This preliminary work is vital to the chefs who will take the final step of creating the dishes. The Chinese restaurant can put out an incredible number of dishes in a small span of time largely because the work has been programmed into a succession of steps and much of the preparation done well before the final stage of cooking.

In cooking from the recipes in this book, the following system is recommended. First, select in advance the dish or dishes you want to prepare and obtain all the necessary ingredients. Second, read the recipe(s) carefully, so that you have a clear idea of the steps to be followed. As part of the cooking preparation, line up the various components of each dish, so that when the cooking stage is reached, everything is at hand and ready to go into the wok, steamer or whatever, in order of use.

The preparation of Chinese dishes makes repeated use of a small number of basic seasonings and other ingredients. Rather than assembling these materials each time Chinese cooking is undertaken, you can keep them together on a tray that can be brought out when needed. The tray should include the following:

thin soy sauce	white vinegar
thick soy sauce	Chinese red vinegar
rice wine	garlic cloves
salt	MSG (monosodium glutamate)
sugar	black peppercorns
sesame oil	cayenne (ground red pepper)
vegetable oil	cornstarch

When cooking, have close at hand a small bowl in which to mix cornstarch and water. A pot with soup stock should be on a back burner, kept warm over a low fire.

In addition to the above, two other groups of ingredients will be used. The first consists of materials that require refrigeration. These ingredients often come in cans, and after being opened should be stored in covered jars in the refrigerator (see Ingredients section for information about storage). They include the following:

black beans	fermented bean curd
fresh ginger	wine lees
sesame paste	pickled mustard greens
Szech'uan hot bean paste	preserved turnip
sweet bean paste	bamboo shoots
oyster sauce	bean sprouts, canned
brown (yellow) bean sauce	plum sauce
Hoisin sauce	water chestnuts

Less frequently used materials that do not require refrigeration can be kept on hand in a drawer or on a pantry shelf. They include:

flower pepper	rice powder
five-flavored spice	bicarbonate of soda
star anise	white and black sesame seeds
rock sugar	peanuts
brown sugar	almonds
malt sugar	dried Chinese dates
hot pepper oil	curry powder
cloud ears	red chili peppers
wood ears	dried shrimp
dried tangerine peel	dried bamboo shoots
black vinegar	gold needles (dried tiger lily buds)
blackstrap molasses	dried mushrooms
water chestnut flour	honey
flour	catsup

Because the ingredients listed above give Chinese dishes much of their authentic flavor, it is important to have them on hand and to use them properly. Substitutions may often be made for main ingredients without compromising a dish, but the seasonings are crucial to the authentic character of a dish.

PROGRAMMING

A good way to approach the preparation of a Chinese dish or an entire meal is to consider it as a problem in programming. What is to be programmed is the sequence of the procedure that must be followed to produce the desired result. The beginner must learn to translate a recipe into steps, and he or she should know how long each step takes, what it requires (for example, vigorous mixing, high heat, judgment about the amount of thickening mixture added) and its relative importance in terms of its effect on the final product. This approach can be practiced on simple dishes prepared singly, and once mastered, extended to the preparation of two dishes and eventually to an entire Chinese meal.

Let us begin with the preparation of a Szech'uan dish, which uses one cooking method, stir-frying.

GREEN PEPPER CHICKEN

1 pound chicken breasts
3 dried mushrooms
Marinade-coating mixture
  2 teaspoons rice wine
  1/2 teaspoon salt
  1 teaspoon grated ginger
  1 egg white
  1 tablespoon cornstarch
3 green peppers
1/4 cup bamboo shoots
2 green onions
1 garlic clove

Seasoning mixture
  1 tablespoon rice wine
  1/2 teaspoon salt
  1/2 teaspoon sugar
  1/4 teaspoon MSG
  1/2 teaspoon Szech'uan hot
    bean paste
About 3 tablespoons soup
  stock
1-1/2 tablespoons water
  mixed with 1 tablespoon
  cornstarch
3 tablespoons vegetable oil

On the day you plan to serve this dish read the recipe carefully, breaking its preparation into steps such as the following:

Step 1: Wash the chicken breasts and remove all skin, membranes and bones. Cut into pieces about the size of mah-jong tiles and put into a bowl. Put the mushrooms in hot water and let stand for at least 15 minutes.

Step 2: Combine all ingredients for the marinade-coating mixture. Put the chicken pieces in it and mix well. Let stand.

Step 3: Wash the green peppers. Halve and then quarter them. Remove stems, seeds and inner membranes. Slice into thin pieces about 2 inches by 1/2 inch. Cut the bamboo shoots into pieces about the same size as the peppers. Remove the mushrooms from the water, squeeze them dry, cut off the stems and cut into quarters. Mince the green onions. Smash the garlic clove with the side of the cleaver, remove the skin and mince. All of these ingredients should be set aside in bowls and lined up in the order of their use in the cooking.

Step 4: Combine all ingredients for the seasoning mixture.

Step 5: Heat up the soup stock. If you have stored portions of stock in the freezer, simply take a portion out, heat it and measure out the required amount. Make the cornstarch paste and stir until smooth.

Step 6: Now you are ready for the actual cooking. This can be postponed for some time (about thirty minutes) after you have completed all the previous steps. However, the meat marinade cannot stand too long because of the egg white and cornstarch in it and the cornstarch paste will have to be stirred from time to time to keep it from solidifying.

Step 7: Put a wok over high heat and when it is very hot add the oil, followed immediately by the garlic and green onion. Stir-fry for a few seconds and add the pieces of chicken. Continue stir-frying until the chicken turns white. Then add the mushrooms, bamboo shoots and green pepper. Stir to coat all ingredients with oil, then add the seasoning mixture. Add the stock and cover the wok.

Step 8: After 1/2 minute uncover the wok. Stir up the cornstarch paste, add to the chicken and vegetables and stir until the sauce thickens, at which point the dish is ready to serve.

If several stir-fry dishes are to be cooked for the same meal, each must be prepared up to the point of cooking and the cooking done for each dish in quick succession. Two or three stir-fried dishes are all that can be managed easily by one cook.

The next recipe illustrates the use of three cooking procedures: deep-frying, stir-frying and short braising.

BRAISED FISH AND BEAN CURD

1 medium-sized eggplant
1 teaspoon salt
1-1/2 cups warm water
4 dried mushrooms
1 large onion
2 green onions
2 cups bean curd, cut into 1-
  by 1/4-inch rectangles
Seasoning mixture
  1 teaspoon grated ginger
  1 garlic clove, minced
  1 tablespoon thin soy sauce
  1 teaspoon sweet bean paste

2 tablespoons rice wine
2 tablespoons water mixed
  with 1 tablespoon
  cornstarch
1 pound fish fillets (cod, haddock, etc.)
1/2 teaspoon salt
Coating mixture
  1/4 cup water chestnut flour
  1/4 cup cornstarch
  1-1/2 cup rich soup stock
  3/4 teaspoon Szech'uan hot
    bean paste

Step 1: Peel the eggplant and cut into strips about 1/2 inch thick and 2 inches long. Dissolve the salt in warm water, place in a bowl and soak the eggplant in this for 20 minutes. Drain the eggplant, squeeze out as much moisture as possible and dry with paper towels.

Step 2: Soak the dried mushrooms for 15 minutes in hot water, squeeze out the water, remove the stems and cut into quarters. Chop the onion and sliver the green onions by cutting them in half lengthwise and then slicing them diagonally into 1/2-inch sections.

Step 3: Place the bean curd in a bowl with boiling water to cover. After a minute remove the bean curd and drain.

Step 4: Combine all ingredients for the seasoning mixture and make the cornstarch paste.

Step 5: Wash and dry the fish fillets. Sprinkle them with 1/2 teaspoon salt and cut in pieces 1 inch by 1 1/2 inches. Pieces that are more than 1 inch thick should be slashed partway through.

Step 6: Combine the ingredients for the coating mixture and use to dredge the pieces of fish, coating them well.

Step 7: Heat up the soup stock. Put enough oil for deep-frying in another pan over high heat. When the oil is about to smoke (about 350°) put in the pieces of fish and fry until they are cooked through and golden-brown on the outside. Turn off the heat. Scoop out the fish, let drain, and arrange on a warm serving plate.

Step 8:   Pour out all but 3 tablespoons oil from the pan (also remove any burned particles) and turn the heat to high. When the oil is about to smoke, add the eggplant, onions, green onions and mushrooms. Stir-fry for 1 minute and add the seasoning mixture. Stir-fry 1/2 minute and put in the soup stock and then the bean curd. Braise until the liquid in the pan is reduced by half. Then add the Szech'uan hot bean paste, stir in the cornstarch paste and cook until thickened. Pour the mixture over the fish and serve immediately.

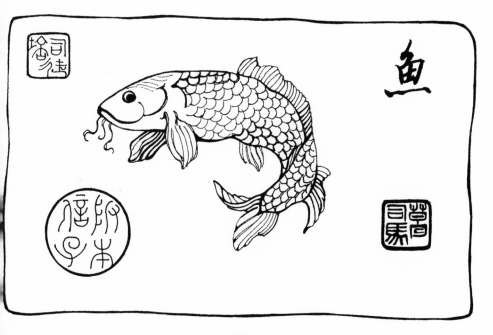

INGREDIENTS

Flavor

In Chinese cooking the appeal of a dish is traditionally characterized by five basic flavors: salt, sour, sweet, hot and fragrant. These are contributed not by the main ingredients but by accessory ingredients. The richness of Chinese cooking is due in great part to the large number of these which can be used to produce variations and different degrees in the basic flavors. Listed below are the most widely used accessory ingredients for each of the five basic flavors.

Salt: Salt, thin soy sauce, thick soy sauce, salted cabbage, preserved mustard greens.

Sour: White vinegar, Chinese red vinegar, black vinegar.

Sweet: White sugar, brown sugar, rock sugar, honey, malt sugar, sweet soy sauce, molasses, Hoisin sauce.

Hot: Black pepper, white pepper, ginger, red pepper (cayenne), red pepper oil, Szech'uan hot bean paste, black bean hot chili pepper, curry powder, *chia ts'ai* (hot preserved turnip).

Fragrant: Onion, five-flavored spice, flower pepper, cinnamon bark, anise, rice wine, brown (yellow) bean, black bean, oyster sauce, garlic, sesame oil, wine lees, Chinese parsley, fennel, tangerine peel, fermented bean curd, sesame paste.

Abalone Available in cans weighing approximately 1 pound from Chinese or Japanese groceries. Once opened, transfer to a jar with a tightly fitting lid and store in fresh water up to 1 week in the refrigerator. The water should be changed daily.

Angelica (*pai chih*)   A fragrant root of the iris family used as a bouquet garni for soups, braised meats and poultry. Available at Chinese groceries or herb dealers.

Anise (*pa chio*), **Chinese star**   A woody, five-pointed spice which adds a fragrance to braised meats and poultry. Sold loose or in 4-ounce plastic packages at Chinese groceries. Stored in a tightly sealed container, it will keep indefinitely.

Bacon, fresh   See Pork, five flower.

Bamboo shoots, canned   Available in cans of varying size. Large pieces of the finest quality are best; do not purchase scraps. Drain and store in a large covered jar filled with water in the refrigerator up to over a week. A little salt will keep them fresh. Change the water daily.

Bamboo shoots, dried   Can be purchased in packages in Chinese groceries. Must be soaked for 1 hour or more before using. Store in a tightly capped large jar or tin.

Bamboo shoots, fresh   Sometimes available in Chinese or Japanese groceries. Place in water, which should be changed daily. A little salt will help keep them fresh. They will keep in the refrigerator for several days.

Bamboo, spring   Available in cans. Store these young, tender shoots the same way as for regular canned bamboo shoots.

Bean curd, fermented   Available in jars. It comes in little squares fermented in wine and is sometimes known as Chinese cheese. Refrigerated, it keeps for months.

Bean curd, fresh (*tofu*)   A soft, whitish cake (about three inches square) made of the water-soluble part of soy beans. It is sold in Chinese and Japanese groceries. Only fresh, sweet cakes without discoloration should be purchased. To store, drain them and place in a large bowl; fill with water to cover and refrigerate up to 2 or 3 days. Change the water daily.

Bean paste, red   A canned sweet paste of red beans used as filling for steamed cakes. Stored in a tightly sealed jar, it will keep for several months in the refrigerator.

Bean paste, Szech'uan hot   A fiery condiment made of chili peppers, yellow soy bean, oil and seasonings which comes in both cans and small bottles. The canned variety should be transferred to a tightly capped jar and both varieties refrigerated. There are several brands, some thinner, some thicker, and they must be sampled to determine the degree of hotness.

Bean sauce, brown   A heavy sauce made of fermented yellow beans, salt and wheat flour, also known as yellow or whole bean sauce. It comes in 1-pound cans. Once opened, it will keep for several months if transferred to a tightly sealed jar and refrigerated.

Bean sprouts   Fresh or canned may be used. If using fresh sprouts, use 1 cup more than the required amount. Fresh sprouts may be bought in bulk and kept in a plastic bag in the refrigerator for a few days. They can also be sprouted at home from dried mung beans. Kits with instructions may be purchased in health-food stores; a large unit that will sprout 2 or 3 cups at a time is desirable. The canned variety will keep a few days if transferred to a covered glass jar filled with water after opening and stored in the refrigerator. Change the water every few days.

Beef   A superior quality of flank steak, sirloin or tenderloin is best for stir-fried dishes. A fine-quality chuck roast is best for braising although other cuts may be used.

Black bean chili sauce   A pungent, hot condiment frequently used in Szech'uan and Hunan dishes which is especially delicious with smoked meats. It comes in a small jar which must be refrigerated after opening, but will keep indefinitely.

Black beans, fermented   Fermented and salt-preserved black soy beans, not to be confused with the dried black beans. Used most frequently in Cantonese cooking, the beans must be rinsed, drained and mashed before using. Refrigerated in a tightly capped jar, they will keep indefinitely.

Broccoli   The Chinese variety, which is more tender and delicate than the Western type, can be purchased in season at Chinese groceries.

Cabbage, celery (*tientsin, napa* [Japanese])   Has long, tightly closed stalks with white stems and light yellow-green wrinkled leaves. Available in many supermarkets and Chinese groceries. Celery may be substituted in stir-fried dishes where crunchiness is important.

Cardamom (*sha jen*)   An herb used in bouquet garni for seasoning soups, braised meats and poultry.

Cashew nuts   The unroasted whole cashew, pale in color and unsalted, can be purchased in Chinese groceries or health-food stores. They can be lightly shallow-fried in a little oil until they rise to the surface, then drained. Do not buy in large quantities because they turn rancid if kept for a long time. Store in covered tins or capped dark jars.

Caul fat (pork omentum)   A thin, fatty tissue used to cover or wrap fish. It imparts a rich flavor to fish.

Cayenne   Available in powdered form in little cans or jars.

Chestnuts, sweet   Available fresh in season or packed in water or syrup in cans. Buy only the best-quality canned whole chestnuts, not pieces. Place fresh chestnuts in 325° oven for 20 to 30 minutes, or until they begin to pop. Remove from the oven and let cool, and then with a sharp paring knife remove the outer shells and inner skins. Rinse the canned variety well before using. Add to dishes just long enough to permit the sauce to permeate the chestnuts.

Chicken   Boned chicken breast is desirable for meatballs because the flesh is free of tendons, etc., and minces into a fine paste. Breast meat is also desirable for stir-fried dishes. Chicken thighs and legs are better suited to braised dishes. A 2- to 3-pound dressed young fryer or pullet is desirable for dishes requiring a whole chicken. For long-braised dishes requiring a whole larger chicken, roasting or stewing chicken should be used.

Chicken fat   Used in many Northern and Eastern dishes, especially those of Moslem origin. To melt, or "render," remove raw solid fat from the inside of a chicken or purchase some from the butcher and put it in a bowl in a steamer over boiling water. Cover and steam for about 1 hour, or until all the fat is melted. Strain and store it in a covered jar in the refrigerator. It will often turn rancid in a short while.

Chrysanthemum greens   The young, edible Japanese variety, with their fragrance and "bite" are delicious used in soup, as a garnish, in salads, or stir-fried with shrimp or chicken. Available in Chinese markets in spring and early summer. Watercress or young spinach leaves are substitutes.

Cinnamon bark   Can be purchased at the spice counter of any grocery. It is used in bouquet garni to season sauces, braised meats and poultry.

Cloud ears   A variety of tree lichen which is a delicate cousin of the wood ear. It is opaque to transparent and needs to be soaked before using. It can be purchased at Chinese groceries. Stored in a covered jar, without refrigeration, it will keep indefinitely.

Cloves, carnation (*ting hsiang*)   Used in bouquet garni for flavoring braised meats and poultry, and also in marinades.

Cornstarch   Generally used for thickening sauces mixed with water in varying proportions. Must be restirred just before using. It is sometimes used to coat poultry or seafood for deep-frying and frequently in a marinade for meats.

Crab   Frozen Alaska king crab meat or any fine-grade canned crab will do. For steamed crab dishes, use whole fresh or frozen crabs.

Crab yellow   The tomalley of the crab is highly prized by the Chinese and is often used in shark's fin dishes. If not available, use a slightly fat pork minced fine as a substitute.

Cucumber   The Oriental variety, obtainable in Chinese and Japanese groceries, is seedless, thin, long, firm and sweet—ideal for cooking. The new seedless variety now available in most supermarkets, if fresh and firm, is excellent.

Curry powder   The varieties found in Chinese, Japanese or herb and spice stores are usually stronger and more flavorful than those found in supermarkets. Keep tightly covered and replace every 6 months for best flavor.

Dates, dried Chinese   Also known as jujube nuts, these are not true dates, but belong to the same family as other drupaceous fruits, such as almonds, and peaches. Somewhat similar to prunes, they are sold by the package in Chinese groceries and must be soaked in cold water before using. Stored in a covered jar, they will keep indefinitely without refrigeration.

Dragon's eye   Available dried or in cans. The raisinlike dried variety is used for flavoring soups and stews. Store in a tightly covered jar.

Duck   Fresh or frozen dressed Long Island duck, about 4-1/2 to 5 pounds, are best. For frozen ducks, follow directions on the wrapping for defrosting.

Duck eggs, preserved   These come in two varieties and are available in Chinese groceries. The lime, salt and ash-coated variety (*p'i tan*) are cured up to a hundred days and need not be cooked. Wash off coating before using. The other variety is preserved in brine and saltpeter and needs to be cooked in simmering water for 1/2 hour. These eggs are served as appetizers sprinkled with a little sesame oil and seasonings. They are also used in dishes such as lobster Cantonese.

Duck fat   Rendered duck fat is often used as a substitute for chicken fat, although its flavor is rather pronounced. See Chicken fat for instructions on how to render it.

Duck sauce (plum sauce)   So called because it is delicious served with duck, this sweet-and-sour sauce is made of plums, apricots, vinegar and sugar. A good substitute is apricot preserves puréed and mixed with half as much catsup, a little white vinegar and a little cayenne. Available in Chinese and Japanese groceries in 1-pound cans. Once opened, transfer to a tightly capped large jar and refrigerate. It will keep for a long period.

Fish   Fresh-water fish are preferred in China, and the grass carp is the favorite. Its thick, sweet, firm flesh is best suited to most Chinese dishes. Substitutes are fresh whole pike, bass and lake whitefish, weighing about 1 1/4 to 1-1/2 pounds. Indications of freshness are clear eyes (no film), pink to red gills, firm flesh and no disagreeable odor. The ideal is to purchase a live fish from a tank in a Chinese market. Above all, do not buy fish that is not fresh. Tell the attendant what kind of dish you are preparing so he can advise you. The fish should be cleaned, scaled (unless otherwise indicated in a given recipe) with head and tail intact.

Five-flavored spice A combination of five finely ground spices: Chinese anise, cinnamon, fennel, flower pepper and clove. The dark, red brown powder adds a very special flavor to pork, chicken and duck. It is often used to season braised meats and in marinades for roast duck and barbecued pork.

Gelatin, meat Formed by straining the liquid left from long, slow braising of fresh ham skin or ham hock. Dissolve a package of gelatin (per pint of liquid) in a little hot water and heat gently. Add to the strained liquid, mix and reheat for a minute. Cool and refrigerate until solid.

Ginger, preserved in brine Red in color and called *benishoga* (rouge ginger) in Japanese. It can be purchased in Japanese food stores and comes in small bottles which should be refrigerated after opening. It keeps for several months.

Ginger, preserved in syrup Comes in tins and ceramic pots. Delicious as a confection or sliced thin and used in sweet-and-sour dishes. Transfer canned ginger and syrup to a covered jar and refrigerate. It keeps for several months.

Ginger root, fresh Not a true root but a rhizome (an underground stem) that is very aromatic and widely used medicinally in the Orient. It is also one of the most common seasonings used in Chinese cooking. After the skin is peeled off, the fibrous yellow meat is grated, minced, slivered, sliced or occasionally juiced.

To make "ginger water" place small pieces of ginger in a garlic press, squeeze out the juice and then add 1 or 2 teaspoons of water.

Ginger is excellent (as are lemon and vinegar) in removing fishy odors and flavors. To store fresh ginger, wash the root and dry it; place it in a jar and cover with any white wine; cap the jar and refrigerate. It keeps for several months.

Gold needles Dried tiger lily buds which must be soaked for 30 minutes in warm water, and then rinsed and the liquid squeezed out before using. They appear most often in vegetarian dishes and also in some special dishes, such as Mu Hsu Pork Hangchou Style (p. 114). Gold needles should be stored in a tightly covered tin or bottle, and will keep indefinitely without refrigeration.

Ham Lean, well-flavored ham on the salty and smoky side is desirable. The Smithfield ham is akin to its Chinese counterparts, Chinhua ham of Chekiang or Yunnan ham.

Ham, fresh Seldom found at packaged meat counters and must be specially ordered from the butcher. They generally weigh about 6 to 8 pounds. The ham comes covered with skin. Delicious when braised slowly for several hours in soy, wine, sugar and seasonings.

Ham hock   Used to prepare meat gelatin. It can also be braised like fresh ham to make fillings (a little lean pork should be added) for steamed cakes and rolls. Ham hock can be bought in smaller pieces and is therefore less expensive than fresh ham.

Hazelnut (filbert)   Can be purchased at Chinese groceries or health-food stores. They must be blanched, air-dried and lightly shallow-fried. Store uncooked nuts for short periods in covered dark jar or tin. Do not buy in bulk, since they may turn rancid and bitter after long storage.

Hoisin sauce   A velvety, thick red-brown sweet sauce made of wheat flour, soy bean, sugar, garlic, chili and vinegar which is most often used as a dip but also in marinades, seasonings and sauces. It is obtainable in cans at Chinese groceries. Once opened, it should be stored in a tightly covered jar and refrigerated. It keeps for long periods.

Honey   Used to coat chicken or duck skin for crispy-skinned dishes. It is also used in sauces, such as Feng Ch'eng Honey Tender Chicken (p. 176).

Lamb   The upper portion of the leg is best. It contains the least sinew and the leanest meat. It is less expensive to buy in bulk. Leftover uncooked meat can be frozen for later use.

Licorice, Chinese (*kan ts'ao*)   An herb and spice used medicinally and in a bouquet garni for flavoring soups and braised meats. Available at Chinese groceries or herb stores.

Miso (Japanese)   Fermented bean paste available from light to dark in little plastic tubs which, refrigerated, will keep for months. Available at Japanese groceries. Can be substituted for wine lees.

Molasses, Chinese   A type of blackstrap molasses which is thick, dark and viscous. It is used in sauces and marinades. Since it is very strong, only small amounts are used.

MSG (monosodium glutamate)   Accent and the Japanese Aji-no-moto are the same. This white powder is used in small amounts and brings out the flavors of ingredients. It is widely used in China but can be considered an optional ingredient here.

Mushrooms, dried black   There are several varieties of dried mushrooms, ranging from dark brown to black and differing in size and thickness, which determine their price. Sold in Chinese groceries in 4- and 5-ounce plastic bags, they will keep indefinitely. Before being used, they must be soaked in warm water for 15 to 30 minutes, depending on size. The best grade should be reserved for dishes in which the mushrooms are cooked whole; the less expensive, for recipes calling for slicing or quartering. Store in tightly covered tins or plastic containers.

Mushrooms, golden   Available in cans. These are a very delicate, long-stemmed, tiny-capped variety.

Mushrooms, straw or grass   Tall, thin mushrooms, available dried or canned in Chinese groceries. The dried variety is crispy in texture, while the canned is smooth and delicate. The dried variety, stored in a covered jar, will keep indefinitely. It must be soaked before using. Once opened, the canned variety will keep for 2 to 3 days in the refrigerator, stored in a covered jar filled with fresh water.

Mustard green, dried   Not to be confused with mustard green preserved in brine or dried *pai ts'ai*. It can be purchased in Chinese groceries and comes in plastic bags either whole or in small pieces. Excellent in soups, with steamed pork or with slow-braised fresh pork.

Mustard green, fresh   A cabbagelike plant with heavy green stalks and dark green leaves. The stalks are especially delicious in soups or stir-fried with meats and poultry. They will keep for a week, wrapped in plastic wrap and stored in the vegetable compartment of the refrigerator.

Mustard green, preserved   Like sauerkraut, which it resembles in flavor, it must be thoroughly washed and the salty liquid squeezed out before slicing. Comes in 1-pound cans in Chinese groceries. Once opened, the contents should be stored in a jar in the refrigerator. Keep up to 1 week.

Noodles, fresh egg   Buy at Chinese groceries, bakeries or noodle shops. They are preferable to dried noodles and can sometimes be purchased frozen. Every 1/2 pound of fresh noodles requires about 1-1/2 quarts of boiling water. For dried noodles, follow cooking instructions on the package. A teaspoon of oil in the cooking water helps keep the noodles from sticking together.

Oil, hot pepper   A very fiery condiment popular in Southwestern cooking which is used in seasonings and dips. To make it, fry 5 dried chili peppers in 1/2 cup vegetable oil over medium heat until they turn dark. Use a fan to eliminate the fumes. Discard the peppers and strain the oil. Add 1 or 2 drops of red food color if the oil is not red. If it tastes too hot, add more oil. Store in a bottle with a tight stopper. An eyedropper is useful for dispensing it.

Oil, sesame   Should be purchased at an Oriental food store not in large amounts but in 6-ounce bottles, as it turns rancid in a few months. Chinese sesame oil, as compared to the lighter Middle Eastern variety, has a distinctive flavor and fragrance and is dark amber in color. Sesame oil is used in seasonings and marinades, and is often sprinkled over dishes just before serving. It need not be refrigerated.

Oil, corn   Used for 95 percent of all Chinese dishes in this book. Corn oil is preferred because it has little or no flavor of its own. In all methods of cooking, including deep-frying, fresh oil is recommended. Peanut oil may be clarified and reused; however, repeated reuse of any oil alters the smoking point and makes it more difficult to estimate and control temperature.

Oyster sauce   A unique sauce concocted by the inventive Cantonese. Fresh oysters, soy sauce, salt and seasonings are slowly cooked until a thick concentrate is formed. It is then strained, bottled and cured. Oyster sauce enriches and blends flavors, imparting a smooth, velvety texture to sauces. Available at Chinese groceries in 8-ounce bottles, it keeps for long periods if stored in the refrigerator.

Pai ts'ai (white vegetable)   A tall, white, many-stalked vegetable with dark green leaves which is popular throughout much of China; called *bok choy* in Cantonese. It is stir-fried with meats, poultry and seafoods and is often found in soups. *pai ts'ai* hearts are used for dishes requiring the tenderest of vegetables (outer leaves may be removed, leaving only the inner heart—reserve the outer leaves for other uses). If not used immediately, trim, wash and wrap in plastic and store in the vegetable compartment of the refrigerator. Dried *pai ts'ai* is used in braised dishes and long-simmered soups.

Parsley, Chinese (coriander)   Widely used in Chinese dishes, this herb imparts a very pungent flavor. It is the same as Italian parsley (cilantro). Available most of the year in Chinese groceries, it is grown from the coriander seed found on the spice shelf in local supermarkets, and can be cultivated in pots at home. Store the fresh sprigs with stems immersed in water in a tall jar in the refrigerator, the leaves covered with plastic wrap.

Peanuts   Introduced to China by the Portuguese in the sixteenth century. Crushed lightly, they are used as a garnish, in fillings, and with braised meats. The raw unroasted variety can be found in Chinese markets, but the kind you buy in jars and tins in supermarkets are easier to use and just as satisfactory.

Pepper, flower (fagara or Szech'uan)   A pungent reddish-brown peppercorn sold loose or in 1-ounce plastic bags in Chinese groceries; used in marinades, seasonings and coatings. As a dip, flower pepper is crushed with a mortar and pestle and lightly pan-toasted (without oil) with a double portion of kosher salt until fragrant. Be careful not to burn the mixture.

Peppers, fresh chili   These little red-hot chili peppers, used frequently in Southwestern cooking, are extremely hot. In removing the seeds and membrane before using, be careful not to touch your eyes or face, and wash your fingers thoroughly afterward. The dried variety can be used interchangeably.

Pepper, black   Whole black peppercorns freshly ground in a peppermill are frequently used in seasonings and dips. For a dip, lightly toast in a pan (without oil) 1 part ground peppercorn to 2 parts kosher salt until fragrant. Be careful not to burn the mixture.

Pork   The universal favorite of the Chinese (with the exception of the Chinese Moslems, who do not eat it). First-quality pork butt with plenty of lean red meat and a layer of crisp white fat on the outside is desirable. The butt may be cut up at home and any unused portion frozen for later use.

Pork, five flower (fresh bacon or pork belly)   Similar to salt pork except that it is unsalted. Not widely available, it usually must be ordered from the butcher. Specify that the rind be left on as required in these recipes. Fresh bacon is well seasoned and cooked in several ways, such as steaming, deep-frying and braising. These methods help break down the fat, leaving a delicious, gelatinous mass much relished by the Chinese. Su Tung Po Pork (p. 116) is a classic example.

Pork steak   A good substitute for a whole pork butt for those who do not do a great deal of Chinese cooking. It must be of the best lean quality with some white fat on the edges. Allow extra weight for bones.

Quail eggs   Miniature eggs the size of a quarter come about twelve per can. They can be purchased at Chinese groceries and are used in soups and noodle dishes primarily as garnish.

Rakkyo   Pickled green onions available in Japanese groceries in small jars. Only the white bulbs are pickled in vinegar, sugar and garlic. Delicious in sweet-and-sour dishes or served as a condiment. Covered tightly and refrigerated after opening, they will keep for many months.

Rice   Long-grained rice is best suited for Chinese food. Japanese rice is short-grained and tends to be "wetter" when cooked. Do not use instant or enriched rice. (See method for cooking rice, p. 6.)

Rice crust   Leftover layer of rice about 1 inch thick. It is intentionally left, uncovered, on the bottom and sides of the pot, and refrigerated overnight before being broken into large pieces. If the rice is not bone-dry, put the crust on a cookie sheet and bake in a 425° oven for 10 minutes, or until thoroughly dried.

Rice, glutinous (sweet rice, or mochi-gome in Japanese)   Used for fillings in steamed cakes. As a coating, it is crushed and mixed with spices, then applied to meats or cakes and deep-fried or steamed.

Rice wine   Japanese *sake* is best for Chinese cooking in American homes because it is easily available and resembles the varieties of Chinese rice wine which are difficult to obtain. A dry sherry can be substituted, in which case double the amount given for rice wine in the recipe.

Rice wine (sweet)   Also known as Japanese *mirin*, this is available in Japanese grocery stores.

Salt   Un-iodized kosher salt is recommended for all recipes. It is lighter and has a clearer, less chemical taste.

Rock sugar   Available in Chinese grocery stores, but quite expensive. Granulated sugar is an adequate substitute.

Sesame oil   See oil, sesame.

Sesame paste   Crushed sesame seeds in oil. Used as a seasoning, it is often referred to as sesame buter. It is available in small jars; refrigerated, it keeps for long periods.

Sesame seeds   Available in white or black varieties in supermarkets. If white seeds turn gray, it indicates they are rancid. Do not buy in large quantities. Store in a tightly capped dark bottle in a cool, dark place. To toast the seeds, place in a dry pan over medium heat and shake the pan until they are golden and begin to pop. Be careful not to burn them.

Shrimp   Fresh green jumbo shrimp of finest quality (about 14 per pound) are best for stir-fried and deep-fried dishes. Medium-sized shrimp, about 20 per pound, are appropriate for dishes requiring mincing, i.e., for shrimp paste, fillings or shrimp meatballs. (For instructions on cleaning and preparing shrimp for cooking see p. 9a.)

Smoke sauce   The regular variety available in supermarkets can be added to meat and poultry marinades, thus omitting the smoking process required by some Chinese dishes. Alternatively, a little of the sauce can be added to a smoking mixture of dried tangerine peel, brown sugar and tea leaves.

Snow peas   Available fresh in most Chinese and Japanese groceries the year round, although they are cheaper in season. The frozen variety now obtainable in most supermarkets should be defrosted completely before using.

Soup stock   Many Chinese recipes call for soup stock, and some designate rich stock (which means a stock made from greater quantities of meat). The quality of the stock makes a difference in the taste of a given dish. Although it is possible to use canned chicken stock or chicken bouillon cubes (beef bouillon is too heavy in flavor), your own homemade stock will add a distinctive dimension to your cooking—you can produce as good a stock as the best Chinese restaurant.

Both the bones and meat of chicken and pork are used for stock. Ham, as well as duck meat, bones and feet, are often included, and various vegetables are also added.

The basic procedure in making stock is to bring some water to a boil, add meat, bones and vegetables, making sure there is enough water to cover them, and reduce the heat to let the stock simmer for about 4 hours. Sediment that rises to the top of the liquid is skimmed off. Should more liquid be needed to keep the solid ingredients immersed, boiling water is added. When done, the stock is filtered through cheesecloth and cooled. After cooling, the excess fat which solidifies on top is removed. Some cookbooks advise that the water be cold when the ingredients are put in, but the method specified here follows the Chinese practice and yields the desired results.

For home use it is usually most convenient to make a large amount of stock and then transfer it to small, uncapped plastic containers, which can be put into the freezer. Then when stock is needed, one or more of the containers can be thawed out.

To make 10 cups of stock, use 1 1/2 pounds of chicken bones and meat, 3 pounds of pork bones and meat and 1 1/2 pounds of ham bones and duck feet to 1 gallon of boiling water.

Soy sauce Comes in two basic forms, thin and thick. Both are made from fermented soy beans added to salted water and then cured for periods which may extend to years. Thin soy is lighter and usually saltier than thick soy sauce, which is used more for its color and pungent flavor. There are many brands of both thin and thick soy sauce and the serious cook will sample as many as possible and then carefully consider the types of dishes each will enhance. Barbecued spareribs call for a dark, thick soy, whereas a bean curd dish could be done with a blander thick soy or with a salty, golden-brown thin soy.

Most soy sauces come from Japan or Hong Kong, but we can look forward to the time when mainland China products are available, especially those from Fukien Province which is said to produce the best. Japanese soy, which is thin, is good for dipping but can be too sweet for some dishes.

Soy sauces come in dark bottles, ranging from 12 to 21 ounces, which can be stored outside the refrigerator, tightly capped.

Soy, red Used as a dip for meats, poultry and steamed cakes and rolls; 1/4 cup brown sugar, 1/4 cup thin soy, a small stick of cinnamon and 3 star anise are slowly simmered over very low heat until the cinnamon flavor is absorbed into the soy and sugar. A few drops of sesame oil may be added.

Spring roll skins (ready-made) Not to be confused with egg roll skins, these are available in both round and square shapes, 10 to 25 skins to a package in Chinese groceries. Wrapped in plastic and then foil, they will keep 3 to 4 days in the refrigerator without drying out.

Spinach, Chinese Less acid than the Western variety, with a lovely cress-like flavor, it is available in season in most large Chinese groceries. Delicious stir-fried in oil, salt and garlic, and in soups. Watercress is an adequate substitute.

Shark's fin Threadlike pieces of dried cartilage from a shark's fin, believed to be very nutritious—high in protein and trace minerals. They are very expensive, the price varying according to the length and thickness of the fins. Stored in covered tins, they will keep indefinitely without refrigeration. Instant shark's fin is an improvement over traditional fins because it shortens cooking techniques and time. Both are available in Chinese groceries.

Sugar White, brown, rock, malt (liquefied) sugars and caramelized sugar are all widely used in small amounts of Chinese cooking.

Caramelized sugar is used as a base for sauces, especially sweet-and-sour sauces. It is made by wiping a little oil on a small frying pan, heating it, adding white sugar and cooking it until it melts and turns golden-brown. Removed immediately to prevent burning, a little hot water is added to thin out the melted sugar.

Rock sugar is preferred for braised meats and poultry, since it gives the skin a glossy dark red color; however, granulated sugar is an adequate substitute. Malt sugar is used to coat Peking duck. Both sugars are available in Chinese groceries.

Turnip, preserved (*cha ts'ai*) Preserved in a hot brine and chili and available in 1-pound cans or 8-ounce plastic bags at Chinese groceries. It is sliced thin or minced and steamed with pork and seasonings or used in fillings. It is also used in soups and stir-fried with pork or beef.

Vermicelli Sold in long packages. There are two types of vermicelli: the pea noodles, made from mung bean flour; and the rice noodles, made from rice flour. Both are semitranslucent and brittle. The recipes in this book call for the rice vermicelli. It can be stir-fried, steamed or deep-fried (when deep-fried, it puffs up into a white cloudlike mass). It must be presoaked for stir-fried or steamed dishes. It is best stored in large tins, and will keep indefinitely.

Vinegar Three vinegars are used: Chinese red vinegar, a mild vinegar made from rice, is most frequently used in flavoring sauces and as a dip. It comes in bottles and should be stored in a dark, cool place. It lasts for a long time. Dark vinegar is sweet in taste and is used mostly for dips. White vinegar, available at any grocery, is used in sweet-sour dishes and in dishes where a sharp flavor is needed.

Water chestnuts A crisp fresh-water plant which grows in the many lakes and ponds of China. The fresh variety can occasionally be found in season at larger Chinese groceries. The rough, outer skin must be peeled; the inside flesh is crisp, sweet and slightly starchy. The canned variety is a good substitute. Store in water in a covered jar and refrigerate. The water must be changed daily. If a film develops or chestnuts turn color, discard them. Do not keep more than 4 to 5 days.

Water chestnut flour   The dried and pulverized flour of the water chestnut. It is excellent for coatings and when deep-fried, it turns very crisp, much more so than other coatings. It can also be substituted for cornstarch as a thickening agent. Available in Chinese groceries in 1-pound bags.

Watercress, fresh   Available in little bunches at most grocers in season. It is used in soup, in stir-fried dishes, as a garnish and in making a bed on serving platters.

Wines for Chinese cooking:

1. Grape: used in few dishes, and generally in those of Moslem origin.
2. *Mirin* (Japanese): a light-colored, heavy sweet wine made from glutinous rice. Used in marinades, seasonings and dips.
3. *Sake* (Japanese): a light-colored, dry rice wine. It most closely resembles the Shaohsing wine used in China.
4. Sherry (dry): a possible substitute for *sake*, although it has a musty or nutty flavor which tends to mask some ingredients as *sake* does not. Also, the volume must be increased to 50 percent more sherry than *sake*.

All these wines are available at any large liquor store. The *mirin* may also be purchased from a Japanese grocer.

Wine lees   A thick paste of fermented rice wine mash sometimes available in Chinese groceries. It is used in seasonings, marinades and sauces. Because this ingredient is difficult to find, Japanese light *miso* may be used as a substitute. Store in a covered jar and refrigerate.

Winter melon   A large squash with a light green rind, white flesh and a center core of seeds which should be removed before the melon is cooked. It is available whole or in slices by the pound at Chinese and Japanese groceries. Wrapped in plastic wrap, it will keep for a week in the refrigerator.

Won ton skins (ready-made)   Not to be confused with spring roll skins, these come either round or square, generally in 1-pound packages available at Chinese groceries. Tightly wrapped in plastic, they will keep 3 to 4 days in the refrigerator.

Wood ear   A dark brown variety of tree lichen that appears crinkled. Wood ear grown on coniferous trees are much prized. Rich in trace minerals, the lichen must be soaked before using. Relished for its crunchy texture, it is available in 2-ounce bags in Chinese groceries. Stored in a covered jar, it will keep indefinitely.

Zucchini   Principally stir-fried with meats and poultry. It can be used as a substitute for cucumbers, but requires more cooking time.

The
NORTH

Northern-style cooking may be classified into regional dishes (which largely represent the provinces of Hopei, Honan and Shantung), palace dishes (which were served at the court in Peking), Moslem dishes and Mongolian dishes.

Regional dishes are rich in the varieties of materials used. Shantung Province has a long coastline yielding abundant crab, shrimp, shellfish and other seafoods. High up in the cliffs along its peninsular coast the precious swallow's nest is harvested for bird's nest soup. In Hopei and Honan provinces, pisciculture has been developed under the People's Republic to such an extent that enormous quantities of fresh-water fish are available from ponds and underwater fields. Flood-control and afforestation programs have transformed Shantung and Honan into rich farmlands producing excellent-quality vegetables, fruits and nuts, as well as poultry and meats.

Shantung cooking is considered the *haute cuisine* of Chinese cooking. Its chefs were the primary chefs at court and in the finest restaurants in Peking, and their influence extended to the eastern cities of Shanghai, Nanking, Suchou and Hangchou.

There are two main styles of Shantung cooking: the Chinan style (Chinan is the provincial capital located in central Shantung); and the Chiaotung style, from the Shantung peninsula region. The Chinan style is characterized by dishes often served with delicate cream sauces or stir-fried with vegetables, crab, shrimp, chicken or meatballs. The Chiaotung style often resembles the Eastern school of cooking (i.e., Shanghai, Suchou, Hangchou and Nanking). This is probably due to their geographical proximity.

Honan Province is famous for Bear's Paw (p. 231) an ancient and unusual dish which was reputed to have been the favorite of Mencius; Hopei Province for its stuffed pancakes and rolls.

The palace dishes are in a category of their own. They originated in various parts of China, were selected and introduced into the imperial kitchens, and were there developed and refined. Others were created by palace chefs, often to cater to the taste of the ruler or to complement some court activity; when tested at the imperial table and favorably commented upon, they joined the ranks of hundreds of other palace dishes. During the last days of the Ch'ing dynasty the life style of the imperial palace was sybaritic and cooking was a large enterprise. There were separate kitchens for the preparation of dinners, teas and picnics. Each kitchen had an individual department for the preparation of meats, vegetables, pastries and rice. There was even a special department which prepared nothing but roast pig and Peking duck. It is said that there were more than three hundred cooks and helpers employed.

Moslem communities exist in virtually every major Chinese city, but the main concentration of the Moslem population is found in the north. Since Moslems do not eat pork, many dishes from the North are based on beef, lamb, poultry and seafood.

The most popular Mongolian dishes are the *Huo Kuo,* or Hot Pot (p. 97) and Mongolian Barbecue (pp. 99–101). Both probably originated somewhere in the northwestern steppes of Asia from which nomadic tribesmen made repeated invasions into China.

NORTHERN RESTAURANTS

In 1925 a restaurant in Pei Hai (North Sea) Park was opened. A number of former palace chefs came out of retirement to join its staff. As they served the same elegant dishes that they had prepared at the palace, the restaurant was named Fang Shan (Imperial-Style Meals). Its offerings range from the simple palace-style stir-fried soft bean curd to the elegant ocean red shark's fin. The Sha Kuo Chu (House of the Earthen Casserole), which opened in 1741, is famous for its large earthen pot, over 4 feet in diameter, in which pork is cooked. During the Ch'ing dynasty pigs were sacrificed to observe the advent of dawn and dusk. Palace watchmen, to whom the slaughtered pigs were given, joined with cooks from the palace kitchens to open a restaurant featuring pork dishes.

Four Moslem restaurants have contributed to this collection. They serve beef and lamb but, of course, not pork. The Yu Yi Shun (Smooth Going Once More) was the favorite of the Dalai and Banchan Lamas when they visited Peking. Its steamed and braised lamb dishes are outstanding. The Hung Ping Lou (Distinguished Guest Pavilion) opened in Tientsin in 1899 and moved to Peking in 1955. The flavor of its older dishes can be appreciated in Hsi Shih's breast in red sauce. The other restaurants are the

Tung En Yuan Chu (Most Gracious Eastern House) and the Moslem Dining Hall.

Shantung cooking is offered by three restaurants, the Ch'un Yuan Lou (Spring Garden Pavilion), the Feng Tze Yuan (Garden of Enrichment) and the Ts'ui Hua Lou (Pavilion of Collected Delicacies), which was highly praised by the Russians when they were welcome in China.

The Yu Hua (Jade Blossom) Dining Hall, though dating back only to 1950, has already earned a notable reputation. Dishes like juicy stuffed rolls indicate why this is so. The Tung Lai Shun (Eastern Prosperity) is perhaps the oldest and best-known Peking restaurant featuring hot pot, the dish that provided the steppes nomads with a complete meal from the ingredients on hand—mutton, spices, herbs, dried vegetables and pot-grown green onions. Another specialty, mongolian barbecue, is prepared by the Barbecue Wan Restaurant. The Peking Hotel Restaurant has contributed dishes for all sections of this cookbook, since its kitchen has chefs specializing in the cooking of virtually all regions of China.

Of the eight great *ch'un* restaurants (that is, restaurants with the word "spring" in their names) famous in the Peking of the 1930s, only one is still open, the T'ung Ch'un Yuan (Spring Garden). Originally, there were also eight Peking restaurants with the word *chu* (house) in their names. Three still remain, two of which have already been mentioned. The third is T'ung Ho Chu (House of Harmony).

Other contributing establishments include the Chu Feng Te (Bountiful Virtue) Meal Shop, and several relatively new dining halls—the Cooperative Dining Hall of Tsingtao, Shantung, the Service Bureau of Peking and the Shantung Bureau of Commerce.

Finally, a number of dishes were originated by well-known chefs and are associated with them more than with restaurants. Among these are Chef Liu Yung Ch'uang, whose forte is dishes requiring precise judgment of timing and temperature; Chef Chao Ch'ang Pin, whose pork with almonds is a classic, and Chef Wang Wen Ch'i. Also represented is Chef Yuan Ch'ao Yin, who specializes in Shantung dishes and adheres to old cooking methods. He has the distinction of having his dishes referred to as "dishes by Yuan."

SWEET ALMOND SOUP

An unusual, rich, sweet soup that can also be served as a dessert. A favorite in Peking, it is typical of the *haute cuisine* of the North. Chilled and garnished with fruit, it is an excellent summer soup. It may be served hot or cold.

2 cups almonds
1/2 cup sugar
1/2 teaspoon salt
1/2 teaspoon vanilla
5 tablespoons water mixed
   with 2-1/2 tablespoons
   cornstarch

1/2 cup cream or half-and-
   half
2 tablespoons finely slivered
   glacéed apricots, lemon
   peel or dried Chinese
   dates

Boil a pot of water and add the almonds. Turn off the heat and allow to cool. Remove almond skins and dry with paper towels. Place the almonds on a cookie sheet in a 200° preheated oven for 5 minutes, or until thoroughly dried. (Do not allow the almonds to turn color; they must remain white.) Place the almonds in a blender and blend evenly into a fine powder.

In a large pan, boil 6 cups water. Add sugar, salt and vanilla, and stir to dissolve the sugar. Sprinkle in the almond powder and whisk until smooth. Slowly add the cornstarch mixture and stir until the soup thickens. Turn off the heat. Add cream and stir.

To serve, pour the soup into a heated tureen or large bowl and garnish with slivered fruit.

If the soup is to be served cold, chill it in the refrigerator before serving. Serves 5–6.

VINEGAR AND PEPPER FISH CHOWDER

This unusual Shantung chowder, often served at banquets, makes a beautiful presentation with a whole fish served in a delicious broth.

1-1/2 pounds whole fish
(scrod, bass or pike is
good)
Vegetable oil for deep-frying
plus 3 tablespoons
1 teaspoon grated fresh
ginger
1 teaspoon white pepper
1 tablespoon rice wine
3/4 teaspoon salt

6 cups Chinese stock (p. 30)
1/4 cup slivered green onion
(cut onions in half lengthwise and slice diagonally
into 1/2-inch sections)
2 teaspoons chopped Chinese
parsley
5 tablespoons white vinegar
1/2 teaspoon sesame oil

Scale and clean the fish, retaining the head and tail. Wash it thoroughly. Put it in a deep, heavy pot and gently pour in enough boiling hot water to cover it completely. Let stand for 1 minute. Carefully pour out the hot water without disturbing the fish and pour cold water over it. Gently remove the fish from the pan and peel off all the skin. Make several diagonal slashes down to the bone on both sides of the fish. Dry thoroughly with paper towels.

In a large wok, heat 3 inches oil to 350°. Lower the fish into the oil and fry for about 5 minutes on each side or until well browned. Carefully remove the fish and drain. Cool the wok, pour the oil out into a can and wash the wok.

Add 3 tablespoons fresh oil to the wok. Heat the oil until it smokes, and add ginger, pepper, wine, salt and chicken stock. Gently place the fish in the wok. When the broth starts boiling, turn the heat to low and gently simmer for 30 minutes, keeping the fish intact.

Add the green onions, parsley and vinegar. Transfer the fish (carefully, to avoid breaking it up) to a serving bowl or tureen. Add the broth slowly, and sprinkle with sesame oil.

Serves 4.

SHRIMP SWIMMING
IN CREAMY CHICKEN BROTH

This is a Shantung-style soup—a favorite banquet dish in Peking.

Chicken cream
  1 egg white
  1 teaspoon water mixed
    with 1/2 teaspoon corn-
    starch
  1/2 cup minced chicken
    breast
Meatballs
  3/4 pound shrimp
  1 egg white
  1/4 pound pork meat,
    minced
  1/2 teaspoon minced fresh
    ginger

3/4 teaspoon salt
1 teaspoon rice wine
4 drops sesame oil
2 teaspoons water mixed
  with 1 teaspoon corn-
  starch
6 cups chicken stock
1 teaspoon rice wine
1/2 teaspoon salt
1/8 pound lean ham, slivered
1/2 cup trimmed watercress

To make chicken cream, beat the egg white with the cornstarch mixture. When foamy but not stiff, add to the minced chicken and mix well.

To make meatballs, shell, devein and wash shrimp. Mince very fine, almost to a paste. In a bowl, beat the egg white until foamy. Mix in the shrimp and pork. Then add the remaining meatball ingredients, mix well and form into balls 1 inch in diameter.

Put the chicken stock in a large pan over high heat and bring to a rapid boil. Remove from heat. Carefully drop the meatballs into the broth. While adding the meatballs skim off the sediment rising to top of the broth.

When all the meatballs are in the broth and it has been cleared, return the pan to low heat. Add wine and salt. Correct the salt seasoning to taste. Turn up the heat and bring to a boil. Add the chicken cream, breaking it up so that it does not stick together in a mass. Stir a few times, transfer to a tureen and garnish with ham and watercress.

Serves 4.

SHRIMP TOAST

Dip
  1 tablespoon flower pepper
  1 tablespoon kosher salt
  1 tablespoon black or white
    sesame seeds
Shrimp paste
  1/2 cup minced shrimp
  1/4 cup minced pork butt
  4 water chestnuts, minced
  1 egg white
  2 tablespoons cornstarch
  1/2 teaspoon rice wine

1/2 teaspoon salt
1 teaspoon finely grated
  fresh ginger
2 tablespoons minced green
  onion
6 slices white sandwich-type
  bread
2 tablespoons minced ham
1 tablespoon minced Chinese
  or regular parsley
Vegetable oil for frying and
  deep-frying

In a dry pan, lightly fry flower pepper and salt until salt is lightly browned and pepper becomes fragrant. Crush together in a mortar with a pestle.

In a dry pan, toast sesame seeds for about 1/2 minute, or until they begin to pop. Set aside.

Mix all shrimp paste ingredients together to form a thick paste.

Remove crusts and cut the slices of bread into 1-1/2-inch squares. Spread the shrimp mixture about 1/4 inch thick on the bread squares and press down firmly. Put the ham and parsley on top of the shrimp mixture and press down lightly.

In a deep-frying pan, heat 2 inches oil to about 350° (use a candy thermometer). Carefully put the squares, shrimp side down, in the pan and fry for 1 to 2 minutes. The paste will become puffy. Turn the squares over and fry for another 1 to 2 minutes. When the squares are golden and thick, remove and drain on paper towels. Sprinkle sesame seeds on top and serve on a heated platter with the dip on the side.

Makes about 36 squares.

KUEI FEI CHICKEN

This famous dish, which might be considered the Chinese version of chicken in wine, was named for Yang Kuei Fei, a court lady of the T'ang dynasty whose beauty is widely cited in Chinese history and legend.

8 green onions
6 dried Chinese dates (soaked
  overnight in water)
Marinade
  1/2 cup thin soy sauce
  6 tablespoons rice wine
  2 teaspoons honey
1 3-1/2-pound frying chicken
1/4 cup cornstarch
1/2 cup water chestnut flour
Vegetable oil for deep-frying
  plus 1 tablespoon

2 cloves garlic, minced
7 cups chicken stock
1/4 cup thin soy sauce
1/4 cup rice wine
1-1/2 teaspoons white vinegar
1 olive-sized piece rock sugar
1/2 teaspoon salt
3 tablespoons red wine
6 water chestnuts, minced

Wash, trim and slice green onions lengthwise in half, then cut them crosswise into 2-inch sections. Wash dates.

Combine the marinade ingredients.

Cut the chicken into serving pieces, and wash and dry them. Place in a bowl with the marinade and rub the marinade all over them. Let stand 10 minutes and drain.

Mix the cornstarch and water chestnut flour and sprinkle over the chicken pieces to coat well.

Heat 3 inches oil to about 375° in a deep frying pan. Deep-fry the chicken pieces until golden-brown. Remove and drain.

Heat 1 tablespoon oil in a stove-top casserole large enough to hold the chicken pieces. Add garlic and green onion, stir-fry 1/2 minute. Put in the chicken pieces, stock, soy sauce, rice wine, vinegar, rock sugar and salt. Bring to a boil, turn down the heat and simmer for 15 minutes, turning the chicken pieces occasionally. Add dates and simmer for 30 minutes more. Add more stock if needed to keep the chicken from sticking to the casserole. The chicken should be tender and the sauce moderately thickened.

Stir in the red wine and sprinkle minced water chestnuts on top.
Serves 4–5.

BRAISED CHICKEN WITH CHESTNUTS

1-1/2 cups fresh chestnuts
5 dried black mushrooms
1/4 cup sliced blanched almonds
1 teaspoon vegetable oil
Marinade
2 tablespoons thin soy
sauce
1 teaspoon grated fresh
ginger
1 tablespoon rice wine
Seasoning mixture
2 tablespoons thin soy
sauce

2 tablespoons rice wine
2 tablespoons sugar
4 cups water
1 tablespoon dragon's eye
(dried longan fruit)
Thickening mixture
1 tablespoon cornstarch
1-1/2 tablespoons water
1 teaspoon thick soy sauce
1/2 teaspoon MSG
3 pounds whole chicken or
chicken parts
Vegetable oil for deep-frying
7 water chestnuts, sliced

Place the chestnuts on a cookie sheet and put them in the oven (preheated to 350°) for 15 to 20 minutes, or until they begin to pop. Cool, and with a sharp paring knife, carefully make a small cut through the skin and remove the outer shells and inner skins. Set aside.

Soak mushrooms in hot water for 15 minutes. Rinse, squeeze out the water, remove the stems and quarter the caps. Add oil to a pan, fry the almonds and drain them on paper towels. Combine the ingredients for the marinade and for the seasoning and thickening mixtures. Wash and dry the chicken, and remove the skin. With a cleaver, cut the chicken into pieces about 2 inches long and marinate for 10 minutes.

Heat about 3 inches oil to 350° in a deep, heavy pot or deep-fryer. Add the chicken pieces in batches and deep-fry until browned.

Put the chicken pieces in a wok and add the seasoning mixture. Bring to a boil, lower the heat and gently braise for 20 minutes. Skim off the excess fat on top.

Add the chestnuts and mushrooms and gently braise for another 10 minutes, being careful not to let the chestnuts crumble. Add the water chestnuts and stir a few times. Add the thickening mixture and stir until the sauce becomes thick. Transfer to a heated platter and garnish with the almonds.

Serves 4.

CHICKEN CUBES WITH SOY SAUCE

This dish is served in a Peking restaurant that features Shanghai cooking. It was created by a chef who went to Russia in 1953 to supervise the cooking in the Dining Hall at the Chinese Agricultural Exhibit and was highly praised by the Russians.

Vegetable oil for frying, deep-frying and braising
1/4 cup shelled walnuts or hazelnuts
5 tablespoons sugar
Several pieces of fresh ginger
1/2 cup green onion (cut in half lengthwise and sliced diagonally into 1/2-inch sections)

1/2 teaspoon salt
1-1/2 cups chicken breast (skinned and boned)
2 egg whites
2 tablespoons cornstarch
3 tablespoons thin soy sauce
1 tablespoon rice wine

Put 1/2 inch vegetable oil in a small frying pan and heat to about 350°. Add nuts and toss with a fork for about 1 minute. Remove, drain and chop coarsely.

Coat a small frying pan with 1 tablespoon oil. Add 4 tablespoons of the sugar and heat over moderate heat. Stir occasionally. When the sugar melts and starts to turn golden, immediately remove from heat. Let cool and mix in a little water so that the sugar liquefies.

Peel several pieces of fresh ginger, place in a garlic press and squeeze out 2 teaspoons juice.

Add salt to 5 cups cold water and soak chicken for 1 hour. With the flat side of a cleaver, gently pound it to press out all water. Dry well with paper towels. Cut into pieces about 1 inch by 1 inch by 1/2 inch.

Beat egg whites until fluffy but not too stiff. Carefully fold in the cornstarch and mix well. Dip the chicken cubes in the mixture, coating well.

Put about 2 inches oil in a wok or deep pot and heat to 350°. Add half the chicken cubes, stirring to keep them apart. Scoop cubes out after 2 minutes and drain well. Maintaining correct temperature, repeat for the other half.

Add 1/4 cup oil to a wok and place over high heat. Add 3 tablespoons soy sauce and listen for the crackle as the water content of the soy sauce decreases. Turn heat down and add 1 tablespoon sugar, wine, ginger juice and caramelized sugar. Stir until a paste forms. Add chicken cubes and stir-fry for about 5 seconds. Turn up heat for a moment and add the green onion. Stir a few times, enough to coat everything. Remove from heat and garnish with the chopped nuts.

Serves 2.

CHICKEN FU YUNG
IN SAUCE SHANTUNG STYLE

1/2 pound boned chicken breast
1/2 pound fish fillets
4 water chestnuts, minced
2 teaspoons minced green onion
1 teaspoon grated fresh ginger
1/2 teaspoon MSG
1-1/2 teaspoons salt
4 teaspoons cornstarch

5 egg whites
3 cups Chinese stock (p. 30)
2 tablespoons water mixed with 1 tablespoon cornstarch
Vegetable oil for deep-frying
1/2 cup slivered green onion (cut in half lengthwise and slice diagonally into 1/2-inch sections)

Mince the chicken breast and fish fillets. Then on a board, with the back edge of a cleaver or other pounding instrument, smash the chicken into a paste. Alternatively, put the chicken through a meat grinder or food processor.

In a bowl, mix the chicken, fish, water chestnuts and minced green onion. Add ginger, MSG, 1 teaspoon salt, and cornstarch and mix well.

Beat egg whites until almost stiff and fold gently into the meat mixture and blend well.

Bring stock to a boil, add 1/2 teaspoon salt and the cornstarch mixture. Stir well until the sauce thickens. Remove from heat and set aside.

In a deep-frying pan, heat 2 inches oil to 350°. Drop the meat-and-egg-white mixture by tablespoonfuls into the hot oil. When fritters float up to the surface, turn each over and fry another 10 seconds.

Remove the pan from heat. Scoop out the fritters and drop them directly into the sauce. Bring to a boil and transfer to a large heated serving bowl. Garnish with the green onion.

Serves 2–3.

RICE CRUST
WITH CHICKEN AND MUSHROOMS

An exceptional dish using a vegetable-and-meat mixture in a slightly hot and sour sauce, along with deep-fried rice crusts. The two are brought to the table sizzling hot and the ceremonial fusion of the two portions is most impressive.

5 dried mushrooms
1 cup canned bamboo shoots, washed and drained
3 cups (packed) dried rice crusts
1 pound chicken breast
Marinade
  1 teaspoon cornstarch
  1 teaspoon rice wine
  1/4 teaspoon salt
  2 teaspoons water
  Pinch of sugar
Seasoning mixture
  2-1/2 tablespoons rice wine
  2-1/2 tablespoons thin soy sauce
  1-1/2 tablespoons Chinese red vinegar
  1-1/2 tablespoons sugar
  1 teaspoon salt

1/4 teaspoon (or to taste) cayenne
1-3/4 cups Chinese stock (pp. 30–31)
Vegetable oil for deep frying plus 3 tablespoons
1 large garlic clove, peeled and crushed
1 cup canned straw mushrooms or canned golden mushrooms, washed and drained
1/3 cup slivered green onion (cut in half lengthwise and slice diagonally into 1/2-inch sections)
2 tablespoons water mixed with 1 tablespoon cornstarch

Soak dried mushrooms in boiling water for 15 minutes. Rinse, squeeze out the water, remove the stems and quarter the caps. Slice bamboo shoots into strips 2 inches by 1/8 inch by 1/8 inch.

Put rice crusts on a cookie sheet in 450° oven for 10 minutes to dry them out.

Slice chicken into strips 2-1/2 inches by 1/8 inch by 1/8 inch.

Combine the ingredients for the marinade and marinate the chicken in it for at least 15 minutes.

Combine the ingredients for the seasoning mixture.

Heat about 3 inches oil to 350° in a deep, heavy pot or deep-fryer. Add the chunks of rice crust. Deep-fry them for 3 to 5 minutes, or until they rise, puffy white, to the surface. Keep oil temperature constant during the entire process. Transfer the rice crusts with a slotted spoon to a very hot large bowl (preheated in the oven). Pour 1 tablespoon of the deep-frying oil over the crusts.

Heat a wok over very high heat. When it becomes very hot, add 3 tablespoons oil, followed by the garlic clove. After 5 seconds, remove and discard the garlic. Quickly add chicken and stir-fry for 1 minute, pressing it down against the sides of the wok with a spatula. Add both kinds of mushrooms and the bamboo shoots. Stir-fry for another minute. Add the seasoning mixture and cover for 1 minute, or until bubbling hot. Remove the cover, add the cornstarch mixture, and stir until thickened. Transfer to another very hot bowl.

Using pot holders to avoid being burned, quickly bring both hot bowls, containing the rice crusts and the meat-and-vegetable mixture, to the table and combine their contents—there should be a hissing sound. Garnish with slivered onion.

Serves 3.

NOTE: The two different portions of this recipe—the rice crusts and the meat-and-vegetable mixture—must be very hot when mixed together in order to produce the ceremonial hissing sound at the table. Be sure to have all ingredients ready, including the heated bowls, before the cooking begins. The rice crusts should be deep-frying while the meat and vegetables are being stir-fried—cooking should be as fast as possible.

SESAME SEED MEATBALLS

1/2 pound boneless pork butt	1 teaspoon sesame oil
2 tablespoons rice wine	1/3 cup white sesame seeds
1/2 teaspoon thin soy sauce	Vegetable oil for deep-frying
1/2 teaspoon salt	1 cup sugar
1 to 2 tablespoons cornstarch	1 cup shredded lettuce

Mince pork with a cleaver, or put through a meat grinder or food processor, until it is almost a paste. Place the pork in a bowl, add wine, soy sauce and salt and mix well. Sprinkle 1 tablespoon cornstarch over the paste and mix. Add sesame oil and mix again. The mixture should hold together well; if not, add extra cornstarch to bind. Form meatballs about 1-1/2 inches in diameter.

Put the sesame seeds in a dry pan over low heat. They should be cooked long enough so that they become fragrant, but be careful not to burn them. When they begin to pop, remove and set aside.

Heat about 3 inches oil in a pan for deep-frying. The temperature should be about 350°. Gently drop the meatballs into the hot oil and fry for about 3 minutes so that the outside is light brown and crisp. Scoop out the meatballs and set aside to drain.

Put a thin layer of oil in a pan over low heat. Add the sugar, turn the heat up to high and stir continually. When the sugar melts and begins to bubble, immediately reduce the heat. After about 2 minutes a thread should form when a spoon is inserted and pulled away. Do not let the caramelized sugar burn or become dark and bitter from overcooking—it should be a golden color.

Take the pan off the heat and very quickly roll the meatballs with a fork or spoon in the caramelized sugar, coating them well. Immediately roll again in sesame seeds. Arrange on a platter of shredded lettuce and serve while still hot.

Serves 2.

RECOOKED LION'S HEAD

This is a variation of a traditional dish called lion's head.

Meatballs
- 1 pound lean pork butt, minced
- 1 egg, beaten
- 4 tablespoons minced green onion
- 1-1/2 teaspoons grated fresh ginger
- 2-1/2 tablespoons cornstarch
- 1 tablespoon thin soy sauce
- 1 tablespoon rice wine
- 1/2 teaspoon salt
- 2 tablespoons Chinese stock (p. 30) or chicken stock

Vegetable oil for deep-frying
- 2 cups Chinese soup stock (p. 30) or chicken stock
- 4-1/2 tablespoons sugar
- 5 tablespoons Chinese red vinegar
- Few drops of sesame oil
- 1/4 teaspoon (or to taste) cayenne
- 2 tomatoes, cut into 12 wedges
- 3 sprigs of Chinese parsley, minced

Place all meatball ingredients in a large bowl, and mix vigorously in one direction. Form into 4 large meatballs.

Heat 4 inches oil to 365° in a deep, heavy pot. Add meatballs carefully, one by one. Fry until they are well browned on the outside, about 4 to 5 minutes.

Transfer meatballs to a ceramic stove-top casserole with a cover and add stock, sugar and vinegar. When boiling begins, skim the residue off the top of the liquid. Cover the pot and simmer over very low heat for 1 hour. Add sesame oil and cayenne, and very gently simmer uncovered for another 30 minutes or until the sauce becomes thick. Stir occasionally to keep the meatballs from sticking or burning.

Add tomato wedges and carefully stir a few times with the sauce and meatballs. Garnish with parsley.

Serves 3.

MU HSU PORK

This Mu Hsu pork dish, created in the cooking classes for cooks and cooks' helpers in Shantung, is one of several versions. The wood ear (tree fungus) adds both a delicate flavor and a crunchy texture. In the United States this dish is often served with pancakes, although in China they are not used. For instructions on preparing these pancakes, see p. 64.

Marinade
  1 teaspoon rice wine
  2 teaspoons thin soy sauce
  1/2 teaspoon cornstarch
  1/2 pound boneless pork butt, cut in strips 2 inches by 1/4 by 1/4 inch
3 dried mushrooms
1-1/2 tablespoons wood ears
Seasoning mixture
  1 tablespoon rice wine
  1/2 teaspoon salt
  1-1/2 tablespoons thin soy sauce

  5 drops sesame oil
  1/4 teaspoon MSG
1/4 teaspoon salt
3 eggs
3 tablespoons vegetable oil
2 slices ginger, slivered
2 green onions, cut in half lengthwise and sliced diagonally into 1/2-inch sections
1/4 cup bamboo shoots, cut in strips 2 inches by 1/4 inch by 1/4 inch

Combine the ingredients for the marinade, mixing well. Add the pork strips and mix thoroughly—the liquid should be absorbed by the meat.

Soak dried mushrooms and wood ears separately in hot water for 15 minutes. Rinse, squeeze out the water, remove the stems and halve the caps. Squeeze the water out of the wood ears, which will have swollen considerably, and cut any large ones into several pieces.

Combine the ingredients for the seasoning mixture.

Add salt to the eggs and beat well.

Put 1 tablespoon of the oil in a wok over medium heat. When the oil is very hot, add the beaten eggs and scramble lightly. Set aside to keep warm.

Clean the wok and put it over high heat. To the hot wok, add 2 tablespoons oil, and then the ginger and pork. Stir-fry until the pork is well cooked, about 2 minutes.

Add the mushrooms, wood ears, green onion and bamboo shoots to the wok and stir-fry for 1/2 minute. Add the seasoning mixture and stir-fry for about 1 1/2 minutes so that everything is well heated. Mix in the scrambled eggs, then transfer to a platter.

Serves 3–4.

QUICK STIR-FRIED BEAN SPROUTS

A pungent bean-sprout dish which takes only a few minutes to cook. The secret is in the proper heat and timing. Everything must be ready in advance, the oil must be hot and the stir-frying done quickly.

5 cups fresh bean sprouts
Seasoning mixture
  1 teaspoon sesame oil
  1 teaspoon rice wine
  2 teaspoons thin soy sauce
  1/2 teaspoon ground black
    pepper

2 teaspoons grated fresh
  ginger
1/4 cup vegetable oil
3/4 teaspoon (or to taste) salt

Wash bean sprouts and drain well. Combine the ingredients for the seasoning mixture.

Place a wok over high heat. When very hot, add oil. Let it smoke, then add bean sprouts and stir-fry for 1/2 minute. Add the seasoning mixture and stir-fry another 1/2 minute. Sprinkle salt over the sprouts, stir once and serve.

Serves 3.

SHARK'S FIN WITH CRABMEAT

4 ounces instant shark's fin
5 cups chicken stock
2 whole green onions, trimmed
2 large slices fresh ginger, peeled
3 tablespoons rice wine
2 tablespoons oil
1/2 cup ham, finely slivered
1-1/2 tablespoons minced green onion

1 cup crabmeat, frozen or canned
1/2 teaspoon salt
1/4 teaspoon sugar
Pinch of white pepper
2 tablespoons water mixed with 1 tablespoon cornstarch
Few drops of sesame oil

Wash and soak the shark's fins overnight in cold water. The next day, rinse several times with cold water in a colander. Place the fins in a pot, add water to cover and bring to a boil. Drain and rinse again in cold water. Repeat this procedure of boiling and rinsing twice more to remove the fishy odor.

Place 2 cups stock, 1 green onion, 1 slice ginger, 1 tablespoon rice wine and the fins in a heatproof bowl and put it in a steamer. Steam vigorously for 30 minutes. Cool, discard the onion and ginger, and drain the stock (use a sieve), saving the fins. Repeat this process of steaming, using the same ingredients, once more.

After the second steaming, drain the fins and set aside. Heat the wok until very hot, add the oil, ham, green onion, crabmeat, fins, 2 tablespoons wine, salt, sugar and pepper. Stir-fry rapidly, coating all ingredients with oil and seasonings, about 2 minutes. Lower the heat.

Add 3 cups stock and braise gently until about 1/4 cup liquid is left. Adjust salt to taste. Add cornstarch mixture and stir until thickened. Sprinkle with a little sesame oil.

Serves 3–4.

SWEET AND SOUR JUMBO SHRIMP

The secret of the unusual flavor of the sauce in this dish lies in the manner in which the sugar and vinegar are introduced. Success depends on having all ingredients prepared ahead of time and lined up ready for use. The stir-frying must be done quickly.

1 pound jumbo shrimp	2 tablespoons chicken stock
Batter	Vegetable oil for deep-frying
1 egg white	plus 3 tablespoons
2 tablespoons cornstarch	1/2 cup chopped green onions
2 teaspoons flour	1/2 teaspoon minced fresh
Thickening mixture	ginger
1/2 teaspoon water mixed	3 tablespoons sugar
with 1/2 teaspoon corn-	1/4 cup white vinegar
starch	

Shell, devein and wash the shrimp. Slice each one lengthwise into halves. Make the batter, mixing well. Add the shrimp and stir to coat well.

Make the thickening mixture and mix thoroughly.

Heat 3 inches oil to 350° in a deep, heavy pot or deep-fryer. Mix the shrimp in the batter again and add about 5 pieces to the oil. Remove when golden and add more shrimp. Maintain 350° temperature. (If the oil is too hot, the outside will brown before the inside is cooked.) Drain the shrimp on paper towels.

Heat a wok over high heat. When very hot, add 3 tablespoons oil, followed by green onion and ginger. Stir-fry for 15 seconds and add the shrimp. Stir-fry 15 seconds. Then sprinkle in the sugar and stir-fry until the sugar melts—a matter of seconds. Quickly add the vinegar, stir a few times and add the cornstarch mixture. Stir until the sauce thickens.

Serves 3.

SHRIMP WITH CROUTONS

A fresh, spicy shrimp dish cooked in the simple style of Shantung which emphasizes color and taste.

3 slices white bread
Vegetable oil for deep-frying
  plus 3 tablespoons
1 pound large fresh shrimp
Marinade
  1 egg white
  1/4 teaspoon salt
  1/4 teaspoon sesame oil
  1/4 teaspoon cornstarch
2 tablespoons sesame seeds

Seasoning mixture
  1-1/2 teaspoons thin soy
    sauce
  1/2 teaspoon Chinese red
    vinegar
  1/2 teaspoon rice wine
  3/4 tablespoon cornstarch
  1/2 cup Chinese stock (p. 30)
    or chicken stock

With a sharp knife, slice the crust off the bread slices and discard. Cut the bread into 1/2-inch cubes. Heat 2 inches oil to 350° in a deep heavy pot. Add the cubes and deep-fry until medium brown and crisp. Scoop out and drain them.

Shell, devein and wash the shrimp. Slice them lengthwise into two pieces. Combine the ingredients for the marinade, add the shrimp and let them marinate for about 10 minutes.

In a small dry pan, lightly brown the sesame seeds. Combine the ingredients for the seasoning mixture and mix thoroughly.

Heat a wok over high heat. When very hot, add 3 tablespoons oil. Add the shrimp and stir-fry until they turn pink, about 1 minute. Transfer to a plate.

Remove the wok from heat; scrape it clean and wash it. Pour the stock into the wok and heat until it boils. Add the seasoning mixture and stir until the sauce thickens. Add the shrimp and mix. Transfer to a heated platter and garnish with croutons and sesame seeds.

Serves 3.

STEAMED CRAB

2 large hard-shelled crabs
(Dungeness type, about 2
pounds each)
Dip
    1/4 cup Chenchiang black
      vinegar
    2 tablespoons thin soy
      sauce
    1/2 teaspoon minced fresh
      ginger
    1/4 teaspoon sesame oil
    1-1/4 teaspoons salt
    1-1/2 tablespoons rice wine

1 teaspoon grated fresh
  ginger
1/8 teaspoon MSG
3 egg whites
2-1/2 tablespoons oil
1 pound string beans, French-
  cut
1/2 teaspoon thin soy sauce
1/4 teaspoon sugar
1/2 cup chicken stock
1/2 cup shredded ham
1 tablespoon minced green
  onion

Wash crabs in cold running water. Place in a steamer and steam for 30 minutes.

Combine the ingredients for the dip.

Carefully remove the crabs from the steamer and let them cool. Remove the shells (Figure 1). Scoop out all organs on top and discard (Figure 2). Carefully pick out the whitish, flaky meat underneath. Put it in a sieve and gently run cold water over it to wash it clean. Press every bit of liquid out so that the meat is very dry. Pick out and discard the small bits of cartilage, and transfer the meat to a large bowl. (There should be about 1 cup crabmeat. If additional crabmeat is needed, canned or thawed-out frozen crabmeat may be used. Squeeze out all liquid before using.) Wash out the shells and dry well.

Add 1 teaspoon salt, 1 tablespoon wine, ginger and MSG to the crabmeat, mixing well. In another bowl, beat egg whites until stiff and gently fold them into the crabmeat. Fill the body cavities and shells with the mixture (Figure 3). Place both body cavities and shells, filling side up, in an already vigorously steaming steamer, using two steamer racks if necessary. Steam for 7 to 8 minutes.

While crabs are steaming, heat a wok over high heat. Add oil, 1/4 teaspoon salt, string beans, soy sauce, sugar and 1/2 tablespoon wine. Stir-fry for 1 minute, coating beans well with the oil and seasonings. Add stock, cover and braise until most of the liquid is reduced and the beans are tender. Transfer to a heated platter. Arrange the stuffed body cavities on top, sprinkle with shredded ham and green onion and cover with the filled shells. Serve with the dip.

Serves 3.

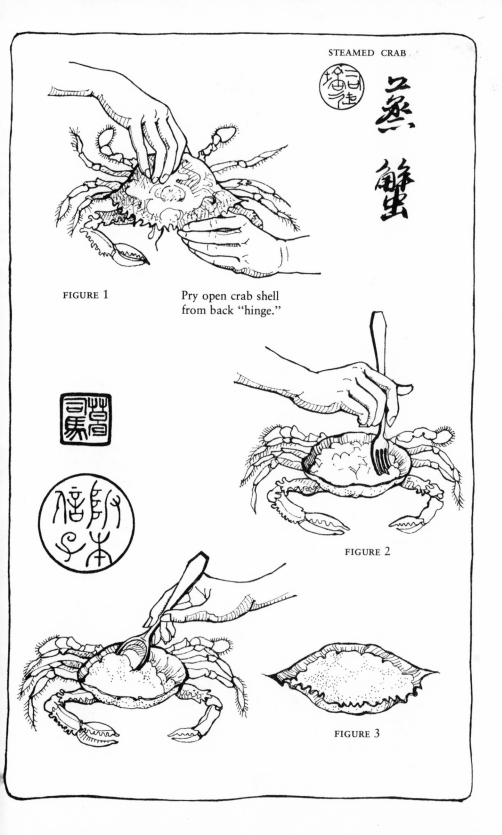

FIGURE 1

Pry open crab shell
from back "hinge."

FIGURE 2

FIGURE 3

JUICY FRIED MEATBALLS

These pork meatballs have a golden crust and a gelatin center, which melts in the cooking and imparts moistness and a delicious flavor. The meatballs must be deep-fried in oil which is just moderately hot so that they have a semimoist golden crust.

Jelly cubelets
  3 cups Chinese soup stock
    (p. 30) or chicken stock
  1 ham-hock skin
  1-1/2 teaspoons thin soy
    sauce
  1-1/2 teaspoons rice wine
  1/8 teaspoon grated fresh
    ginger
  Few drops of sesame oil
  1 package unflavored gelatin melted in 1/2 cup hot
    water

Meatballs
  1-1/4 pounds lean pork
    butt, ground or finely
    minced
  2 egg whites
  7 tablespoons cornstarch
  1/2 teaspoon salt
Dip
  1 tablespoon salt
  1 tablespoon ground black
    pepper
  1 tablespoon five-flavored
    spice
  1/2 cup bread crumbs
  Vegetable oil for deep-frying
  3 or 4 lettuce leaves

To prepare jelly cubelets, boil stock, add ham-hock skin and reduce liquid down to 1 cup. Discard skin. Add all other cubelet ingredients and mix well. Pour into a 9-inch-square cake pan and refrigerate overnight to set. Cut jelly into 1/4-inch cubelets.

Mix all meatball ingredients in a large bowl until firm in consistency. Divide the mixture into 24 pieces. On a board lightly dusted with cornstarch, press into a circle about 3 inches in diameter. Place each jelly cubelet in the center and wrap the pork mixture around it to encase it. Gently roll each piece of the meat mixture into a ball about 1 1/2 inches in diameter.

Mix all the dip ingredients together.

Roll the meatballs in bread crumbs. Heat oil to 325°–340° in a deep, heavy pot or deep-fryer. (Do not let the oil exceed this temperature and begin to smoke.) Add batches of four or five meatballs at a time. Deep-fry, turning three or four times until they are golden. Drain and place on top of lettuce leaves arranged on a platter and serve while hot with the dip.

Serves 4–5.

SWEET AND SOUR
SQUIRREL-LIKE FISH

This is a classic Northern-style sweet-sour dish. A whole fish is boned, dipped in batter and deep-fried until it turns a golden-brown and twists into a shape resembling a squirrel, hence the name of the recipe.

1-1/2 pounds fresh whole fish
(pike, scrod, shad, lake
trout or snapper are
good)—reserve the head
and tail
5 large dried black
mushrooms
1/2 cup green peas
Seasoning mixture I
2/3 cup water
2/3 cup sugar
2/3 cup white vinegar
Seasoning mixture II
2 tablespoons thin soy
sauce
3 tablespoons rice wine
1/4 teaspoon white pepper

7 tablespoons catsup
1/2 teaspoon sesame oil
2-1/2 tablespoons corn-
starch
1 teaspoon salt
1-1/2 tablespoons rice wine
Batter
1 large egg
6 tablespoons flour
5 tablespoons cornstarch
6 tablespoons cold water
Vegetable oil for deep-frying
plus 2 tablespoons
2 medium-sized tomatoes, cut
into 6 wedges
3 tablespoons chopped
parsley

Wash the fish and pat it dry. Soak the mushrooms in boiling water for 15 minutes. Rinse, squeeze out the water, remove the stems and quarter the caps. Parboil the peas for 2 minutes and drain.

Mix all ingredients of seasoning mixture I. Place the mixture in a pan and bring to a boil. Remove from heat and stir until the sugar is dissolved. Combine the ingredients for mixture II, mixing until all lumps of cornstarch are dissolved.

Lay the fish on a board and split lengthwise with a sharp knife, but do not cut through the back. Spread it open and carefully remove the backbone and ribs. Make XX's all over on the flesh side if it is more than 1/2 inch thick and sprinkle salt on it. After 15 minutes, rub off the salt (don't wash off) and moisture. Sprinkle with wine and let stand for 5 minutes more.

In a large bowl, make the batter by beating the egg and slowly adding flour and cornstarch, a little at a time, alternately with water. Put the fish in the batter and coat it well.

Heat 3 inches oil to 350° in a large wok. Deep-fry the fish until golden-brown, about 3 or 4 minutes. Turn once or twice. (The body will twist, since there is no backbone or ribs to help hold its shape.) Remove, drain and arrange on a heated platter.

Heat 2 tablespoons oil in a wok until it almost begins to smoke. Add mushrooms and peas, and stir-fry for 1 minute. Add mixture I and stir-fry, then add mixture II, continuing to stir. Add tomatoes as the sauce thickens. Pour over the fish and garnish with parsley.

Serves 3–4.

SWEET AND SOUR
BEEF LIVER HONAN STYLE

The secret of this delicious dish lies in the thinness of the liver slices and the timing of the cooking.

1 teaspoon white sesame
  seeds
1/2 head lettuce
Seasoning mixture
  2 large garlic cloves,
    crushed, peeled and
    minced
  1 teaspoon minced
    fresh ginger
  4 drops sesame oil
  1 tablespoon rice wine
  2-1/2 tablespoons thin soy
    sauce

1 teaspoon thick soy sauce
2-1/2 tablespoons Chinese
  red vinegar
2 tablespoons brown sugar
  or crushed rock sugar
Dash of cayenne or to taste
3 tablespoons vegetable oil
1 pound fresh beef liver, cut
  into slices 2-1/2 inches by 1
  by 1/8 inch
1 tablespoon minced green
  onion

Lightly toast sesame seeds in a dry pan. Slice the lettuce and arrange on a platter. Combine the ingredients for the seasoning mixture.

Heat a wok over high heat. When very hot, add oil, followed by the slices of liver. Stir-fry for 1/2 minute, add the seasoning mixture and stir-fry for 1 minute. Place on top of the lettuce on a serving platter, sprinkle with sesame seeds and then with green onion.

Serves 3.

PEKING DUCK

The making of Peking duck is a demanding specialty for which no exact recipe exists. It is a dish that is exclusively limited to restaurant cooking. The process itself can be observed and described, but in practice the special judgment, materials and equipment make the dish very difficult to produce in the home kitchen. So that the reader can appreciate the real thing, we offer a description of how Peking duck is prepared in the Ch'uan Chu Te and Pien Yi Fang restaurants in Peking.

Peking duck is made with a certain kind of duck raised in Peking especially for this dish. With short wings and legs, it has a wide, long back and plentiful breast meat. Its meat is different from that of other ducks in that it has layers of white fat between the meat fibers. Because of this fat, the roasted pinkish-white meat is very tender and succulent.

The duckling is first allowed to feed by itself and later is force-fed for about thirty days, until it is 7 or 8 pounds for a male and 5 or 6 pounds for a female. The entire cycle from hatching to roasting takes about a hundred days.

When the duck is ready to be used, it is killed by cutting its neck, and the internal organs are removed from the anal opening. Care is taken to avoid injuring or breaking the skin, since this is the chief attraction when the finished dish is brought to the table. The wing tips are cut off and an air pump is used to force air between the skin and the body. This inflation separates the skin from the underlying flesh and will permit the skin to become crisp when roasted. After this step the duck must be handled by its legs, wings or neck because touching the body will damage the skin. A metal hook is inserted in the loose, uninflated flesh of the neck, and the duck is hung over a pan or sink. A thin stick, like a chopstick, is wedged between the duck's wings to spread them apart and keep them from touching the body while the skin is being prepared for roasting.

To tighten the skin, three scoops of boiling water are poured over the duck, one over each wing and the third from the neck down over the whole body. If more than three scoops of water are used, fat will emerge from the pores and the sugar coating to be applied next will not stick well to the skin.

The sugar syrup coating gives the skin the glossy reddish color and flavor characteristic of Peking duck. The basic method for making the sugar syrup is to melt 1 pound of malt sugar until it becomes yellowish, add a bit of salt to aid the sugar in dissolving, and then put in about 2-2/3 cups of water. The sugar is completely dissolved by stirring and heating and then the mixture is stored in a jug for a month.

Two applications of syrup are made; the second is put on only after the first has thoroughly dried and hardened. If too much sugar coating is used the skin will become black as it roasts and taste charred; too little coating will produce an unevenly colored skin. The coating mixtures are made up of different proportions of syrup and water. The rule is to decrease the amount of syrup gradually from summer to fall, and to increase it from winter to spring, thus following the temperature-humidity cycle of Peking weather. The sugar coating is done by pouring three scoops of the appropriate syrup-water mixture over the duck in the same fashion as described above for the application of boiling water. The first coating mixtures are:

Winter   10 ounces syrup and 32 ounces water

Summer   on sunny days, about 3/4 ounce more syrup; on cloudy days, 1 ounce more syrup.

And for the second coating:

Winter   6 1/2 ounces syrup and 43 ounces water

Summer   4 1/2 ounces syrup and 43 ounces water

After the sugar coatings have been applied, the duck is hung up to dry, usually outdoors if it isn't freezing. This takes about 3 hours. In winter the duck is usually hung indoors, and the drying takes two or three days. After drying, the duck is wrapped in a towel and stored in a cold place until the oven is ready.

Peking duck is roasted by hanging it in a large brick oven with an open door through which the cook watches and manipulates the duck inside. There is a wood (or sometimes coal) fire on the floor of the front half of the oven and the duck is hung from a bar in the rear half of the oven, away from the fire. Fat drips down from the duck onto a metal plate and runs out of the oven into a bucket. The cook stands at the door of the oven and manipulates the duck with a long rod, half of which is iron-coated to prevent scorching when it is extended into the oven.

The cook judges the oven's heat without benefit of a thermometer and his constant job is to adjust the fire and the position of the duck with respect to the fire. If parts other than the breast begin to change color first, or the skin shrinks and becomes wrinkled soon after it is put in the oven, then the fire must be increased. Too little time in the oven results in underdone meat, and too long causes so much of the fat to melt away that the skin becomes thin and the meat tough. A duck weighing 4 or 5 pounds when it is put into the oven should lose at most 2 to 3 ounces of fat. The meat will then be tender and the skin thick and crisp.

The roasting time depends on the season of the year and the size of the duck. In Peking a 4-pound duck takes 40 minutes in winter and a little more than 30 minutes in summer.

After the oven is prepared and preheated, the duck is made ready for the roasting. The wing stick is removed and a piece of sorghum stalk some 3 inches long is put into the anal opening from the inside to close it. The stalk should have a joint (a raised ring) on it to close the opening tightly. Just before being put in the oven the duck is filled from the neck opening 75 percent full of boiling water.

The duck is put in the oven and the heat causes the water inside it to boil. In order to brown the skin evenly, during the roasting the position of the duck is changed so that its four sides face toward the fire for varying periods. The right side gets about 10 minutes, the left 5 to 7 minutes, the right front 5 to 6 minutes, the left front 5 to 6 minutes, and the back 5 to 6 minutes, in that order. Finally, if necessary, different parts of the duck are brought closer to the fire to make them turn just the right color. This finishing touch is called singeing; it is done wherever the color isn't quite right. The finished color should be a glossy red. Experienced cooks don't have to do much singeing because they know when to turn the ducks in the oven at the right time to color the skin evenly.

With the duck out of the oven, the business of carving and serving gets underway. The sorghum stalk is removed and the water drained from the duck. The hook is removed from the neck and the duck is placed breast side down on a special platter. The platter is metal, with a raised rim surrounding a wooden plaque. The fat and juices which run out of the duck resting on the plaque will collect below the rim of the platter and so the skin of the duck will remain dry. Diners are given a choice between eating the skin and meat separately or together, and the duck is sliced accordingly. The order of slicing is to do the left breast first and then work back along the backbone, doing the left wing and leg while they are attached to the duck. After the left side is done, the right is carved the same way. The yield from a 3- to 4-pound duck can fill four serving plates. As each plate is filled it is presented to the diners. Finally, the rear end of the duck and a piece of the backbone are put on a plate and shown to the diners to indicate that the duck has been completely sliced.

Thin pancakes are served with Peking duck. A pancake is put on a plate; duck skin and/or meat is put in its center; some green onion sections, crushed garlic and bean paste are added; and the pancake is rolled up and eaten. Those who like sweet things dip the end of the rolled pancake into sugar.

PEKING DUCK HOME STYLE

This dish is a close approximation of the classic Peking duck described in the preceding pages. A more practical version, it originated not in China but in our own kitchen. Be sure to make up the pancakes, green onions and sauces ahead of time so that everything is ready when the duck is served.

Pancakes
  2 cups flour
  1 cup boiling water
  2-1/2 teaspoons sesame oil
8 green onions
Sauce I
  1/2 cup fava bean paste or
    Japanese *miso*
  3 large garlic cloves,
    crushed and minced

Sauce II
  1/3 cup Hoisin sauce
  3 large garlic cloves,
    crushed and minced
  1/2 teaspoon sesame oil
  1 tablespoon thin soy sauce
1 4- to 5-pound duck, fresh-
    killed if possible
  1/2 cup malt sugar or granu-
    lated sugar
  2/3 teaspoon salt
Few drops of red food color-
    ing

PREPARATION OF PANCAKES

Put flour in a large bowl. Add boiling water gradually and knead into a soft, smooth dough. Cover with a damp towel and let stand for 15 minutes.

On a floured board, roll the dough into a long roll at least a foot long (Figure 1). Slice 3/4-inch pieces from the roll and flatten each one with your palms until it is about 1/4 inch thick. Brush the top of each piece with a little sesame oil.

Place two pieces of dough with their oiled sides together (Figure 2). Dust the top with a little flour, and then using a rolling pin, roll each piece out into a pancake of uniform thickness about 5 inches in diameter (Figure 3). While rolling, press down evenly, and turn the pancake to make the thickness even. Repeat until all the dough is used up.

Heat an unoiled griddle or heavy frying pan over medium-low heat and fry each pancake separately. In about 1/2 to 1 minute, when the pancake bubbles and is only slightly browned on the bottom, turn it over and fry the other side for about 1/2 minute. If you overcook the pancakes they will become brittle—they should be pliable. Remove each pancake from the pan and pull apart the two layers to produce two thin pancakes (Figure 4). Place them one on top of the other, oiled side up, on a heatproof

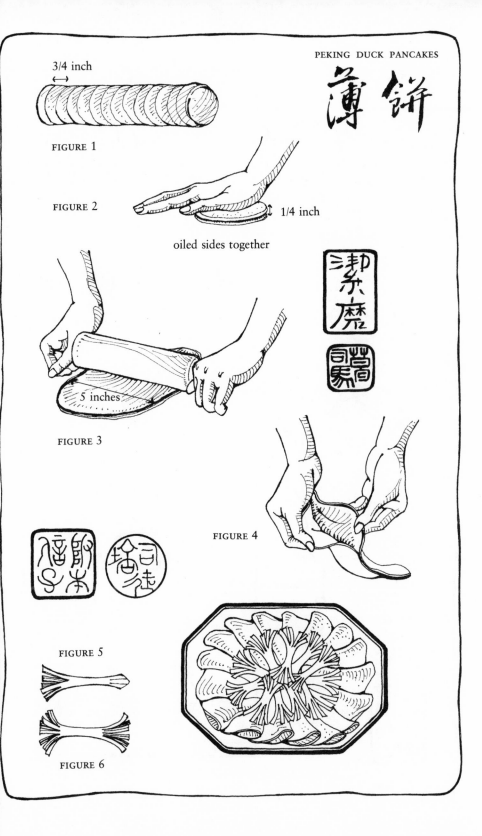

3/4 inch

FIGURE 1

FIGURE 2

1/4 inch

oiled sides together

5 inches

FIGURE 3

FIGURE 4

FIGURE 5

FIGURE 6

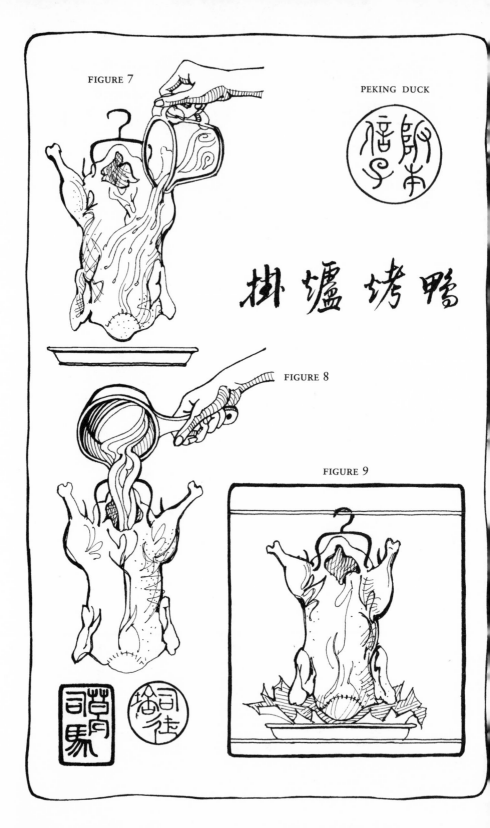

FIGURE 7

PEKING DUCK

掛爐烤鴨

FIGURE 8

FIGURE 9

pie plate. Keep the pancakes covered with a damp cloth so they won't dry out.

Makes about 16 pancakes.

PREPARATION OF GREEN ONIONS

Trim off the green part of the onions and cut the white part into 2-inch sections. Make a cross-shaped cut into each end, about 1/3 inch deep (Figure 5). Place the onion sections in ice water for one hour. The ends will open outward in a flowerlike shape (Figure 6).

PREPARATION OF SAUCES

Mix separately the ingredients of Sauces I and II. Sauce I is the traditional Chinese accompaniment for Peking duck, but Sauce II makes a good substitute—or serve both if you like.

PREPARATION OF DUCK

Wash the duck well. If it is frozen, defrost it completely. Be careful not to break the skin. Cut off the wing tips and wedge the wings apart with a stick so they don't touch the body. Form a double S-shaped hook from a section of a heavy wire clothes hanger and hook the duck solidly through the flesh around the anal opening. Then hang the duck, neck down, over a pan. Carefully sew up the neck opening (sew over the opening twice) into the body cavity so that the inside will hold water without leaking. Seal must not leak!

Put a pan over medium heat and add the sugar and salt. When the sugar starts to melt, add 2/3 cup hot water and stir until the sugar dissolves completely. Add red food coloring. Let the syrup cool before using.

Boil about 2 cups water. Pour 1/2 cup over the left side of the hanging duck, from the leg down. Pour another 1/2 cup similarly over the right side. Then pour about 3/4 cup from the top so that it runs down the front and back of the duck (Figure 7).

Pour the syrup over the duck in three motions (using about 1/3 cup each time), as with the boiling water, trying to make the syrup cover the entire skin area. Save the syrup which drips into the pan for a second coating.

Next the duck must be well dried for 6 hours or more. In cold (but not freezing) weather hang it outdoors in a well-screened area or, if indoors, use an electric fan. Then hang the duck back over the pan and apply a second coating of syrup in the same way as the first one. Let the duck stand for 30 minutes. It need not be completely dry this time.

Preheat the oven to 300° for 20 minutes. Fill the duck three-quarters full with boiling water just before carefully hanging it in the oven (Figure 8).

Prepare the oven by removing all but two racks, in the highest and lowest positions. Place a shallow pan on the bottom rack to catch drippings. The duck will be suspended in the front part of the oven from the top rack. (Ideally, it should hang in the oven, but since most ovens are not large enough, it may be necessary to have the duck's lowest part resting on the pan.) Take care so that water in the duck does not spill out. If the duck touches the pan, put a piece of aluminum foil between them to prevent the duck from sticking (Figure 9). Roast it for 1-1/2 hours, then turn the heat up to 450° and let the skin brown. This may take from 10 to 20 minutes. Watch the duck during this period so that it doesn't scorch, and using hot pads or mitts, remove it when completely browned. Carefully tip the duck and pour out the hot water.

SERVING

Before serving the duck, place the plate of pancakes in a steamer and steam for 10 minutes. Place the duck on a board, and when cooled enough to handle, carve the meat along with the skin and cut it into serving pieces. Serve the duck with the pancakes, green onions and sauces. Each diner puts a pancake on his plate, places some meat and/or skin in its center, adds green onion sections and sauce, and then rolls up the pancake.
Serves 4–6.

JUICY STUFFED ROLLS

These delicious rolls are made of thin flour wrappings generously stuffed with a filling of meat and seasonings. When served piping hot, the meat gelatin melts, flavoring the filling and impregnating the roll with a delectable sauce.

1-1/2 pounds fresh ham, with skin	4 cups all-purpose flour
1/2 pound fresh ham skin	1/2 teaspoon baking soda
3 slices fresh ginger	Hoisin sauce for dip
3 whole green onions	Soy dip
2 chicken legs	1/4 cup thin soy sauce
2 tablespoons rice wine	1/2 teaspoon Chinese red vinegar
1 teaspoon salt	1/2 teaspoon shredded ginger
1/4 teaspoon white pepper	1/2 teaspoon minced garlic
3 tablespoons thin soy sauce	1/2 teaspoon sugar
1 teaspoon grated fresh ginger	2 teaspoons rice wine
1/4 cup chopped green onion	4 drops sesame oil

Remove the skin from fresh ham. Wash both the ham with skin and the additional skin and place in a large pot. Cover with water, and bring to a boil for 2 or 3 minutes. Drain the hot water and rinse the ham and skin in cold water.

Return the ham and skin to the pot and add 5 1/2 cups water. Add ginger slices and whole green onions. Bring the water to a boil, then reduce the heat and simmer for 2 hours. Add chicken legs and simmer for another hour, or until everything is very tender. Cool and transfer meats and skin to a board. Reserve the stock. Remove the skin from the chicken legs and discard.

With a sharp knife, cut the ham and chicken into 1/3-inch cubes. Mince the ham skin into a paste. Discard ginger and green onions, and add the paste to the stock. Boil down the stock until it becomes thick and sticky (make sure it does not burn).

Mix together the wine, salt, pepper, soy sauce, grated ginger and chopped green onion. Add this mixture and ham and chicken cubes to the stock paste and mix well. Simmer gently (a double boiler is good for this

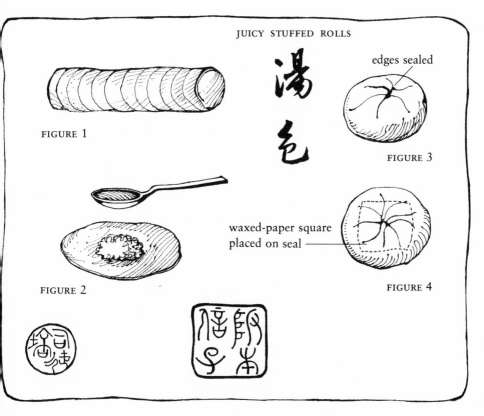

JUICY STUFFED ROLLS

FIGURE 1

edges sealed

FIGURE 3

FIGURE 2

waxed-paper square placed on seal

FIGURE 4

purpose) for 15 minutes. Cool and refrigerate, stirring occasionally so it forms a homogeneous gelatin.

Place flour in a large bowl. Combine baking soda with 1 tablespoon water. Add this mixture to 2 cups water. Then add the water to the flour, a little at a time, mixing well until a slightly sticky dough is formed. Flour a board and your hands generously. Knead the dough lightly on the board, turning frequently. Continue kneading until the dough is well formed (not sticky) and elastic. Add a little flour if needed. Divide the dough into 2 equal portions. Form each into a long roll about 12 inches long and 1-1/4 inches in diameter. Cut 12 equal slices out of each roll (Figure 1). With a floured rolling pin, roll the slices into flat circles about 4-1/2 inches in diameter.

Cut waxed paper into 6-inch squares and stack the circles of dough by placing the waxed paper between them to keep them from sticking together.

Bring out the filling from the refrigerator and stir it. Remove one circle of dough at a time and place about 1-1/2 tablespoons of filling in its center (Figure 2). Pull up the edges and pinch to close. Edges may be moistened with a little water for a tighter seal (Figure 3).

Cut 1-1/2-inch squares out of the waxed-paper squares and place on the seal (Figure 4)—this keeps the rolls from sticking to the steamer tray. Cover with a moist cloth without letting it touch the rolls. Let them rest for 15 minutes.

Combine the ingredients for the soy dip.

Arrange the rolls, sealed side down, in a steamer, allowing room between them so they don't touch. If steaming is to be done in batches, lightly sprinkle with water the rolls waiting to be steamed and cover loosely with plastic wrap. Steam vigorously for 8 minutes. Turn off the heat and allow the steamer to cool a bit. Take out the rolls, remove the waxed paper and serve with Hoisin sauce and soy dip.

Makes about 24 rolls.

SKEWERED SUGAR-GLAZED
CRAB APPLES

For hundreds of years the little *shan li hung,* a red mountain fruit resembling small apples, was used for this recipe. Crab apples make a good substitute. The sugar-glazed fruit was threaded on long wooden skewers and sold by street vendors in the late fall and winter months.

2 dozen small, firm crab apples	1/2 cup corn syrup
2 cups sugar	1 teaspoon cinnamon
3/4 cup water	1 tablespoon red food coloring

Remove the stems and wash and dry the apples.

Fill the bottom part of a large double boiler one-third of the way up with hot water and bring to a boil. Reduce heat and cover.

Put sugar, water, corn syrup, cinnamon and coloring into the top part of the double boiler. Place over medium heat and stir until the sugar dissolves. Keep stirring until the liquid begins to bubble. Put the pot on top of the bottom part of the double boiler and turn up the heat. Continue stirring until a fine thread forms when a little syrup is dropped from a spoon.

Stick a long wooden chopstick or skewer into each apple, dip it completely in the syrup and put it on a well-oiled platter to cool.

When the apples are cool, thread through the center of the fruit with a long, thin skewer until there are about 12 apples on each skewer.

Serves 6.

Palace Dishes

The following dishes have been handed down by the chefs who were employed at the Imperial Palace in Peking before the fall of the Ch'ing dynasty in 1912.

After the establishment of the People's Republic in 1949, some of the chefs were invited to join the staffs of famous restaurants. Scores of original palace dishes were re-created by them for the enjoyment of the people, and were passed on to a new generation of chefs. Thus a repository of old recipes and cooking techniques has been preserved.

GREEN AND WHITE SAUCED CHICKEN BREAST

Chicken balls
  4 egg whites
  3/4 pound boneless chicken
    breast
  1/3 teaspoon salt
  1 tablespoon cornstarch
Vegetable oil for deep-frying
2 cups clear Chinese stock
  (p. 30) or chicken stock

1 tablespoon rice wine
1/2 teaspoon salt
1-1/4 tablespoons water
  mixed with 1/2 tablespoon
  cornstarch
2/3 cup green peas
1 teaspoon melted chicken fat
1/2 cup slivered ham

Beat egg whites vigorously with a whip until foamy, and set aside. Chop the chicken breast into very small pieces. With the dull edge of a cleaver,

72

mash the chicken thoroughly into a paste. While mashing, add 1 table-spoon cold water and mix until it is absorbed.

Place the chicken in a bowl, and while mixing (in one direction only) add egg whites a little at a time so that they are thoroughly absorbed. Add salt and cornstarch, and mix well. Add a little more cornstarch if the mixture is too soft. The consistency of the chicken paste should be such that when a chopstick is inserted into it and pulled out, the paste doesn't stick to the chopstick. Form pieces of the paste into pea-sized balls.

Heat about 2 inches oil to 350° in a deep, heavy pot. Drop the balls in the oil, frying in small batches so that they don't stick together. Fry the balls for 1 minute, then scoop them out and drain them on paper towels.

Put the stock in a bowl. Add wine, salt and the cornstarch mixture. Add more salt if necessary. Pour into a pan and cook over high heat, stirring until the sauce becomes milky. Add peas. When the sauce boils, add the chicken balls, stir once and add chicken fat. Garnish with slivered ham. Serves 2.

CRAB-AND-PORK BALLS

Crab-and-pork balls
1/2 pound crabmeat, shredded
1/4 pound pork butt, finely chopped
4 water chestnuts, finely chopped
1/2 teaspoon grated fresh ginger
1/2 teaspoon minced green onion
1 egg
1 teaspoon rice wine
1/2 teaspoon salt
1/2 tablespoon cornstarch

Vegetable oil for deep-frying
1 cup rich Chinese stock (p. 30) or chicken stock
1/2 teaspoon rice wine
1/4 teaspoon salt
1 tablespoon water mixed with 1/2 tablespoon cornstarch
2 cups shredded lettuce
1 teaspoon melted chicken fat or few drops of sesame oil
2 tablespoons slivered ham
1 tablespoon chopped Chinese parsley

To prepare the balls for cooking, mix together the crabmeat, pork, water chestnuts, ginger and green onion in a large bowl. Add egg, wine and salt, and mix well, stirring in one direction. Sprinkle cornstarch over the mixture and mix, again stirring in one direction. If the mixture does not hold together well, add a bit more cornstarch. Shape into walnut-sized balls.

Heat 3 inches oil to 350° in a deep, heavy pot. Add the balls and fry for about 3 minutes, or until they have a firm outer crust. Scoop out the balls and place in a heatproof bowl. Pour 1 tablespoon stock over them, place the bowl in a steamer and steam for 15 minutes.

Pour the remaining stock into a pot and heat over medium heat. Add wine, salt and the cornstarch mixture, and stir well until the sauce is thickened.

Arrange the lettuce on a platter and place the balls on top. Pour the sauce over the balls, sprinkle with chicken fat or oil, and garnish with ham and parsley.

Serves 2

STIR-FRIED HAZELNUTS WITH BROWN BEAN SAUCE

This dish was served regularly at court during the winter months when fresh vegetables were difficult to obtain.

1/3 cup fresh hazelnuts, shelled
1 tablespoon baking soda
Seasoning mixture
   1-1/2 teaspoons rice wine
   2-1/2 teaspoons thin soy sauce
   Pinch of MSG
   1/4 cup Chinese soup stock (p. 30) or chicken stock
Vegetable oil for deep-frying plus 2 tablespoons for stir-frying

3/4 pound lean pork butt, cut into 1/4-inch cubes
1 teaspoon chopped green onion
1/2 teaspoon grated fresh ginger
2-1/2 teaspoons brown bean sauce
1 tablespoon water mixed with 1/2 tablespoon cornstarch
4 water chestnuts, sliced
Few drops of sesame oil

Place hazelnuts in a pot of boiling water, then remove the pot from heat. Add baking soda. Allow the water to cool, remove the nuts and rub off their skins. Rinse well and air-dry them on paper towels.

Combine the ingredients of seasoning mixture.

Heat 2 inches oil to about 350° in a deep, heavy pot, and deep-fry the nuts until they float to the surface. Remove with a slotted spoon and drain on paper towels.

Put a wok over high heat. When very hot, add 2 tablespoons oil. Add the pork and stir-fry for about 2 minutes. Add green onion, ginger and bean sauce, and stir-fry for 1minute more. The bean sauce will be absorbed and its aroma will dominate. Add the seasoning mixture and mix well.

Add the cornstarch mixture to thicken the sauce, and stir several times. Remove the pot from heat. Add hazelnuts and water chestnuts and stir to coat all ingredients.

Transfer to a serving platter and sprinkle with sesame oil. Serves 2–3.

STIR-FRIED CUCUMBER
WITH BROWN BEAN SAUCE

3 large dried mushrooms
Seasoning mixture
   1-1/2 teaspoons rice wine
   2 teaspoons thin soy sauce
   Pinch of MSG
   1/4 cup Chinese soup stock
     (p. 30) or chicken stock
2 tablespoons vegetable oil
1/2 pound pork tenderloin
   cut into 1/2-inch cubes
2 tablespoons finely chopped
   green onion
1 teaspoon grated fresh
   ginger

1 tablespoon brown bean
   sauce
3-1/2 cups fresh cucumber,
   peeled (leave some of the
   green for color) and cut
   into 1/2-inch cubes*
1/2 tablespoon water mixed
   with 1/4 tablespoon cornstarch
Few drops of sesame oil
1/2 teaspoon crushed flower
   pepper

Soak mushrooms in hot water 15 minutes. Rinse, squeeze out the water, remove the stems and quarter the caps.

Combine the ingredients for the seasoning mixture.

Put a wok over high heat. When very hot, add oil. Add pork and stir-fry for several minutes. Add mushrooms, green onion, ginger and bean sauce and stir-fry for 1 minute. The bean sauce will be absorbed, and its aroma will become quite strong. Add the seasoning mixture.

Add the cucumber, stir a few times and add the cornstarch mixture to thicken the sauce. Stir several times and turn off the heat.

Transfer quickly to a heated platter, and sprinkle sesame oil and flower pepper over the dish. Serves 2.

---

* If firm and almost seedless cucumbers cannot be found, substitute zucchini.

PALACE-STYLE
STIR-FRIED SOFT BEAN CURD

2 medium-sized dried
mushrooms
4 cakes soft, fresh bean curd
3 tablespoons vegetable oil
2 tablespoons minced green
onion
1 teaspoon grated fresh
ginger
1/4 cup minced water
chestnuts
1-1/4 teaspoons salt

1 tablespoon rice wine
Pinch of MSG
1/3 cup chicken stock
1 tablespoon water mixed
with 1/2 tablespoon corn-
starch
2 teaspoons melted chicken
fat
1/4 teaspoon crushed flower
pepper

Soak mushrooms in hot water for 15 minutes. Rinse, squeeze out the water, remove the stems and sliver the caps.

Rinse the bean curd and, with a fork, mash them in a bowl into a thick paste.

Heat the oil in a wok over medium heat and stir-fry the green onion only until it is translucent. Add ginger, mushrooms and water chestnuts, and stir-fry for 1/2 minute. Add salt, wine and MSG, and stir-fry another 1/2 minute. Add bean curd and stir until well blended. Add the stock and braise gently for 1 or 2 minutes. Add the cornstarch mixture and stir until the sauce is thickened.

Transfer to a platter, sprinkle with melted fat and flower pepper. Serves 2–3.

OCEAN RED SHARK'S FIN

1/4 pound instant shark's fin
4 tablespoons vegetable oil
1/4 cup thinly sliced carrot
1 drop of red food coloring
2 medium-sized dried
  mushrooms
1/2 cup crab yellow or finely
  minced pork with some fat
2 tablespoons rice wine
5 pinches of salt
5 pinches of MSG
1 green onion, cut into 4 equal
  pieces

1 large slice fresh ginger
5 to 6 cups Chinese stock
  (p. 30) or chicken stock
1 tablespoon water mixed
  with 1/2 tablespoon cornstarch
1/4 cup slivered ham
1/4 cup slivered cooked
  chicken breast
2 tablespoons slivered green
  onion (cut in half lengthwise and slice diagonally
  into 1/2-inch sections)

Wash and soak the shark's fin overnight in cold water. The next day, rinse several times with cold water in a colander. Place the fin in a pot, add water to cover and bring to a boil. Drain and rinse again in cold water. Repeat boiling and rinsing two more times to remove the fishy odor. In a pan, heat the oil, add the carrot and sauté gently over medium heat until soft. Remove from heat. Drain off the oil, add food coloring to it and reserve. Discard the carrots.

Soak the mushrooms in hot water for 15 minutes. Rinse, squeeze out the water, remove the stems and sliver the caps.

If using crab yellow, wash by gently running water over it in a strainer and drain it well.

Put the fin in a heatproof steaming bowl. Add 1 tablespoon wine, 1 pinch of salt, 1 pinch of MSG, 1 piece of green onion and the ginger. Add enough stock to cover the fin, place the bowl in the steamer and steam for about 1-1/2 to 2 hours, or until tender. To test for tenderness, use a fork to cut through the fin; if it cuts through easily, it is done.

Transfer the fin to a pot, discarding the ginger, onion and liquid. Add enough stock to cover the fin, 1 pinch of MSG, 1 pinch of salt, 1 green onion piece, and bring to a boil. Simmer a few minutes, then discard the stock and onion. Repeat this process two more times. After final draining, keep the fin hot while preparing the sauce.

Heat half of the reserved oil over medium heat. Add crab yellow or pork, mushrooms, 1 tablespoon wine, 1 pinch of MSG, 1 pinch of salt and 1/3 cup stock. Gently simmer for about 10 minutes so that the flavor of the oil, seasonings and stock permeates the pork or crab yellow. Add the cornstarch mixture and stir until the sauce thickens. Remove the pan from heat. Add the remaining half of the reserved oil, stir a bit, and pour the sauce over the fin. Garnish with slivered ham, chicken and green onion.

Serves 2–3.

PALACE SWEET AND SOUR FISH SLICES

The delicate flavor of fresh-water fish is much favored in Peking. In this dish, the pungent sweet-and-sour sauce just lightly coats the fish, unlike similar dishes of other provinces which are less delicate in flavor and are prepared with a heavier sauce.

1 pound fresh-water fish
  fillets
Seasoning mixture
  2-1/2 tablespoons thin soy
    sauce
  1 tablespoon Chinese red
    vinegar
  5 teaspoons sugar
  4 teaspoons rice wine
  1/8 teaspoon MSG

1 tablespoon water mixed
  with 1-1/2 teaspoons
  cornstarch
Vegetable oil for deep-frying
  plus 3 tablespoons for
  stir-frying
1/2 cup water mixed with 1/4
  cup cornstarch
1/3 cup chopped green onion
1 teaspoon grated fresh
  ginger

Wash and dry the fish fillets. Cut into pieces about 2 inches by 1 inch by 1 inch.

Combine the ingredients for the seasoning mixture.

Heat 3 inches oil to 350° in a deep-frying pan. Dip the fish slices in the cornstarch mixture, coating them well. Deep-fry the fish slices about 2 to 3 minutes, or until they are golden-brown. Separate the pieces while frying. Drain on paper towels.

Place a wok over medium heat. When hot, add oil. Add green onion and ginger and stir-fry until the onion is translucent. Turn up the heat and add the seasoning mixture. Stir until the sauce thickens.

Remove the wok from heat and add fish pieces to the sauce. Carefully turn them over, coating the fish slices well with the sauce. Quickly transfer to a heated platter.

Serves 2–3.

BUDDHA'S HAND

The imperial chefs took great care in creating novel dishes such as this one for the delight of the court during the Ch'ing dynasty. The crisp golden wrapping is intended to resemble the Buddha's hand.

Filling
- 1/2 pound pork butt, minced or finely ground
- 1 teaspoon minced green onion
- 1 teaspoon grated fresh ginger
- 1-1/4 tablespoons water mixed with 1-1/2 table-spoons cornstarch
- 1-1/2 tablespoons rice wine
- Pinch of MSG
- 1/2 teaspoon salt
- 1/8 teaspoon sugar
- 1/2 teaspoon thin soy sauce

Batter for wrappings
- 5 large eggs
- 3 tablespoons water mixed with 1/2 tablespoon cornstarch
- 1/2 tablespoon vegetable oil

Binder mixture
- 1 egg
- 3 tablespoons water
- Vegetable oil for frying and deep-frying
- 1 teaspoon flower pepper
- 2 teaspoons kosher salt
- 1 cup fresh spinach leaves, washed and trimmed
- 1/4 cup thinly sliced fresh radishes

Mix together all ingredients for the filling and set aside. Mix together the batter ingredients and set aside. Blend the binder mixture.

Heat a 12-inch griddle over medium heat. Brush ample oil all over the pan. When the pan is hot, pour in half the batter to cover about two-thirds of the pan, making a circle about 10 inches in diameter. Tip the pan to spread the batter evenly. When the bottom is done, air bubbles will form on top. With a spatula and your fingertips, gently loosen the wrapping from the pan, flip it over so that the top side cooks for a few seconds, and then transfer to a well-oiled plate. Clean and oil the pan, and repeat the process for the second wrapping.

Brush the binder mixture over each circle. Put a 3-by-6-inch row of filling on the middle third (Figure 1). Fold the sides over and brush the binder on top of the flaps (Figure 2). Fold the bottom third over and brush the binder on top (Figure 3). Close by bringing the upper third down and seal (Figure 4).

Gently turn both cakes over with a spatula and put them on a cutting

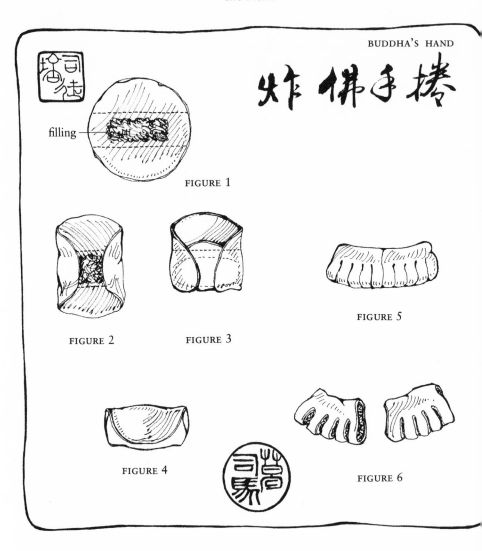

BUDDHA'S HAND

炸佛手捲

filling

FIGURE 1

FIGURE 2

FIGURE 3

FIGURE 5

FIGURE 4

FIGURE 6

board. With a sharp knife make slashes on each cake about 2-1/4 inches long and about 1/2 inch apart, leaving about 3/4 inch uncut. On the fifth slash, cut *all the way through*. This will make 2 "hands" with 10 fingers (Figure 5). Gently spread the fingers apart (Figure 6).

Lightly brown the flower pepper and kosher salt together (do not burn). Place in a mortar and grind fine with a pestle.

Heat 3 inches oil to 350° in a deep-frying pan. Carefully lower one "hand" into the oil and deep-fry for about 1 minute. If it begins to darken, turn it over or take it out temporarily with a slotted spoon. Add the other "hand" and repeat. Then reheat both together for another 2 to 3 minutes. (When done, they should be a light golden-brown.) Drain them.

Place the "hands" on a bed of spinach leaves and radishes, and serve with the flower pepper and salt to be used as a dip.

Makes 4 "hands."

SU TS'AO MEATBALL SOUP

Su ts'ao is a combination of herbs that for centuries have been relied upon by the Chinese for their restorative properties. In this ancient and unique dish, the herbs are tied up into a small bouquet garni and steeped in soup stock, giving it a distinctive and delicious flavor. Angelica, woodwort and licorice root are available in Chinese groceries or herb stores, and in the small amounts required for this recipe must be measured out by the grocer or herbalist.

Meatballs
1 pound lean pork butt, minced or finely ground
6 to 7 water chestnuts, minced
1 teaspoon minced green onion
1/2 teaspoon grated fresh ginger
1/2 teaspoon salt
2 teaspoons thin soy sauce
2 teaspoons rice wine
1/4 cup cornstarch
1 cake fresh bean curd

Su ts'ao—equal parts cardamom, cloves, angelica, woodwort, licorice root to make 1/4 ounce
Vegetable oil for deep-frying
4-1/2 cups Chinese stock (p. 30) or chicken stock
1 teaspoon thin soy sauce
1 teaspoon rice wine
1/4 pound Japanese chrysanthemum greens or spinach leaves, washed and trimmed

In a large bowl, mix together all ingredients for the meatballs except cornstarch. Sprinkle the cornstarch over the mixture and blend well. Form into small meatballs about 1 inch in diameter.

Cut bean curd into 1-inch cubes.

Wrap the *su ts'ao* in a small cloth bag and tie with string.

Heat 2 to 3 inches oil to 375° in a deep-frying pan. Add the meatballs and stir with chopsticks to keep them from sticking together. Fry for 2 to 3 minutes, or until a crust forms on the balls. Remove them with a slotted spoon. Turn up the heat and return the meatballs to the pan. Refry for 2 minutes or until they are well browned and firm. Remove and drain on paper towels.

Pour stock into a large pot. Heat almost to boiling, then reduce heat and add soy sauce and wine. Add *su ts'ao* bag to the stock and reduce the heat to a simmer.

Carefully add the meatballs and gently simmer for 5 minutes, adding the chrysanthemum greens or spinach for the last 3 minutes. Add the bean curd for the last 2 minutes. Remove the *su ts'ao* bag, adjust the salt and transfer the soup to a heated tureen or bowl.

Serves 4.

MT. T'AI EGG FU YUNG

This dish is a representation of T'ai Shan (the sacred mountain in Shantung Province), and should be presented as a *pièce de resistance*. It takes the form of a rising mountain peak with fluffy white clouds around its summit, the peak represented by a steamed egg fu yung and the clouds by a puffy white mass of vermicelli.

8 large fresh shrimp
Marinade
   1/2 teaspoon thin soy sauce
   1/2 teaspoon rice wine
   Pinch of salt
   1/4 teaspoon sugar
Fu yung mixture
   2 tablespoons water mixed with 1 tablespoon cornstarch
   1/4 cup ham shreds
   1/4 cup cooked pork cut into 1/4-inch cubes
   1/4 cup chopped onion
   4 sliced canned water chestnuts
   1-1/2 cups fresh bean sprouts or 1 cup well-drained, packed canned sprouts
   2 tablespoon chopped green onion
   5 large eggs

Seasoning mixture
   1/4 teaspoon thin soy sauce
   1/4 teaspoon rice wine
   1/2 teaspoon salt
   Pinch of MSG
Sauce mixture
   1-1/2 cups Chinese stock (p. 30) or chicken stock
   1 teaspoon thin soy sauce
   1/4 teaspoon salt
   1/8 teaspoon sesame oil
   1 tablespoon water mixed with 2 teaspoon cornstarch
15 3-inch lengths of rice vermicelli
Oil for deep-frying plus 1 teaspoon

Shell, devein, wash and split the shrimp lengthwise. Combine the ingredients for the marinade and marinate the shrimp for 15 minutes.

Start the steamer with plenty of water before assembling the ingredients for the fu yung mixture. Put the shrimp, ham, pork, onion, water chestnuts, bean sprouts and green onion in a large bowl. In another bowl, beat the eggs, add the seasoning mixture and cornstarch paste; mix well and pour into the other bowl. Mix the ingredients together and put the mixture into a well-oiled 1 1/2-quart heatproof bowl. (A large bowl in the shape of a ceramic Chinese rice bowl—with sharply sloped, not curved, sides—will help the "peak" to rise.)

When the steamer begins to steam vigorously, remove it from heat and carefully take off the cover. Place the bowl containing the fu yung mixture in the steamer and steam over high heat for 30 minutes.

While the fu yung is steaming, place the ingredients for the sauce in a pan, and heat and stir until thickened. Heat about 2 inches oil in a small, heavy pot until it begins to smoke. Add vermicelli (it will burst into a fluffy white "cloud"). Remove immediately to avoid darkening the color. Put aside and drain.

When the fu yung is done, remove from the steamer and let it air-dry for 10 minutes. Dry off the "peak" and paint about 1 teaspoon oil all over it. Brown the fu yung for a few minutes under a preheated broiler until it becomes a deep, golden-brown. Garnish with the "clouds" and serve with the heated sauce.

Serves 4–5.

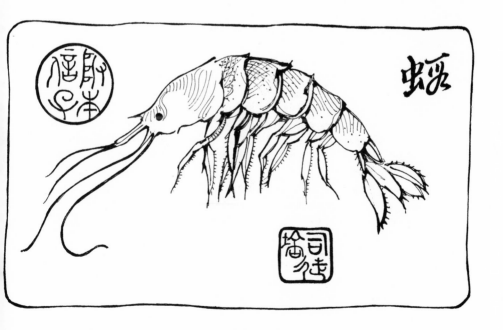

PORK WITH ALMONDS

This palace dish is a combination of tender pork and almonds. The almond flavor permeates the rich brown sauce. The Chinese use fresh unsalted bacon, which is rather fatty but yields the most tasty result. Fresh bacon can generally be purchased from a butcher if ordered ahead, but good-quality pork butt with some fat is an adequate substitute.

8 almonds
Seasoning mixture
   1 tablespoon grated fresh
     ginger
   3 tablespoons minced green
     onion
   1 tablespoon thin soy sauce
   3 tablespoons rice wine
   1 tablespoon water
   2 tablespoons oil
   2 tablespoons crushed rock
     sugar (2 tablespoons granu-
     lated sugar may be substi-
     tuted)

1 pound fresh unsalted bacon
   or fat pork butt, cut in
   1-inch cubes
1 tablespoon water mixed
   with 1/2 tablespoon cornstarch
2 tablespoons slivered green
   onion (cut in half lengthwise and slice diagonally
   into 1/2-inch sections)

Blanch the almonds by dropping them into boiling water and boiling for about 1 minute. Drain and remove skins. Split almonds in half and tie them up in a small cheesecloth bag.

Combine the ingredients for the seasoning mixture.

Heat a wok over high heat. Add 1 tablespoon oil and 1 tablespoon rock sugar. When the sugar turns a light brown (be careful not to let it burn), add the bacon or pork and stir-fry. Add the seasoning mixture and bag of almonds. Stir-fry until the meat is cooked through, about 2 to 3 minutes. Add 1 tablespoon rock sugar and stir-fry another minute or so. Remove the wok from heat.

Remove the almonds from the bag and put them on the bottom of a steaming bowl. Place the meat on top of the almonds. Remove and discard excess fat from the juices in the wok and pour 2 tablespoons of the remaining juice over the meat. Reserve the rest of the juice for later use. Cover the steaming bowl with foil, seal the edges tightly and place it in a steaming tray. Steam for 30 minutes.

Carefully remove the bowl from the steamer and transfer the meat to a heated plate. Arrange the almonds on top of the meat. Pour the steaming-bowl juices into a pan with the reserved stir-frying juices. Heat and slowly stir in the cornstarch mixture to thicken. Pour this sauce over the meat and almonds and garnish with green onion.

Serves 2–3.

Moslem Dishes

BEEF IN BUDDHIST ROBES

An interesting characteristic of this dish is a wrapping which suggests the Buddhist monk's saffron-colored robe. The meat filling is fragrant and spicy. These morsels can be served as appetizers or as an entrée.

Batter for wrappings
  6 large eggs
  2 tablespoons water mixed
    with 1 tablespoon corn-
    starch
  1/2 teaspoon salt
  1/2 teaspoon water
  1 teaspoon oil
Vegetable oil for frying and
  deep-frying
Filling
  1/2 pound lean ground beef
  1 teaspoon grated fresh
    ginger

1 tablespoon crushed
  flower pepper
1 tablespoon minced green
  onion
1/2 teaspoon sesame oil
1/2 teaspoon salt
1 tablespoon thin soy sauce
2 tablespoons water mixed
  with 1 tablespoon corn-
  starch
1/2 pound watercress or
  spinach leaves, washed and
  trimmed

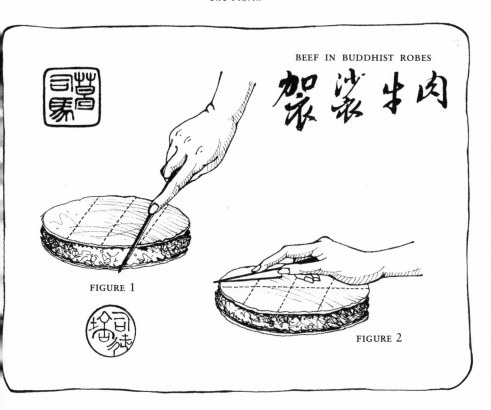

BEEF IN BUDDHIST ROBES

FIGURE 1

FIGURE 2

Mix together all ingredients for the batter.

Oil a 9-inch frying pan and place over low heat until hot. Remove from heat and pour in enough batter to cover two-thirds of the bottom of the pan, making a thin circle about 6 inches in diameter. Move the pan in a circular motion to set the batter evenly. (It should set in about 1/2 minute.) If too thin, add a little more batter before it sets. Turn it over and heat for a moment to ensure complete setting. Transfer to a well-oiled plate. Repeat the process to make five more wrappings. (There should be some batter left to use as a sealer.) Oil the top of each wrapping and stack one on top of the other on a plate.

Mix together all ingredients for the filling.

Place three wrappings on a board and brush half of the remaining batter on top. Spread a layer of filling over each wrapping and smooth the top by pressing with the side of a cleaver. Brush the rest of the batter on the remaining wrappings and place them wet side down on top of the filling. Press the wrappings down firmly so that they adhere to the filling. With a sharp knife, cut each circle in half. Then cut the semicircles again lengthwise into strips (Figure 1) and slice across the strips (Figure 2). Take care that the filling does not come out.

Heat about 2 inches oil to 350° in a deep-frying pan. With a spatula, carefully lower the strips into the oil. When done (2 to 3 minutes), the wrappings should be golden with edges light brown and slightly crisp. Scoop out and drain. Serve on a bed of watercress or spinach leaves. Serves 2–3.

STEAMED LAMB

2 pounds leg of lamb (shank portion, trimmed and boned)*
Seasoning mixture
    4 tablespoons thin soy sauce
    1 teaspoon Chinese red vinegar
    4 teaspoons rice wine
    2-1/2 teaspoons brown sugar
    5 large Chinese star anise
4 tablespoons Hoisin sauce

2 green onions, cut into 2-inch sections
1 large garlic clove, peeled and mashed lightly
2 large slices fresh ginger
2 tablespoons water mixed with 1 1/2 tablespoons cornstarch
2 cups finely slivered lettuce
1 tablespoon melted chicken fat
1 tablespoon minced Chinese parsley

Wash the lamb, pat dry and cut into 4 large pieces.

Combine the ingredients for the seasoning mixture.

Place the lamb in a large pot and cover with water. Bring to a boil and simmer for 30 minutes.

Drain and place the lamb in a steaming bowl. Pour the seasoning mixture and Hoisin sauce over the lamb and add the onion, garlic and ginger. Seal the bowl securely with aluminum foil and punch four or five holes on top.

Place the bowl in a steamer and steam for 1 1/2 to 2 hours. Test the lamb for tenderness and transfer to a heated platter. Pick out the anise, garlic and ginger pieces and discard. Reserve the liquid from the steamer bowl and strain into a pan. Heat and thicken with the cornstarch mixture until a thick gravy is formed.

---

* Generally the shank portion of a leg of lamb weighs about 4 pounds. For this recipe, have the butcher saw the shank in half. The other half can be frozen and used later.

Arrange the lettuce around the lamb, and spoon first the chicken fat and then the gravy over it. Garnish with parsley. Each person cuts off his own chunk of lamb and takes some lettuce and gravy with it.

Serves 4.

QUICK FRIED BEEF

3/4 pound flank steak
Marinade
    1/2 cup water mixed with
        1/4 cup cornstarch
    1 tablespoon thin soy sauce
Seasoning mixture
    2 tablespoons white vin-
        egar
    1 tablespoon thin soy sauce
    1 tablespoon rice wine
    1 teaspoon water
Vegetable oil for deep-frying

1/2 to 3/4 cup cornstarch
1/2 teaspoon crushed, peeled
    and minced garlic
1 cup slivered green onion
    (cut in half lengthwise and
    slice diagonally into
    1/2-inch sections)
1 teaspoon finely chopped
    Chinese parsley
1/2 teaspoon crushed flower
    pepper

Remove the thin membrane from the outer surface of the steak. With a sharp knife, slice the steak along the grain into matchstick-sized strips. (It is important that the strips be very thin.)

Mix the marinade ingredients together and carefully add the meat strips. Don't allow the strips to become tangled.

Combine the ingredients for the seasoning mixture.

Heat about 3 inches oil to 375° in a pan for deep-frying. Remove 6 or 7 meat strips from the marinade and coat them lightly with cornstarch. Add them to the hot oil, stir gently to keep them separated from each other, and remove as soon as they are crispy and curled. Drain on paper towels. Continue this process until all the meat is cooked.

Carefully remove and discard all but 2 tablespoons oil, free of food particles, from the pan. Reheat the oil over moderate heat, add garlic and meat and stir-fry for 1/2 minute. Add the seasoning mixture and stir a few times over high heat. Turn off the heat, add green onion and mix several times.

Serve on a heated platter, garnished with Chinese parsley and flower pepper.

Serves 2–3.

BRAISED LAMB WITH SAUCE

This dish is traditionally served with rolls, which are essential for the Mongolian barbecue. It can be enjoyed with rice, of course, but if you prefer rolls, follow the recipe on p. 100, but reduce the ingredients by half.

2 pounds lamb, cut from the
  leg
Dip
  1 tablespoon Chinese red
    vinegar
  1/2 teaspoon sesame oil
  1 teaspoon thin soy sauce
  1/4 teaspoon salt
1 teaspoon salt

4 tablespoons chopped green
  onion, white part only
2 large slices fresh ginger
2 large garlic cloves, peeled
  and sliced
3 large Chinese star anise
5 kernels flower pepper
1 tablespoon minced Chinese
  parsley

Wash the lamb, pat it dry and cut it into pieces about 2 by 2 inches by 1 inch.

Combine the ingredients for the dip.

Cover the lamb with water in a heavy pot. Bring to a boil and skim off the top several times if necessary.

Add salt, onion, ginger, garlic, star anise and flower pepper. Return to a boil, lower the heat and gently braise until the meat is tender and the liquid is reduced to 1/2 to 3/4 cup.

Transfer the lamb to a heated platter, spoon the sauce over it and garnish with parsley. Serve with the dip.

Serves 4.

PHOENIX-TAILED SHRIMP IN CLOUDS

8 fresh jumbo shrimp
Cornstarch, enough to coat
　shrimp
Batter
　2 large eggs
　4 tablespoons water-
　　chestnut flour or corn-
　　starch
　1 tablespoon cold water
　1 tablespoon rice wine
　1/2 teaspoon salt

Dip
　1 teaspoon Chinese red
　　vinegar
　2 tablespoons thin soy
　　sauce
　1/2 teaspoon shredded
　　fresh ginger
　4 drops sesame oil
Vegetable oil for deep-frying
1-1/2 cups 4-inch lengths of
　rice vermicelli
2 cups fresh spinach leaves,
　washed and trimmed

For the preliminary steps in preparing the shrimp for deep-frying, follow the illustrated instructions on page 9b, and then lightly coat the shrimp with cornstarch and set aside on a platter to air-dry.

Combine the ingredients for the batter. Mix together the ingredients for the dip.

Heat about 3 inches oil to about 350° in a wok and add vermicelli. It should suddenly puff up into a mass of white noodles. Quickly toss to make sure all noodles are fried. Remove them immediately from the heat to avoid browning them. Drain, and arrange on a warm platter.

Remove all food particles from the oil in the wok and add another inch of fresh oil. Reheat the oil to 350° and maintain it within 5° or so (use a candy thermometer).

Coat a shrimp thoroughly with batter and, holding it by the tail, slide it into the hot oil (see illustrated instructions on p. 9c). Deep-fry 2 shrimp at a time in the wok until all are done. Drain the shrimp and arrange them, tails up, on a bed of fluffy vermicelli, and arrange spinach leaves on the outer margin. Serve with the dip.

Serves 2–3.

MOSLEM CHICKEN SOUP

Chinese dishes using milk are usually of Moslem origin as this one is, or recently developed. In the past, the use of dairy products in classic Chinese cuisine was rare.

1/3 pound fresh fish fillet
2-1/2 tablespoons water
    mixed with 1 tablespoon
    cornstarch
4 tablespoons milk
1-1/4 teaspoons salt
4 egg whites
2 tablespoons melted chicken
    fat
1-1/2 cups boned, cooked and
    thinly sliced chicken breast
2 tablespoons water chestnut
    flour or cornstarch

1/4 cup thinly sliced carrots
    (cut crosswise)
2 tablespoons fresh Chinese
    parsley leaves
6-1/2 cups chicken stock
1 tablespoon rice wine
Pinch of MSG
1/4 cup slivered green onion
    (cut in half lengthwise and
    slice diagonally into
    1/2-inch sections)

Mash the fish into a paste with the back edge of a cleaver or put through a meat grinder or food processor. Put the paste in a bowl. Slowly add the cornstarch mixture, milk and 1/2 teaspoon salt, and mix well in one direction. Beat egg whites in a large bowl until stiff and slowly fold them into the fish paste. Add 1 tablespoon chicken fat and blend well.

Lightly oil the bottom of a 6 1/2-by-6 1/2-inch heatproof pan. Arrange the chicken slices in it so that they form a bottom layer. Sprinkle water chestnut flour over the chicken slices and spread the fish paste evenly over them. Arrange carrot slices and Chinese parsley leaves on top in alternate rows. Place the pan in a steamer and steam vigorously for 15 minutes. (The result will be a cake.)

Take off the steamer lid and allow to cool. Remove the pan and, with a sharp knife, carefully slice the cake into 2-by-1-inch pieces. Arrange the pieces on the bottom of individual soup bowls, with carrots and parsley on top.

Heat the stock in a large pot over high heat. Add 3/4 teaspoon salt, wine and MSG, and bring to a boil. Add 1 tablespoon chicken fat and stir. Adjust salt if necessary. Pour the broth gently over the pieces of cake. Garnish with 1/2 teaspoon slivered green onion per bowl.

Serves 6.

HSI SHIH'S
BREAST IN RED SAUCE

This ancient Moslem dish was named for the famous beauty Hsi Shih, who lived at about the time of Confucius. In preparing the fish dumplings, take care to mix the ingredients in one direction. They should be soft, yet must hold together.

5 large dried black mushrooms
Vegetable oil
Seasoning mixture
   2 tablespoons sugar
   1/2 teaspoon grated fresh ginger
   1/2 teaspoon salt
   2 tablespoons white vinegar
   1 tablespoon thin soy sauce
   2 tablespoons rice wine
   1/2 teaspoon MSG
   2 teaspoons white sesame seeds
1 pound white fish, haddock or cod fillets
1-1/2 teaspoons salt
1 teaspoon rice wine
1/4 teaspoon white pepper

1-1/2 tablespoons melted chicken fat
2 egg whites
1 to 2 tablespoons cornstarch
3 cups chicken stock
1-1/2 tablespoons vegetable oil
2 large slices fresh ginger
1/2 cup onion slices, cut 1 inch thick
1 tablespoon thin soy sauce
1/2 cup carrot slices, cut crosswise 1/8 inch thick
6 water chestnuts, cut in slices 1/8 inch thick
1/2 cup cucumber slices, cut crosswise 1/4 inch thick
1/2 teaspoon sesame oil
1 tablespoon water mixed with 1/2 tablespoon cornstarch

Soak mushrooms in hot water for 15 minutes. Rinse, squeeze out the water, remove the stems and quarter the caps.

To make the seasoning mixture, put a thin layer of oil in a small pan over low heat. Add sugar, turn up the heat and stir continually. When the sugar melts and begins to bubble, immediately reduce the heat or temporarily remove from the burner. The liquid should turn amber-colored and thicken slightly; do not let it burn or become dark and bitter from overcooking. Carefully add 1 tablespoon hot water, reheat and stir to dissolve. Remove from heat and add to the remaining seasoning-mixture ingredients.

In a dry pan, lightly toast sesame seeds until they are golden and begin to pop.

Remove any skin or bone from the fillets. Wash, pat dry and chop into a fine paste, or put the fish through a meat grinder or food processor. Put the paste in a bowl, add 5 tablespoons cold water and mix well. Transfer the paste to a strainer and press out all liquid. Remove any connective tissue and discard.

Put the paste back into the bowl, add salt, rice wine, pepper and chicken fat, and mix well in one direction only. Add about 1/4 cup cold water, using only as much as the paste will absorb without becoming watery. Continue mixing in one direction. Sprinkle cornstarch on the paste a little at a time and mix in one direction. Use just enough to hold the paste together. Beat egg whites until stiff and fold into the paste. Mold into little dumplings about 1-1/2 inches in diameter.

Bring the stock to a boil in a frying pan about 9 inches in diameter. Turn the heat down to a simmer and carefully slide a few dumplings into the hot stock. Gently poach until firm, about 2 minutes, and add another batch. Continue until all the dumplings are poached.

Transfer the dumplings and stock to a large heat-resistant casserole or equivalent. Place in a steamer and steam vigorously for 5 minutes. Remove the casserole from the steamer and carefully transfer the dumplings with a spatula to a lightly oiled plate. Reserve 1 1/2 cups of the stock.

Heat a wok over moderate heat. Add oil, ginger and onion, and stir-fry until the onion turns golden. Add the soy sauce and reserved stock. Simmer 1/2 minute and discard the onion and ginger.

Add the seasoning mixture and mushrooms to the wok and simmer 1/2 minute. Carefully slide in the dumplings and simmer gently for another 1/2 minute, taking care not to break them. Lower the heat if necessary to keep the simmer gentle. Spoon the sauce repeatedly over the dumplings. Slide the dumplings to one side, add carrots and water chestnuts, and continue simmering another 1/2 minute. Add cucumber for the last 15 seconds.

Sprinkle sesame oil over the dish and carefully thicken with the cornstarch mixture, taking care not to break up the dumplings. Remove the dumplings, vegetables and sauce to a heated serving platter, and garnish with sesame seeds.

Serves 3–4.

STUFFED PANCAKES

Eaten as a snack, this pancake with its very thin skin and pungent meat-and-vegetable filling might be termed Peking's answer to our American hot dog or hamburger. The pancakes can be made up in quantity, stuffed and quick-frozen uncooked for later use.

2 cups flour
1/4 teaspoon salt
3/4 cup water
Filling
    2 cups chopped celery cabbage, firmly packed (before measuring, put in a dishtowel and squeeze out the excess moisture)
    1/2 pound ground beef
    1-1/2 tablespoons thin soy sauce

1/2 tablespoon rice wine
1/4 teaspoon salt
1/4 cup chopped green onion
2 teaspoons grated fresh ginger
1/2 tablespoon sesame oil
2 tablespoons vegetable oil
1/3 cup Hoisin sauce*

Place flour and salt in a large bowl, and slowly add water. Dust your fingers with flour and mix until a dough is formed. Transfer the dough to a floured board and knead for about 5 minutes, or until it becomes elastic. Put it back in the bowl, cover with a moist towel and put it in a warm place. It should rise in about 15 minutes.

In a large bowl, thoroughly mix together all the ingredients for the filling.

Flour a board and shape the dough into a long roll about 2 inches in diameter, then cut into 20 equal pieces. Form each piece into a ball. Flour the board again and use a rolling pin to flatten the balls into pancakes about 4 to 5 inches in diameter. (The edges should be rolled thinner than the center so that, when pinched together to seal the pancakes, they will be thin enough to cook through readily.)

Place about 1-1/2 tablespoons filling in the middle of each pancake. Pull up the edges gently, pinching them firmly together to seal, and moisten with a little water if necessary.

Heat vegetable oil in a large frying pan or griddle until hot. Place the

* As a substitute for the Hoisin sauce, try a sauce made of 1 teaspoon minced fresh ginger, 3 tablespoons thin soy sauce, 1 teaspoon Chinese red vinegar, 1/4 teaspoon sesame oil, 1/2 teaspoon rice wine and 1/4 teaspoon sugar.

stuffed pancakes, sealed side down, in the pan. Lower the heat and flatten each pancake gently with your fingers. Fry for 3 minutes over medium heat. Brush a little oil on top of the pancakes, turn them over and fry for another 3 to 4 minutes. Turn them over again and fry for 2 minutes. (The cakes must be well browned and crisp on both sides.) It may be necessary to fry the pancakes in several batches if the pan is not large enough. Remove and serve while piping hot with Hoisin sauce and hot tea.

Serves 4.

Mongolian Dishes

Both the hot pot (*huo kuo*) and the barbecue have been modified and re-fined over the years, with the addition of a wider range of ingredients. But the use of a single pot and the basic simplicity of the cooking procedure still suggest the nomadic way of life.

MONGOLIAN HOT POT
(HUO KUO)

The Mongolian hot pot is a simple but festive way to entertain. Much of the preparation is done ahead of time and each person does his or her own cooking. A distinctive charcoal-burning pot called a *huo kuo*, sold in many Oriental specialty stores, is traditionally used for this dish. Electric models of the pot are also available, but an electric frying pan serves nicely as a substitute. Although the authentic Mongolian hot pot is made only with lamb and a few vegetables, the main ingredients can include different kinds of meat, poultry and seafood, as well as a variety of vegetables.

Broth
12 cups water
3-1/2 pounds chicken wings
1 pound lamb shanks or
  shoulder
4 green onions, sliced in
  1-inch pieces
1 large slice fresh ginger
Few drops sesame oil
Salt
Condiments
1 cup thin soy sauce
1/4 cup sesame oil
1/4 cup sugar
1/2 cup Chinese red vinegar
1/8 cup dry mustard mixed
  with enough water to
  make a thick paste

2 tablespoons Szech'uan
  hot pepper oil or hot
  bean paste
2 tablespoons grated fresh
  ginger
2 tablespoons mashed
  garlic mixed with 1 teaspoon white vinegar
1 cup chopped green onion
1/2 cup chopped Chinese
  parsley
4 pounds boned and rolled
  leg of lamb
2 pounds celery cabbage
2 pounds fresh spinach
1/2 pound snow peas, aspara-
  gus or broccoli
4 cups rice vermicelli, broken
  into 4-inch lengths

The broth can be prepared a day in advance and stored in the refrigerator until ready to use. Bring water to a boil in a large pot. Add chicken, pork, green onion and ginger. Bring the soup to a boil, reduce the heat and simmer, covered, for 2 to 3 hours. Cool and discard all solids. Strain the soup, and add sesame oil and salt to taste. Fill the *huo kuo* with the broth and heat it. Reserve the extra broth.

Put each of the condiment ingredients in an individual bowl and place on a large tray.

Slice the lamb as thinly as possible.* Wash and trim the celery cabbage, spinach leaves and snow peas. If necessary, cut the vegetables into bite-sized pieces. Arrange the vegetables and lamb on plates for each diner and give each person a bowl in which to mix their condiments.

At dinner time bring the *huo kuo* to the table along with the individual servings of the vegetables and lamb. Also put the tray of condiments on the table. Each person picks up a slice of meat or vegetable and plunges it briefly into the piping hot broth until just done. (Cooking time is slightly longer for meat.) Then the diner dips the food into his or her own blend of seasonings and sauces.

Near the end of the meal, the broth is brought to a boil, and the vermicelli is cooked in it for 3 to 5 minutes, or until they are fluffy and white.

---

* In order to do this, wrap the lamb in aluminum foil and put it in the freezer for 1 hour or more until it is firm enough (but not frozen solid) to be sliced very thin (about 1/8 inch thick). Some butchers will do both the freezing and slicing for you.

Each person helps himself to the cooked noodles accompanied by the broth. As the broth begins to run out, add more to keep the *huo kuo* full at all times.

Serves 6 to 8.

MONGOLIAN BARBECUE

A truly native meal, typical of the diet of the rugged Mongolian nomad. The thin-sliced meat is dipped in a spicy sauce, quickly grilled and then wrapped in a sesame roll. A gruel-like millet soup is eaten between sandwiches, and the meal is topped off with draughts of heated sorghum whiskey. Transposed to the West, this meal is ideal for an outdoor barbecue.

Millet soup
   1/2 cup millet
   Lamb bones
   10 cups cold water
   Salt
2 pounds boneless lamb
   taken from the upper part
   of the leg*
2 pounds boneless beef sirloin
2 cups slivered green onion
   (cut in half lengthwise and
   slice diagonally into
   1/2-inch sections)

2 cups Chinese parsley leaves
Dip
   1 cup thin soy sauce
   1/2 cup Chinese red vinegar
   1/2 cup rice wine
   1/2 cup fresh ginger juice**
   2 tablespoons flower
      pepper salt (p. 28)
   1/4 cup hot pepper oil
   1/4 cup sesame oil
   2 tablespoons garlic
      paste***

Soak the millet overnight in cold water. The next morning, put the lamb bones in a large pot. Add water and bring to a boil. Reduce the heat and simmer for several hours, adding water to maintain the original volume. Skim off the fat, remove the bones and strain the stock. Drain the millet, rinse several times, add to the stock and simmer slowly for 1 to 2 hours, or

---

* Ask the butcher to bone a leg of lamb. Use the bones to make the soup and freeze the shank portion for later use.
** Smash 5 large slices of fresh ginger with the end of a cleaver handle and put them in 1/2 cup water for 2 hours. Squeeze out the juice from the ginger slices.
*** Peel and crush 4 large garlic cloves into a paste, and add a little rice wine or vinegar to moisten.

until the grains break up and the soup is thickened. Salt to taste. Turn off the heat and set aside.

While the stock is simmering, trim off all fat and skin from the beef and lamb. Wrap the meat well and place in the freezer for 2 to 3 hours, or until it becomes firm, but not frozen hard. (This makes it easier to slice the meat very thinly.)

Using a very sharp knife or cleaver, carefully cut against the grain of the meat to make slices about 1/8 inch thick. Cut each slice into strips about 2 by 4 inches. Arrange the beef and lamb in layers on separate platters. Cover and refrigerate until ready to use.

Put the green onion and parsley in separate bowls, cover and refrigerate until ready to use.

Put each dip ingredient in a separate bowl, place the bowls on a large tray, cover and set aside. Prepare the rolls.

Rolls

2 cups lukewarm milk	1/2 cup melted shortening
1/3 cup sugar	7 cups flour
1/2 teaspoon salt	1/4 cup blackstrap molasses
2 cakes compressed yeast	1/4 cup sesame seeds
2 large beaten eggs	

Mix the milk, sugar and salt together in a large bowl. Crumble the yeast and mix it in. Stir in the eggs and shortening. Using a whip, beat until foamy. Add flour in 3 or 4 parts, stirring well after each addition. (The dough should be slightly sticky, but workable.) Turn the dough out onto a lightly floured board and knead gently a few times. Put it in a lightly oiled bowl, cover with a damp cloth, and keep in a warm, draft-free place for about 1 hour, or until it has doubled in volume.

On the floured board, roll the dough into a large rectangular piece about 10 by 35 inches. Then slice into strips about 2 by 7 inches. Fold each strip in half so the rolls measure about 2 by 3 1/2 inches. Brush molasses on top of each roll and sprinkle with sesame seeds. Place the rolls about 2 inches apart on ungreased cookie sheets. Bake in a 375° oven for 15 to 20 minutes. The rolls are ready when they have risen and are firm and golden-brown on top. Place the rolls in a large basket or on a tray and cover with a cloth to keep warm.

Makes 25 rolls.

SERVING THE BARBECUE

While the dough is rising, start a fire in your barbecue grill. By the time the rolls are baked the fire should be very hot. Place the grill about 3 inches from the hot coals.

When ready to serve the meal, bring out the hot soup, meat platters, greens, dip tray and rolls.

Each person fills a bowl with any combination of dip ingredients to make his own sauce creation, then dips a slice of meat in the sauce and quickly cooks it on the hot grill just long enough to lightly scorch the meat on each side. A roll is split open and the meat sandwiched into it, garnished with greens.

The bowl of soup served between sandwiches is made purposely bland to contrast with the spicy meats and pungent greens. The choice of meats and the variety of sauces and seasonings offer a challenge to each diner to find the "perfect" blend.

The
EAST

Eastern Chinese cooking developed in and around the cities of the lower Yangtze delta: Hangchou, Shaohsing, and Ninpo, in the province of Chekiang; Suchou, Chenkiang, Yangchou and Nanking, in Kiangsu; and the municipality of Shanghai. From the sixth century on, these towns grew and prospered both economically and culturally. High government officials, emperors, princes, dukes and wealthy merchants all gravitated to this region to create what has been termed a "heaven on earth."

In the past the cooks of the great villas made good use of the region's abundant foodstuffs to compete with each other in creating many remarkable dishes. The final culinary flowering of the region came with the appearance of the imperial chefs from the south. Since a general culinary standard had already been established, the influx of this new element resulted in what some purists of the time complained of as unnecessarily elaborate dishes and overly opulent banquets.

On the one hand, the purists initiated such dishes as *hsi hu* vinegar fish and *su tung po* pork, fresh ginger chicken and braised *pai ts'ai* hearts. The imperial chefs created, in contrast, such elaborate and decorative dishes as bright moon red pine chicken.

Shanghai has its own characteristic cuisine. Braising (or red-cooking), using the triad of soy, wine and sugar, is its tour de force, with ginger root, green onion and, occasionally, fennel or tangerine peel as its seasonings. The meat is never browned initially (although at times it may be lightly deep-fried), and ultimately it turns a beautifully glazed reddish brown. The sauce is not thickened but is reduced through long braising into a delicious concentrated gravy.

In Chinese homes braised dishes are usually cooked in an unglazed ceramic casserole which provides the slow, even cooking essential to the absorption of flavors and tenderizing of meats. Some fine examples of Shanghai braising are braised fresh pork with rock sugar, braised pork with vegetables and shrimp soy dip, and duck in sauce Shanghai style. Quick braised dishes made of fish, vegetables with meatballs or small pieces of meat or fowl are not uncommon in restaurants and government-sponsored dining halls which cook large numbers of small, disposable casserole dishes for workers who wish to have a hot, nourishing meal at midday.

Suchou, just west of Shanghai, is noted for its superb pastries made according to recipes that are centuries old. To the north lies Chenkiang, known for its excellent seafood dishes as well as for the superior dark vinegar used almost exclusively as a dip. Just across the Grand Canal from Chenkiang is Yangchou, famous for its bite-sized pastries and noodles, and for the finest example of Chinese egg roll.

The cuisine of Nanking, the old Ming capital, includes a wide variety of braised dishes, seafood dishes and, especially, smoked meats and poultry. Nanking cuisine has been greatly influenced by the Moslem population, whose dietary prohibitions, such as the ban against pork, have survived through the centuries. With the lack of a good source of fat, chicken and seafood dishes predominate. Chicken fat is liberally used, as are ground pepper, flower pepper and sesame seeds. Phoenix-tail shrimp, fried shrimp balls and egg *shao mai* soup (p. 00) are all Moslem dishes.

Hangchou cuisine may be regarded as the *haute cuisine* of the East, since that city has a long heritage of imperial residences and great wealth. Here some of the most famous Chinese dishes were created: shrimp and rice crust, spiced steamed chicken and stuffed steamed duck.

In nearby Shaohsing, the excellent salted and pickled vegetables are used in such dishes as dried mustard green with pork.

EASTERN RESTAURANTS

Hangchou is represented in this collection by three restaurants and a cooking class. The Hangchou Chiu Chia is a wine house which offers wines with its tasty dishes, an example of which is spiced steamed chicken. The Lou Wai Lou (The Pavilion Beyond) is over a hundred and forty years old and is known for both its cuisine and its location on Ku Shan (Lonely Mountain) island in magnificent West Lake. Its upstairs dining rooms overlook weeping willows and peach trees on the lakeshore, with gently rolling hills dotted with the bright tiled roofs in the distance. Dishes like Hsi Hu (West Lake) vinegar fish make good use of the lake's abundant supply of fish. The T'ien Hsiang Lou (Heaven's Fragrance Pavilion) and the Food Service Organization of Hangchou have also contributed.

Shanghai is represented by a number of distinguished restaurants. The

Lao Yung Shun (Old Splendor) is located near a famous temple and is favored by the throngs of temple visitors. The Te Hsing Kuan (Virtue and Glory Hall) is patronized by workers from the surrounding market areas. The Ta Chia Li (Great Benefit) Western Dining Hall was located until 1926 on Lake T'ai and specialized in serving those on outings in colorful pleasure boats. The tea cakes of the Wu Fung Chai (Five Fragrance Vegetarian) Tea Cake Shop are famous throughout the area. Other contributing restaurants are in the Lin Fu Chai (Lin's Blessed Vegetarian Restaurant), Yi Chi Fu Hsing (The Righteous Reprospering), the Yung Chiang Chuang Yuan Lou (Imperial Scholar's Pavilion of Yung Chiang), the Fu Ch'un (Blessed Spring) Tea House and the Food Service Organization of Shanghai.

Nanking restaurants cannot be neglected. The specialty of the Liu Hua Ch'un (Spring Flower) is vegetable dishes simmered in ceramic pots. The Sze Ho Ch'un (Four Crane Spring) is highly regarded in the area. Two Moslem restaurants are represented: the Ma Hsiang Hsing and the Hua Lo Yuan (Happy Garden).

Yangchou pastries are the specialty of the Lu Yang Ts'un (Green Willow Village). The Ts'ai Ken Hsiang (Fragrant Vegetable Root) and the Yangchou Dining Hall, which was originally named Yueh Ming (Bright Moon), have both contributed recipes of Yangchou dishes.

Suchou is represented by four establishments. The Ch'en Ta Ch'eng has a reputation throughout China for its tea cakes. Also contributing are the Sung Ho Lou (Pavilion of Pine Trees and Cranes), known for its braised duck, the Yung Hua Lou (Glorious Flower Pavilion), famous for its pastries and snacks, and the City Cooking Class of Suchou.

Finally, Chenkiang is represented by the Chenkiang Restaurant, and by the Shen Lung (Great Prosperity) Dining Hall of Peking, which is known for its dry-fried shrimp with tomato sauce.

EGG SHAO MAI SOUP

Filling
3/4 cup minced fresh
   shrimp (about 1/2 pound,
   unshelled)
1/2 teaspoon salt
1/2 teaspoon MSG
2 tablespoons minced green
   onion, white part only
1 teaspoon water mixed
   with 1 teaspoon corn-
   starch
1 teaspoon rice wine
2 teaspoons melted chicken
   fat

Batter for wrappings
4 large eggs, beaten
1/4 teaspoon sugar
2 teaspoons water mixed
   with 1/2 teaspoon cornstarch
3 drops sesame oil
1/4 teaspoon salt
1/2 teaspoon MSG
4 cups chicken stock
Vegetable oil for light frying
1 teaspoon water mixed with
   3/4 teaspoon cornstarch

Mix all the ingredients for the filling, blending well. Mix all the batter ingredients for making the wrappings. Add salt and MSG to the stock.

Lightly oil a small (6 or 8 inch) skillet, and heat it over a medium flame. Add 1 to 1-1/2 tablespoons batter to the skillet, tilting the pan so that the batter flows evenly over the bottom of the pan. As soon as the bottom side of the wrapping is cooked (the upper side should be moist and not completely cooked), carefully remove it from the skillet and set aside on a lightly oiled plate. Continue making the wrappings until all but 2 tablespoons of the batter are used.

Place about 2 teaspoons of the filling in the center of the moist side of each wrapping. Wet the edges with a little batter and fold half of the wrapping over the other half, enclosing the filling. Squeeze the edges together gently to seal. When all the dumplings are made, put them on the oiled plate, place it in a steamer and steam for 10 minutes.

Heat the soup, add the cornstarch mixture and stir until slightly thickened, salting to taste if necessary. Place a few dumplings in each soup bowl and pour the soup over them.

Serves 3.

FRAGRANT CRISPY CHICKEN LEGS

This tender chicken dish has a definite bite to it and is common to both Eastern and Northern Chinese cooking.

2 pounds chicken legs	2 tablespoons rice wine
Marinade	1 tablespoon minced fresh
1 teaspoon five-flavored	ginger
spice	Dip
2 tablespoons sugar	1 teaspoon flower pepper
3/4 teaspoon salt	2 teaspoons kosher salt
1/2 cup thin soy sauce	1/3 cup cornstarch
1 teaspoon sesame oil	Vegetable oil for deep-frying

Wash the chicken legs and wipe them dry. Combine the marinade ingredients, mix well and marinate the chicken legs for several hours.

To make the dip, follow instructions given under Pepper, flower, on p. 28.

Put the chicken legs and marinade in a steaming bowl, mix well and cover with aluminum foil. Pierce the foil in several places with a fork. Put the bowl into a steamer and steam for 1 hour. If necessary, add more boiling water to the steamer periodically.

Remove the bowl and take out the chicken legs. Shake the moisture off the legs, dry with a towel and air-dry them for several hours.

Dredge the chicken legs with cornstarch.

Heat 3 inches oil to about 360° in a deep, heavy pot or deep-fryer. Put two chicken legs in at a time and fry until they are golden-brown and crisp. Serve with the dip.

Serves 3.

SPARERIBS WITH DIPS

The secret of how these tender ribs turn out to be so juicy inside and crisp outside is that they are fried three times.

2 pounds spareribs, cut from
    the back
Marinade
    3 tablespoons thin soy
        sauce
    5 tablespoons rice wine
1/2 cup cornstarch
Dipping sauce
    1-3/4 teaspoons thin soy
        sauce

3-1/2 tablespoons water
3-1/2 tablespoons sugar
3 tablespoons white vin-
    egar
1 tablespoon water mixed
    with 1/2 tablespoon
    cornstarch
Vegetable oil for deep-frying
Black pepper salt dip (p. 29)

Wash and dry the ribs. Cut the rack, across the ribs, into strips 2 to 2 1/2 inches wide, and then separate out the individual rib pieces.

Mix the marinade ingredients in a large bowl. Add the ribs and mix well. Remove them from the marinade, sprinkle cornstarch over them and put them back in the marinade.

Combine the ingredients of the sauce mixture in a pan, heat and stir until thickened.

Heat about 4 inches oil in a large, deep pot or deep-fryer. When the oil reaches 340°, remove the ribs from the marinade and add half of the ribs, one at a time, to the oil. Deep-fry for 1/2 minute and drain on paper towels. Regulate heat as needed to maintain proper temperature. Add the second half of the ribs and again fry for 1/2 minute and drain.

Repeat the above process for both batches again, keeping the oil at 340° at all times and clear of food particles. Then heat the oil to 350°, add all the ribs at once and deep-fry for about 1 minute. Remove and drain on paper towels. (This method of deep-frying helps maintain better tempera-ture control and results in more even frying. The ribs should be cooked and tender inside and crispy outside.) Transfer the ribs to a large bowl.

Reheat the sauce if necessary, and pour into a small bowl. Serve the ribs with the sauce and the black pepper salt dip.

Serves 3.

SWEET AND SOUR SPARERIBS

The recipe for these succulent ribs originated in the cooking classes sponsored by the city of Suchou to instruct the chefs of the people's dining halls.

2 pounds meaty spareribs
Marinade
   1 tablespoon thin soy sauce
   5 tablespoons rice wine
   1/2 cup cornstarch
   2 tablespoons water
Seasoning mixture
   1/3 cup sugar
   1 tablespoon thick soy
     sauce
   2 tablespoons thin soy
     sauce
   3 tablespoons lemon juice
   1/2 teaspoon sesame oil

2 whole Chinese star anise,
   finely crushed
1 tablespoon sesame seeds
Vegetable oil for deep-frying
   plus 1 tablespoon
1 large garlic clove, crushed
1 large onion, sliced
1/2 cup chicken stock
2/3 cup *rakkyo* (Japanese-
   style pickled green onions)
2 tablespoons water mixed
   with 1-1/2 tablespoons
   cornstarch

Wash the spareribs, pat dry and cut across the ribs into 2-inch-wide strips. Separate individual rib pieces out of the strips.

Mix the marinade ingredients together, place the ribs in a large bowl and pour the marinade over them. Mix well, coating all surfaces, and marinate for about 15 minutes.

Combine the ingredients of the seasoning mixture.

Lightly toast the sesame seeds in a dry pan.

Heat 3 to 3 1/2 inches oil in a deep, heavy pot or deep-fryer until the oil is about 340°. Remove half of the ribs from the marinade and add, one at a time, to the oil. Fry for 1/2 minute, regulating the heat so that it doesn't vary. Remove the ribs with a slotted spoon, and fry the second half. Repeat the process for both batches. Finally, keeping the oil at a constant temperature, add all the ribs and fry for about 1 minute. Remove and drain well on paper towels. (The ribs should be crisp on the outside and tender inside.)

Place a wok over high heat. When it is very hot, add oil and garlic, and brown until golden. Discard the garlic. Add the onion slices and stir-fry for 1/2 minute. Add the seasoning mixture and simmer for 1/2 minute. Add the stock and bring to a boil. Add *rakkyo* and thicken the sauce with cornstarch paste. Add spareribs, mix well and transfer to a heated platter. Garnish with sesame seeds.

Serves 3.

SMOKED HAM WITH
SNOW PEAS AND ALMONDS

The unusual and delicious flavor of this dish is derived from specially smoked ham, stir-fried with snow peas and garnished with almonds.

Seasoning mixture
3 pieces dried tangerine
  peel, soaked in water for
  15 minutes
2 tablespoons crushed rock
  sugar
2 teaspoons thin soy sauce
1/2 teaspoon sesame oil
1/2 cup water

2 tablespoons barbecue
  smoke sauce*
2/3 pound snow peas
1/3 cup sliced almonds
3 tablespoons vegetable oil
1 1-pound boneless ham slice,
  with some fat
1/2 teaspoon salt
1 teaspoon rice wine

Combine the ingredients of the seasoning mixture. Parboil the snow peas in boiling water for 1/2 minute. Drain and quickly rinse them with cold running water. Put the peas in a bowl and allow the water adhering to them from the cold-water rinsing to collect in the bottom of the bowl.

Lightly fry the almonds in 1/2 teaspoon oil in a small frying pan.

Put 1 tablespoon oil into a large frying pan, add ham and slowly heat for 1 minute. Add the seasoning mixture and simmer very gently, turning occasionally until the liquid is reduced. Remove the ham and discard the remaining liquid. Slice the ham into strips about 2 inches by 1/2 inch.

Put a wok over high heat. When very hot, add 2 tablespoons oil, followed by salt, then snow peas (along with any water collected in the bowl) and wine. Stir-fry until well coated with oil for about 1 minute. Add the ham and stir twice. Transfer to a heated platter and garnish with almonds.

Serves 3.

* Available in most supermarkets.

BRAISED PORK AND VEGETABLES
WITH SHRIMP SOY DIP

2 pounds fresh ham
Seasoning mixture
  1 tablespoon thin soy sauce
  1 tablespoon rice wine
  1/2 tablespoon sugar
  1/4 teaspoon salt
  1/4 teaspoon MSG
2 large pieces canned bamboo
  shoot
Shrimp soy dip
  1 tablespoon dried shrimp

1/3 cup thin soy sauce
1/2 teaspoon grated ginger
1 tablespoon minced green
  onion
1/4 teaspoon sesame oil
1/4 teaspoon white pepper
1/4 teaspoon MSG
1 tablespoon rice wine
4 medium carrots
1/2 pound string beans

After removing the skin,* wash and dry the ham.

Combine the ingredients for the seasoning mixture. Slice the bamboo shoot into quarters lengthwise, put the pieces in a colander and pour several cups of boiling water over them.

To make the dip, first soak the shrimp in warm water for 10 minutes, then drain it and put it in a small pot with all the other dip ingredients except rice wine. Bring to a boil, reduce heat and simmer for 5 minutes. Add wine, turn off heat and cool for 30 minutes. Transfer to a serving bowl.

Place the ham in a heavy pot and add just enough water to cover. Add the seasoning mixture and bring to a boil. Lower the heat and simmer about 2 hours, or until the liquid is reduced by half. Turn the meat from time to time.

Transfer the meat and liquid to a ceramic flameproof casserole. Arrange carrots and bamboo-shoot pieces in separate sections around the meat, leaving room for the string beans. Cover the casserole and gently braise for 20 minutes. If additional liquid is needed, add another 1/2 cup water or stock. Add the string beans to the casserole, cover and braise for 10 to 15 minutes. Serve with the shrimp soy dip.

Serves 4–5.

---

* Store the skin in plastic wrap in the refrigerator for use in other Chinese dishes.

MU HSU PORK HANGCHOU STYLE

This version of *mu hsu* pork can be served alone or with the traditional pancakes, green onion and Hoisin sauce of the original.

Seasoning mixture
1 tablespoon thin soy sauce
1 tablespoon rice wine
1/4 teaspoon MSG
1 cup loosely packed gold needles (dried lily buds)
1/4 cup loosely packed wood ears
3 large eggs
1/4 teaspoon salt
1/4 cup vegetable oil
1 pound pork loin (with some fat), cut in slices 2 inches by 1/4 inch

2 tablespoons Chinese stock (p. 30) or chicken stock
1-1/2 cups slivered green onion (cut in half lengthwise and slice diagonally into 1/2-inch sections)
1/4 teaspoon sesame oil
Pancakes (optional), p. 64
8 green onions, white part only, cut in 1-inch sections (optional)
2/3 cup Hoisin sauce (optional)

Soak gold needles and wood ears in warm water for 20 minutes. Combine the ingredients of the seasoning mixture.

Rinse the gold needles and wood ears and squeeze out the water. Cut both the gold needles and wood ears into 1-inch sections.

Break the eggs into a bowl, add salt and beat well.

Heat 1 tablespoon of the oil in a wok over moderate heat. Add the beaten egg and scramble lightly. Remove and set aside. Quickly scrape the sides of the wok with a spatula.

Add the remaining oil to the wok, and when the oil is very hot, add the pork and stir-fry for 1 minute. Add the seasoning mixture, stock, gold needles and wood ears and stir-fry about 2 minutes.

Add green onion slivers and stir-fry for 1 minute. Turn off the heat, add scrambled eggs and mix lightly. Sprinkle sesame oil over the dish, and transfer to a heated platter.

If desired, serve with pancakes, green onions and Hoisin sauce. Each person takes a pancake, adds some *mu hsu* pork and green onion and rolls the pancake up. It is then dipped into Hoisin sauce and eaten.

Serves 4.

DRIED MUSTARD GREENS WITH PORK

The best dried mustard greens come from Chekiang Province. When fresh, the greens are salted and dried outdoors, which is why they may be somewhat sandy. In this recipe the mustard greens impart an almost astringent taste to the braised pork, rendering it less oily. Delicious served with hot rice and green tea.

1-1/4 pounds pork butt with some fat	Seasoning mixture
	1-1/2 tablespoons thick soy
1/2 cup (firmly packed) whole dried mustard greens	sauce
	1-3/4 teaspoons sugar
1-1/2 cups water	2 teaspoons rice wine

Cut the pork into 1-inch cubes. Soak the mustard greens for 1 hour in warm water, then wash and rinse very thoroughly until all sand is removed. Discard the tough parts and cut the stems into small pieces. Keep the leafy parts whole.

Put the pork into a large pot, add water and the seasoning mixture. Bring to a boil, reduce heat and braise, stirring occasionally, for 30 minutes, or until the liquid is reduced to about 1/3 cup. The pork should appear glossy red. Remove the pork and set aside. Add the mustard-green stems to the sauce and stir. Transfer them to a steaming bowl and arrange the pork cubes evenly over them. Cover the pork with mustard leaves. Add 2 tablespoons water to the sauce in the pan and spoon it over the leaves. Place the bowl in a steamer and steam for 30 minutes.

Serves 3.

SU TUNG PO PORK

This ancient recipe, beloved by all Chinese, is attributed to the Sung dynasty poet and gourmet Su Tung Po. He lived in exile during the latter part of his career and advocated living a simple life, which included plain cooking. This is such fare, for it uses the humblest ingredients, simply flavored and cooked, but it is a most remarkable dish. Braised and then steamed, the pork becomes as soft as bean curd and tastes indescribably delicious.

1-1/2 pounds five flower pork
1/2 teaspoon salt
Seasoning mixture
    4-1/2 teaspoons crushed
      rock sugar
    3 tablespoons thin soy
      sauce
    3 tablespoons rice wine

2 slices fresh ginger
1 tablespoon chopped
    green onion
1/2 head lettuce, shredded
1 tablespoon slivered green
    onion (cut in half length-
    wise and slice diagonally
    into 1/2-inch sections)

Sprinkle the pork with salt and let stand for 20 minutes. Rub off all moisture and salt.

Place the pork in a pot, cover with water and boil for 10 minutes. Remove and wash with cold water. Cut the pork into pieces 2 inches by 1/2 by 1/2 inch. Put the pieces back in the pot, add the seasoning mixture and 1 cup water. Bring to a boil, reduce heat and gently braise for 2-1/2 to 3 hours, or until the liquid is reduced to a thick sauce (do not allow to stick or burn).

Transfer the pork and juices to a heatproof bowl, put it in a steamer and steam vigorously for 30 minutes. Remove from the steamer, discard the ginger and onion and skim off the oil. Arrange the pork pieces on a bed of shredded lettuce. Spoon the sauce over the pork, garnish with slivered green onion and serve with hot rice.

Serves 3.

BRAISED PORK WITH ROCK SUGAR

Here fresh ham is slowly braised to produce the traditional "red-cooked" meat. The flavor is reminiscent of the home-style cooking of the Suchou-Wuhsi area. Any leftover meat may be refrigerated and reheated later with various vegetables to be served for several meals.

5 to 6 pounds fresh ham
1/3 cup rice wine
1/3 cup lightly crushed rock sugar
1/4 cup vegetable oil
1/4 cup thin soy sauce
5 whole pieces Chinese star anise
1/4 teaspoon fennel seeds
3 green onions, sliced in half crosswise

4 slices fresh ginger, cut 1/4 inch thick
4 cups chopped vegetables (such as carrots, potatoes and turnips) or 1 pound celery cabbage, sliced diagonally about 3 by 2 inches, or 1 pound whole string beans, trimmed

Wash and dry the meat. With a sharp knife, make slashes down to the bone in parts where the meat is thick, to facilitate cooking.

Put the meat, skin side down, in a large flameproof casserole or heavy iron pot with a cover. Add enough water to cover, bring to a boil and skim off the scum. Add all the remaining ingredients except vegetables and bring to a boil. Reduce the heat to low and simmer for 30 minutes. Turn the meat over, cover and simmer for 3 or more hours, or until it is very tender. Transfer it to a heated platter and keep it warm.

Check the amount of liquid left. If necessary, add enough water to total about 4 cups liquid. Stir well and bring to a boil. Lower the heat, add the vegetables and cook until tender, stirring from time to time to avoid burning. Remove the vegetables and continue to simmer the sauce until it is reduced to about 1 1/2 cups and is thick and glossy. Just before serving, reheat the meat and vegetables in the pot.

Place the meat on a large platter and arrange the vegetables around it. Serve the sauce in a bowl and spoon it over the sliced meat.

Serves 6.

PORK SPRING ROLLS
YANGCHOU STYLE

These delectable, puffy deep-fried rolls should be eaten whole, the ends dipped into plum or Hoisin sauce or a combination of thin soy sauce and hot mustard.

Seasoning mixture
  2 tablespoons rice wine
  1 tablespoon thin soy sauce
  2-1/2 teaspoons sugar
  Pinch of salt
  1/2 teaspoon MSG
  1/4 teaspoon black pepper
  1/3 cup Chinese stock
    (p. 30) or chicken stock
Binder paste
  3 tablespoons cornstarch
  1/4 cup boiling water
  2-1/2 cups thinly (diagonally)
    sliced celery cabbage
Vegetable oil for deep-frying
    plus 3-1/2 tablespoons
4 large slices fresh ginger

1/4 cup green onions cut in
  3-inch sections
3/4 cup minced pork butt
1/2 cup shredded bamboo
  shoots
2 tablespoons water mixed
  with 1 tablespoon corn-
  starch
6 water chestnuts, minced
1/2 cup roughly crushed
  cashew nuts
Wrappings*
  2 cups plus 2 tablespoons
    flour
  1/2 teaspoon salt
  1 cup warm water
  1 teaspoon vegetable oil

Combine the ingredients for the seasoning mixture. Make the binder paste by mixing the cornstarch and boiling water and stirring the mixture over heat until it thickens. Wrap the cabbage in a large dishcloth and squeeze out as much liquid as possible.

Prepare the filling. Heat a wok until very hot and add 3 1/2 tablespoons oil, and then the ginger and green onions. Stir-fry until golden and discard the vegetables but leave the oil in the wok. Add pork and stir-fry until lightly browned. Add cabbage, bamboo shoots, and the seasoning mixture and bring to a boil. Add the cornstarch mixture and stir until it thickens. Add the water chestnuts and cashews. Set aside to cool.

To make the wrappings, first mix flour and salt together in a bowl. Combine water and oil and add to the flour, a little at a time, mixing well. The dough will begin to separate from the sides of the bowl. If it is very

* Ready-made spring roll skins are available in Chinese grocery stores and may be used in this recipe.

sticky, add a little flour; if dry and powdery, add a little warm water. On a lightly floured board, gently knead the dough for 3 to 4 minutes, or until it is elastic and stops sticking to your fingers. Leave the dough on the board and put it in a warm place, cover with a damp cloth and let it sit for 20 minutes.

On a floured board, shape the dough into a roll about 1-1/4 inches in diameter and slice it into 14 equal pieces. Form each piece into a ball and flatten it out. With a rolling pin, roll each piece into a circle about 5 inches in diameter. The edges of the circles should be a little thinner than the center.

Heat a lightly oiled large skillet over moderate heat. When the skillet is slightly hot to the touch, place a wrapping on the skillet for a second only, or until it turns barely firm and whitish. Take great care to see that the wrapping is cooked yet remains pliable enough to be easily wrapped around the filling. Transfer to an oiled plate and cover with a moist cloth. Repeat the process for the remaining wrappings.

Place a wrapping on a board. Spoon about 2 tablespoons filling in the center and spread it into a rectangle about 1-1/2 by 3 inches (Figure 1). Fold the left and right sides over and apply ample binder paste along the top of these edges (Figure 2). Fold the edge nearest you up and over the filling (Figure 3) and apply the binder to the top side of this edge. Spread the binder on the underside of the top edge, then fold this edge over the filling

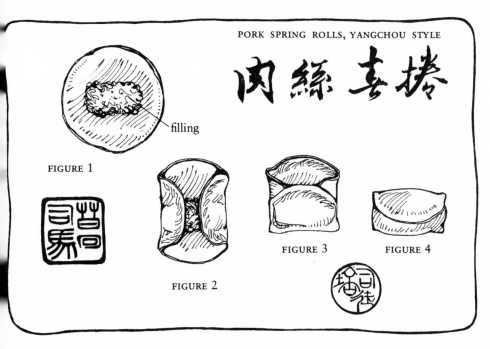

PORK SPRING ROLLS, YANGCHOU STYLE

filling

FIGURE 1

FIGURE 2

FIGURE 3

FIGURE 4

to close firmly (Figure 4). Be generous with the binder to make sure the rolls stay closed.

Heat 3 inches oil in a wok to about 350°. Carefully lower two rolls at a time into the oil and deep-fry for 2 to 3 minutes, turning them from time to time until they are puffy and golden. Maintain the temperature in the range of about 330° to 350°. Drain the rolls well and serve while they are still hot and puffy.

Makes 14 rolls.

NOODLES WITH TENDER CHICKEN

This delicious thick soup can be prepared quickly, and is ideal for lunch or a snack. The Chinese enjoy dipping the noodles into a dip.

Seasoning mixture
  1 tablespoon thin soy sauce
  1/2 teaspoon MSG
  1-1/2 teaspoons salt
Dip
  1/4 cup Chinese red vinegar
  1/4 cup thin soy sauce
6 to 8 cups Chinese stock
  (p. 30) or chicken stock
3 tablespoons vegetable oil
2 cups *pai ts'ai* hearts cut
  diagonally into 1/2-inch
  slices

1/2 pound fresh or packaged
  Chinese noodles
1 teaspoon sesame oil
1/2 pound shredded, cooked
  chicken
2 large hard-boiled eggs,
  halved lengthwise
1 cup slivered ham or barbecued pork

Combine the ingredients for the seasoning mixture. Make the dip.

In a pot, bring the stock to a rapid boil, turn down the heat and let it boil gently.

Put a wok over high heat. Add vegetable oil and then the *pai ts'ai* hearts, and stir-fry for about 1 minute, or until the leaves turn dark green.

Add the boiling stock to the hearts, then add the noodles. When the liquid comes to a boil, skim off the top. Add 1 teaspoon sesame oil and continue boiling until the noodles are almost cooked, or when you can easily snip a noodle in half with your fingernails. Add the seasoning mixture and chicken. Stir, lower the heat and simmer for 1 to 2 minutes.

When the noodles are cooked and the soup is thick, transfer to individual bowls. Place half an egg, slivered ham or pork on top of each soup bowl, and serve with the dip in individual bowls.

Serves 4.

SPICED STEAMED CHICKEN

1 3-pound chicken
2 teaspoons sesame oil
1 teaspoon plus salt to taste
3 green onions, cut into
  2-inch sections
1-1/2 tablespoons minced
  fresh ginger
12 kernels flower pepper,
  ground
3 tablespoons rice wine

Dip
  2 tablespoons thin soy
    sauce
  1 teaspoon fresh ginger
    shreds
  2 teaspoons rice wine
  1/4 teaspoon sugar
1 bunch fresh watercress,
  trimmed and washed, or
  1/2 head lettuce,
  washed, drained and
  shredded
Pinch of MSG

Remove giblets from the chicken. With a sharp cleaver, cut the chicken open along the backbone, leaving the breast side whole. Wash and dry it thoroughly with paper towels, and let it air-dry for 10 minutes.

Smear the inside and outside of the chicken with sesame oil, then sprinkle with salt all over. Make a few cuts into the thicker parts of the legs. Put the onion, ginger, flower pepper and wine inside the chicken and place it in a large heatproof bowl.

Mix together the ingredients for the dip.

Place the bowl with the chicken in a steamer and steam for 30 minutes over high heat.

Remove the bowl from the steamer and carefully transfer the chicken to a board, saving the liquid in the bowl. When the chicken is cool enough to handle, cut it into serving pieces (see illustrated instructions for carving and serving fowl on p. 9) and arrange on a bed of watercress or lettuce.

Strain the liquid in the bowl. Add MSG and salt to taste, and pour it over the chicken. Serve with the dip.

Serves 4.

DELICIOUS WINED CHICKEN

1 2-1/2- to 3-pound frying
  chicken
Marinade
  2 green onions, chopped
  1 teaspoon salt
  2 large pieces cinnamon
    bark
  3 large pieces Chinese star
    anise
  2 tablespoons sugar

1-1/2 tablespoons wine lees
  or 3 tablespoons Japa-
  nese white *miso*
5 drops sesame oil
1 teaspoon salt
1 tablespoon rice wine
1/2 head lettuce, sliced
1 tablespoon chopped
  Chinese parsley

Wash and dry the chicken. With a sharp knife, cut through the skin around the leg and thigh joint so that the skin will not split during boiling.

Mix the marinade ingredients in a large bowl.

In a large pot, bring enough water to a boil to cover the chicken. Add the chicken and boil gently for 3 minutes. Pour off the water.

Add more water to cover the chicken and bring to a boil. Lower the heat, cover and simmer for 20 minutes. Remove the chicken and drain well. Save the hot stock.

Add 1/2 cup of the reserved hot stock to the marinade, stirring to dissolve the wine lees. Add 1 1/2 more cups stock, mix well and cool.

To carve the chicken, see the illustrated instructions on p. 9. Sprinkle salt and wine over the chicken and let stand for 1 hour.

With a fork, pierce the chicken pieces and immerse completely in the marinade. Cover and refrigerate for at least 3 hours or overnight.

On a serving platter, assemble the chicken parts on a bed of lettuce to approximate the original shape of the fowl. Spoon some of the sauce over the chicken and reserve the rest for individual use. Garnish with parsley.

Serves 3.

FRESH GINGER CHICKEN

1-1/2 cups chicken breast, cut
   into strips 1-1/2 inches by
   1/2 inch
Batter
  2 egg whites
  2 tablespoons cornstarch
  1/2 teaspoon salt
1 tablespoon slivered fresh
  ginger
1/3 cup Chinese stock (p. 30)
  or chicken stock

1 teaspoon salt
3 tablespoons rice wine
Vegetable oil for deep-frying
1 teaspoon water mixed with
  1/2 teaspoon cornstarch
4 drops sesame oil
1/4 teaspoon freshly ground
  black pepper
1 teaspoon minced green
  onion

Mix the ingredients for the batter and coat the chicken with it. Put the ginger in a bowl, pour boiling water over it. Let stand for 1 minute and drain.

Mix the stock, salt and wine together.

Heat about 3 inches oil in a wok over moderate heat to about 350°. Separate the strips of chicken and add them to the oil a few at a time, using a fork to keep the pieces apart. Deep-fry about 2 minutes or until golden. Scoop out and drain.

Carefully pour out all but about 3 tablespoons oil from the wok. Reheat the oil and add the stock mixture and ginger. Bring to a boil, add the cornstarch mixture and stir until thickened. Add the chicken and stir lightly.

Quickly transfer the chicken to a heated platter. Sprinkle sesame oil and black pepper over the dish and garnish with green onion.

Serves 3.

KUEI FEI CHICKEN WINGS

6 large dried black
  mushrooms
20 chicken wings
2 medium-sized onions
5 tablespoons vegetable oil
1 teaspoon minced fresh
  ginger

2 teaspoons sugar
2-1/2 tablespoons thin soy
  sauce
2-2/3 cups chicken stock
Pinch of salt
2 teaspoons red wine

Soak the mushrooms for 15 minutes in hot water. Rinse, squeeze out the water, remove the stems and quarter the caps.

Cut off and discard the wing tips. Cut the wings at the joint into two sections.

Mince 1 onion and slice the other.

Heat a wok over high heat. When very hot, add 4 tablespoons oil. Add ginger, minced onion and chicken. Stir-fry for about 1/2 minute. Add 1 teaspoon sugar, 1-1/4 tablespoons soy sauce and stir-fry for 4 minutes, or until the wings appear reddish.

Transfer the contents of the wok to a large flameproof casserole. Add the stock and salt. Cover and, stirring occasionally, simmer over very low heat for 30 minutes, or until tender (the meat should come off the bones easily).

Heat 1 tablespoon oil in the wok over moderate heat. Add the onion slices and stir-fry until lightly browned, then add the mushrooms and stir. Add the onion-mushroom mixture to the casserole along with 1 teaspoon sugar and 1-1/4 tablespoons soy sauce. Cover and braise for another 15 minutes. Skim off the excess oil and add wine just before serving.

Serves 5.

CHICKEN CONGEE

A whole chicken is simmered until tender, cut into serving pieces and eaten with gruel made by simmering rice for several hours in chicken broth until it is very soft.

1 3-pound frying chicken	1 cup sliced lettuce
1-1/4 teaspoons salt	5 radishes, sliced
1-1/2 cups rice (do not use in-	1-1/2 tablespoons minced
stant rice)	Chinese parsley
1/2 cup thin soy sauce	1/4 cup green onion
Pinch of MSG	1 tablespoon minced fresh
3 tablespoons sesame oil	ginger
3 tablespoons vegetable oil	

Clean, wash and dry the chicken. Rub the cavity with 1/4 teaspoon salt. Make cuts in the thickest part of the thigh and breast for even cooking.

Wash the rice in cold water until the rinse water runs clear. Drain.

Put the soy sauce in a bowl, add MSG and stir to dissolve. Set aside.

In a large pot, bring to a rapid boil enough water to cover the chicken, then reduce the heat to low and gently boil the chicken for 30 minutes. Pierce the thighs and breast to check for doneness. The meat should not be pink and no blood should appear. Cook an additional 5 to 10 minutes as needed.

Remove the chicken, saving the liquid, and soak it in cold water. Drain and dry it thoroughly. Put it in a bowl with sesame oil, and rub the oil all over the skin so that it is shiny and put it in the refrigerator.

Add the rice to the reserved chicken broth. Add 1 teaspoon salt and the vegetable oil to the broth. Bring the rice to a boil and lower the heat so that it simmers. Stir occasionally for the first 20 minutes to prevent the rice from sticking to the pot. Continue simmering for 1-1/2 to 2 hours, stirring occasionally. The gruel should have a thick, creamy consistency.

Cut the chicken into serving pieces (see the illustrated instructions on p. 9) and arrange the pieces, skin side up, on a platter. Put the lettuce and radishes around the chicken. Sprinkle with Chinese parsley and serve with the gruel in individual bowls. Each person dips chicken into the soy sauce, then sprinkles it with green onion and ginger.

Serves 5–6.

BRIGHT MOON RED PINE CHICKEN

A decorative dish portraying a favorite theme of the T'ang poets and artists—a solitary moon shining through the pines.

Chicken breast, gently braised until deep red, is sliced into strips and arranged on a platter radiating outward to resemble pine-tree trunks. One or more stir-fried green vegetables placed around the center represent the foliage. Traditionally, half of a preserved salted duck egg placed in the center represents the full moon, but a hard-boiled chicken egg serves nicely as a substitute.

1 hard-boiled egg	Sauce mixture
Pork seasoning mixture	1 teaspoon thick soy sauce
1-1/2 teaspoons rice wine	1 teaspoon thin soy sauce
1/2 teaspoon sugar	1-1/4 teaspoons rice wine
Pinch of salt	1 teaspoon sugar
1 teaspoon water mixed	1/2 teaspoon grated fresh
with 1/2 teaspoon corn-	ginger
starch)	1/2 cup Chinese stock
1/2 pound minced pork butt	(p. 30) or chicken stock
Vegetable seasoning mixture	2-1/2 tablespoons cornstarch
2 teaspoons rice wine	1/2 pound chicken breast
Pinch of salt	3/4 pound fresh spinach
1 teaspoon sugar	leaves or broccoli cut in
5 drops sesame oil	1-1/2-inch pieces
	3-1/2 tablespoons vegetable
	oil

Slice the hard-boiled egg in half crosswise.

Combine the ingredients for the pork seasoning mixture, add to the pork and stir well until the mixture becomes a paste.

Stir together the ingredients for the vegetable seasoning mixture and do the same for the sauce mixture.

On a board sprinkled with 1 tablespoon cornstarch, gently pound the chicken until it is of even thickness throughout, about 1/2 inch. Spread the pork paste evenly and firmly over the chicken fillet. Sprinkle 1-1/2 tablespoons cornstarch on top of the pork and press down with a spatula.

Parboil the spinach or broccoli for 1 minute. Drain well.

Heat 2 tablespoons oil in a frying pan over moderate heat. Gently fry the meat, chicken side down, for about 3 minutes, or until golden. Carefully turn it over and fry the pork-paste side for another 3 minutes.

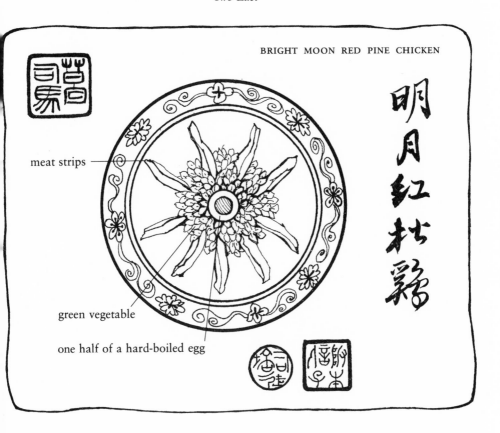

BRIGHT MOON RED PINE CHICKEN

meat strips

green vegetable

one half of a hard-boiled egg

明月红松鸡

Add the sauce mixture to the meat, bring to a boil, lower the heat and braise for 30 to 40 minutes, or until the liquid is almost absorbed. Spoon the sauce over the meat from time to time. The meat should become dark reddish brown.

Carefully transfer the meat to a board, pork side up. With a very sharp knife, cut the fillet into long strips 1/2 inch wide. On a large platter, arrange the strips pork side up, radiating outward like spokes of a wheel.

In a wok over high heat, stir-fry the spinach or broccoli in 1-1/2 table-spoons oil for 1 minute, coating well with the oil. Add the vegetable seasoning mixture and stir-fry another minute.

To serve, assemble the dish in the manner shown by the illustration below. Half a teaspoonful of the hot oil may be poured over the egg.

Serves 2–3.

CHICKEN LEGS OF FIVE FLAVORS

This hearty Suchou dish gets its name from the sauce, which is fragrant, hot, sweet, sour and salty.

2-1/2 pounds chicken legs,
  with thighs
1 medium-sized potato
1 medium-sized onion
Seasoning mixture
  1/4 cup catsup
  1 tablespoon sugar
  1 tablespoon rice wine
  1 teaspoon salt
  1/4 teaspoon MSG
  1-1/2 cups Chinese stock
    (p. 30) or chicken stock

2 tablespoons cornstarch
  mixed with 5 tablespoons
  water
2 cups water
1 tablespoon rice wine
2 green onions
3 slivers fresh ginger
1/4 cup vegetable oil
1-1/2 teaspoons curry powder
1 tablespoon chopped
  Chinese parsley

Wash the chicken legs. Cut through the joint to separate the upper and lower parts. Chop off about 1 1/2 inches of the lower leg bone so it will not protrude after the meat is cooked.

Wash and peel the potato and cut into about 8 chunks. Peel and slice the onion.

Combine the ingredients for the seasoning mixture.

Boil enough water in a pot to cover the pieces of chicken. Put them in and boil for 2 minutes. Remove and cool them with cold water. Put the chicken in a heat-resistant bowl, add 2 cups water, rice wine, green onions, and ginger, and cover the bowl. Put potatoes in a small heatproof bowl. Place the bowls on two tiers of a steamer and steam vigorously for 5 minutes. Reduce heat and continue steaming for 1 hour.

Meanwhile, put oil in a wok over medium-low heat. Add onion and stir-fry until translucent and limp. Discard the onion and save the oil.

Remove the chicken and potatoes from the steamer. Mash the potato well. Heat the reserved oil in a wok over high heat. When the oil begins to smoke, add curry powder and stir-fry for a few seconds until it becomes fragrant. Add the mashed potato and mix well. Add the seasoning mixture and the chicken and let the sauce boil. Pushing the chicken aside with a spatula, add the cornstarch mixture and stir for a few minutes until the sauce thickens. Transfer to a heated serving platter and garnish with parsley.

Serves 3–4.

BRAISED DUCK SUCHOU STYLE

1 4-1/2-pound duck, washed
and dried
Seasoning mixture
  2 tablespoons rice flour
  1/4 cup thin soy sauce
  1 tablespoon rice wine
  1 teaspoon cinnamon
  2 olive-sized pieces rock
    sugar
  1 teaspoon grated fresh
    ginger

1/4 teaspoon salt
1 tablespoon minced drag-
  on's eye
1/4 cup slivered blanched almonds
1/4 teaspoon vegetable oil
3 tablespoons sugar
2 tablespoons water mixed
  with 1 tablespoon corn-
  starch
1/2 head lettuce, shredded

Combine the ingredients for the seasoning mixture. Lightly pan-fry the almonds in oil.

Put the duck in a large pot with just enough water to cover. Add the seasoning mixture. Bring to a boil, reduce the heat to moderate, cover the pot and simmer for about 1 hour. Regulate the heat so that the liquid does not boil over.

Carefully turn the duck, lower the heat and simmer for 1/2 to 1 hour more, or until the duck is tender. (Check the area between the thighs and the body—if a thigh pulls away easily, it is done.) Put the duck in a colander to drain, then place it on a board and let it cool.

Reserve 2-1/2 cups of the cooking liquid. Skim off the excess fat. Add sugar and simmer, stirring occasionally, for about 10 minutes. Add the cornstarch mixture and heat until the sauce is thickened.

Cut the duck into serving pieces (see illustrated instructions on p. 9) and arrange on a bed of shredded lettuce on a heated platter. Pour the sauce over the duck and garnish with almonds.

Serves 3–5.

WEST LAKE DUCK

1 4-1/2- to 5-pound duck
Marinade
  1 tablespoon honey
  1 tablespoon thin soy sauce
  1 tablespoon rice wine
Stuffing
  5 dried black mushrooms
  1 cup shredded ham
  3 cups thinly sliced celery
  1/2 cup sliced water
    chestnuts
  1/2 cup shredded bamboo
    shoots
Steaming mixture I
  1-1/2 teaspoons thin soy
    sauce
  1/2 teaspoon minced fresh
    ginger
  1 teaspoon rice wine
  1/2 teaspoon sugar
  Pinch of MSG
Steaming mixture II
  1 tablespoon rice wine
  1/8 teaspoon salt
  1/8 teaspoon MSG

Stuffing seasoning
  1 tablespoon thin soy sauce
  1 teaspoon rice wine
  1/4 teaspoon MSG
  3/4 cup Chinese stock
    (p. 30) or chicken stock
  1/8 teaspoon white pepper
Sauce seasoning
  2 teaspoons thin soy sauce
  1/2 teaspoon salt
  1/2 teaspoon MSG
  1 teaspoon rice wine
  1/8 teaspoon white pepper
3 tablespoons slivered
  blanched almonds
Vegetable oil for deep-frying
  plus 1/4 cup
4 tablespoons water mixed
  with 2 tablespoons cornstarch into a paste
Salt
3 cups shredded lettuce
1 teaspoon minced parsley

Wash and dry the duck thoroughly. Cut off the wing tips and skin flap at the neck opening. Cook them together with the giblets and neck in 5 cups water over moderate heat for 30 minutes or more. Skim off the fat and reserve the stock.

Make the marinade by mixing together the ingredients and rub the duck all over with it, inside and out. Hang the duck to air-dry (see illustration). Be sure to put a bowl underneath to catch the drippings.

To make the stuffing, first soak dried mushrooms in hot water for 15 minutes. Rinse, squeeze out the water, remove the stems and cut the caps into very thin slices. Place the stuffing ingredients in separate sections on a platter.

In separate bowls, mix the ingredients for steaming mixtures I and II, the stuffing seasoning and the sauce seasoning.

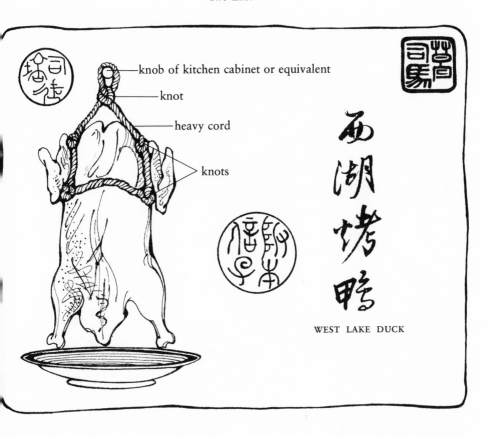

knob of kitchen cabinet or equivalent

knot

heavy cord

knots

WEST LAKE DUCK

Lightly oil a small frying pan and pan-fry almonds until golden.

In a deep, heavy pot or deep-fryer, heat to 375° enough oil for deep-frying the duck. Wipe off the excess marinade from the duck and deep-fry for about 6 minutes on each side to brown it all over. Remove and drain in a colander.

Place the duck in a large heatproof bowl and pour in enough of the reserved hot giblet stock to reach a point two-thirds of the way up. Add steaming mixture I. Place the bowl in a steamer and steam vigorously for 1 hour, or until the duck is done (test by moving a leg up and down—if it moves freely, the duck is ready).

Remove the duck and let it cool. Skim off the fat from the steaming stock and pour 2 cups of the stock into a pan. Heat the stock, add the sauce seasoning and thicken with 3 tablespoons of the cornstarch paste. Add salt if needed and set the sauce aside.

Bone the duck by following the illustrated instructions on p. 8.

Place duck halves skin side up on a 9-inch heat-resistant plate and sprinkle with steaming mixture II. Put the plate in a steamer and steam vigorously for 15 to 20 minutes.

Meanwhile, heat a wok until very hot. Add 1/4 cup oil, and when hot, add the ham shreds and stir-fry for 1/2 minute. Add mushrooms, celery, water chestnuts and bamboo shoots and stir-fry 2 to 3 minutes. Add the stuffing seasoning and stir a few times. Cover the wok and cook for 1 minute. Remove the cover and thicken the sauce with the remaining 1 tablespoon of the cornstarch paste. Remove from heat and keep warm until the duck is ready.

When the duck is done, carefully remove it from the steamer with a spatula and tongs and put it on a board, skin side up. Carve the duck for serving by following the illustrated instructions on p. 9.

Place the stuffing on a bed of lettuce on a large platter and place the legs and wings at the four corners of the platter. Rearrange on top of the stuffing the other pieces of duck so that they form the duck's original shape.

Reheat the sauce and spoon it over the entire dish. Garnish with almonds and parsley.

Serves 4.

DUCK IN SAUCE SHANGHAI STYLE

1 4-1/2-pound duck	5 tablespoons sugar
1 tablespoon salt	3-1/2 tablespoons thin soy
Bouquet garni	sauce
2 slices fresh ginger	1/2 teaspoon salt
2 pieces dried tangerine	2 tablespoons minced water
peel	chestnuts
1 teaspoon fennel seed	1 tablespoon sesame oil
Seasoning mixture	4 sprigs parsley
2 tablespoons rice wine	

Wash the duck and plunge it in and out of boiling water to harden the skin. Drain and rub salt all over the duck, inside and out.

Tie the ingredients of the bouquet garni in a cheesecloth bag.

Combine the ingredients of the seasoning mixture.

Bring 6 cups water containing the bouquet garni to a rapid boil, reduce heat and simmer 15 minutes. Discard the bouquet garni. Put the duck in the water, add the seasoning mixture and simmer, covered, over medium heat until the duck is tender. Turn occasionally while cooking.

Transfer the duck to a platter and let it drain and cool a few minutes. Place the duck on a board and rub sesame oil all over the duck. Carefully cut it, skin side up, into serving pieces and arrange them on a platter.

Continue simmering the seasoned water in the pot until it becomes a thick and glossy sauce. Skim off the oil on top and pour the sauce over the duck. Garnish with water chestnuts and parsley.

Serves 4.

CLAM, SHRIMP, AND BEAN CURD STEW

2 6-1/2-ounce cans chopped
clams
10 jumbo shrimp
2 fresh bean curd cakes, cut
in 1-inch cubes
2 tablespoons vegetable oil
2-1/2 cups Chinese stock
(p. 30) or chicken stock
1 piece chicken skin about 3
inches square, minced
3/4 cup sliced (1 1/2 inches
by 1/4 by 1/4 inch) canned
bamboo shoots
1/4 teaspoon salt
1-1/4 teaspoon thin soy sauce

Sauce
1-1/2 tablespoons vegetable
oil
1 large garlic clove, minced
2 teaspoons minced
Chinese parsley leaves
1/4 teaspoon salt
1/3 cup Chinese stock
(p. 30) or chicken stock
1-1/2 teaspoons water mixed
with 1/2 teaspoon corn-
starch
1/2 teaspoon rendered
chicken fat
1/4 teaspoon ground black
pepper

Drain the clams, saving the juice. Shell, devein and wash the shrimp, then cut into 4 sections. Put the bean-curd cubes in boiling water for 1/2 minute, then carefully drain.

Heat the oil in a wok over moderate heat until it almost begins to smoke. Add the clams and shrimp and stir-fry for 1 minute. Remove them from the wok and set aside. Add the stock, clam juice, chicken skin, bean curd, bamboo shoots, salt and soy sauce. Bring to a gentle boil, reduce heat to low and simmer for 10 minutes.

While the stew is simmering, make the sauce. Heat the oil in a pan over medium heat. Add garlic and cook until it turns golden. Add parsley and stir-fry about 1 minute. Add salt and stock and bring to a boil, then reduce heat and thicken with the cornstarch mixture. Pour the sauce into a small bowl. Transfer the stew from the wok to a large bowl, sprinkle with chicken fat and ground black pepper, and serve with the sauce.

Serves 2–3.

FRIED SHRIMP BALLS

This delicate Moslem dish makes an excellent hors d'oeuvre.

Shrimp balls
1-1/2 pounds fresh shrimp
1 teaspoon salt
8 water chestnuts, minced
2 eggs, beaten
2-1/2 tablespoons glutinous
rice flour
2 teaspoons rice wine
1/4 teaspoon MSG
2 tablespoons water-
chestnut flour
1/4 cup water-chestnut flour
for coating

Rendered chicken fat for
deep-frying
1 cup watercress or parsley
sprigs
Black peppercorn salt dip*
Tomato dip
1/4 cup catsup
1/2 teaspoon vinegar
1/2 teaspoon sugar
Cayenne to taste

Shell, devein, wash and dry the shrimp. Sprinkle salt over them and let them stand for 5 minutes, then mince them. Add the remaining shrimp-ball ingredients to the shrimp and mix well in one direction. (The mixture will be slightly sticky.)

Flour your hands and a board with water chestnut flour and make walnut-sized balls with the shrimp mixture. Gently roll the balls in flour, coating them well.

Mix the tomato dip and put it in a small bowl.

Heat about 2 inches chicken fat in a wok over high heat until it reaches 310 to 320°. Add three or four balls at a time to the oil and deep-fry for about 2 minutes, or until they become puffy and golden. Use a wooden fork to turn the balls and to keep them from sticking. Drain and arrange them on a bed of watercress or parsley on a platter. Serve with the black peppercorn salt dip and the tomato dip.

Makes about 24 balls.

* See Pepper, black (p. 29) for the recipe.

SHRIMP AND FRESH MUSHROOMS

2 slices fresh ginger
1 green onion, cut into 2
    pieces
24 large fresh mushrooms,
    halved
2 egg whites
1/4 teaspoon salt
3 tablespoons cornstarch
16 fresh jumbo shrimp,
    shelled, deveined and
    halved lengthwise
Sauce mixture
    1 teaspoon rice wine
    3/4 teaspoon salt

1/2 teaspoon MSG
1/3 cup Chinese stock
    (p. 30) or chicken stock
2 tablespoons peanuts
2 cups plus 1 teaspoon vege-
    table oil
2 teaspoons water mixed
    with 1 teaspoon corn-
    starch
3/4 teaspoon sesame oil
1 tablespoon slivered green
    onion (cut in half length-
    wise and slice diagonally
    into 1/2-inch sections)

Put ginger slices and the 2 pieces of green onion in boiling water, add mushrooms and boil for 1 minute. Remove the mushrooms, drain and dry.

Thoroughly mix together the egg whites, salt and cornstarch and coat the shrimp with the mixture.

Combine the ingredients of the sauce mixture.

Lightly pan-fry peanuts in 1 teaspoon oil.

Put enough oil for deep-frying in a deep, heavy pan or deep-fryer over high heat. When the oil is about 350°, add half of the shrimp and fry for about 2 minutes, or until almost cooked. Remove from the pan and fry the remaining shrimp. Reserve 3 tablespoons of the oil.

Put a wok over high heat. When very hot, add the reserved deep-frying oil and then the mushrooms. Stir-fry for about 1 minute. Add the sauce mixture and heat until it becomes very hot. Add the shrimp.

Thicken the sauce with the cornstarch mixture. Sprinkle with sesame oil. Transfer the contents of the wok to a heated platter and garnish with peanuts and slivered green onions.

Serves 3–4.

FRIED SHRIMP WITH SHELLS

This shrimp dish is prepared with shells and tails left on, to retain the natural juices and keep the shrimp tender and moist. To eat them, hold the shrimp by the tail, suck out the sauce, and then work the flesh out of the shell.

14 fresh jumbo shrimp	1 cup quartered onions
Seasoning mixture	3 tablespoons Chinese red
1/4 cup thick soy sauce	vinegar
1 tablespoon rice wine	1 tablespoon chopped green
3-1/2 teaspoons sugar	onion
Oil for deep-frying	

Prepare the shrimp for deep-frying by following the illustrated instructions on p. 9c. Combine the ingredients for the seasoning mixture.

Heat about 2 inches oil in a wok over high heat. When the oil begins to smoke, add the shrimp in batches of four or five, and deep-fry for about 10 seconds. (The moisture in the shrimp should disappear, making a spattering sound, and the shells will start to separate from the meat.) Remove from the wok and drain immediately.

Carefully empty all but 1 teaspoon of oil from the wok. Turn up the heat, and when the oil is almost smoking, add onions and stir-fry for 1 minute. Add the seasoning mixture and stir, then put the shrimp back in the wok.

Add vinegar, stirring two or three times, just enough to coat the shrimp. Quickly transfer to a heated platter and garnish with green onion.

Serves 3–4.

DRY-FRIED SHRIMP WITH TOMATO SAUCE

This dish of shrimp cooked in their shells is a Northern favorite. The shells help to keep the natural juices in, and the meat becomes succulent. It is customary to suck the juices out of the shells, then work out the meat as you would with a lobster.

20 fresh jumbo shrimp
Seasoning mixture
  2 tablespoons rice wine
  1-1/2 teaspoons white vin-
    egar
  1/2 cup catsup
  1/2 teaspoon salt
  2 teaspoons sugar
  1/3 cup Chinese stock
    (p. 30) or chicken stock

1/4 cup vegetable oil
1 teaspoon grated fresh
  ginger
1 large garlic clove, minced
1/2 cup chopped green onion
1-1/4 cups sliced onion (cut
  about 1/4 inch thick)
1/4 teaspoon (or to taste)
  cayenne

To prepare the shrimp for frying, follow the illustrated instructions on p. 9c.

Combine the ingredients for the seasoning mixture.

Heat a wok over high heat. When very hot, add 3 tablespoons of the oil. When it almost begins to smoke, add ginger and garlic, and then the shrimp. Stir-fry, using a spatula to turn over and press down the shrimp. After about 2 minutes, add green onion and the seasoning mixture.

Turn the heat down, add the onion and simmer slowly until most of the liquid is gone. Stir to keep from scorching. Add cayenne and the remaining oil and stir a few times.

Serves 3–4.

SHRIMP AND RICE CRUST

10 to 12 fresh jumbo shrimp,
   shelled, deveined and
   washed
3/4 cup cornstarch
Marinade
   3 tablespoons cornstarch
   2 tablespoons water
   1 tablespoon rice wine
   1/4 teaspoon salt
Seasoning mixture
   1-1/3 cups Chinese stock
     (p. 30) or chicken stock
   1/2 teaspoon thin soy sauce
   1/2 cup catsup
   1/2 tablespoon rice wine
   1/8 teaspoon salt
   1/4 teaspoon white pepper
Oil for deep-frying plus 3
   tablespoons

1 large garlic clove, peeled
   and lightly crushed
1/4 pound pork butt meat,
   minced
1 small green pepper, sliced
   into wedges 2 inches by 1/2
   inch
1/3 cup bamboo shoot strips
   (2 inches by 1/2 inch)
2 tablespoons water mixed
   with 1 tablespoon cornstarch
2 cups rice crusts (p. 29)
2 tablespoons slivered green
   onion (cut in half lengthwise and slice diagonally
   into 1/2-inch sections)

Dry the shrimps thoroughly and dust well with cornstarch.

Mix together the ingredients for the marinade, add the shrimp and marinate for 15 minutes.

Combine the ingredients for the seasoning mixture. Place two large heatproof bowls in 350° oven to preheat. Have two thick potholders on hand.

Heat about 3 inches oil in a deep, heavy pot or deep-fryer. When the oil is about 350°, add three or four shrimp to the oil to deep-fry. Stir to prevent sticking. In about 2 minutes, when the shrimp turn golden, scoop them out and drain them. Continue until all the shrimp are deep-fried. Clear the oil of food particles and turn the heat to low.

Put a wok over high heat. When very hot, add 3 tablespoons oil and garlic, followed by the pork, and stir-fry for 1 minute. Add green pepper and bamboo shoots and stir-fry another minute. Add the seasoning mixture and bring to a boil.

Turn the heat under the deep-frying oil in the pot to high.

Add the shrimp to the wok, then add the cornstarch mixture. Stir until the sauce thickens and put the shrimp and sauce into one of the preheated bowls.

When the oil in the deep-fryer is about 360°, add rice crusts. They should puff up, turn white, and rise to the surface when done, in 1 to 2 minutes. Scoop out the crusts, place them in the other hot bowl, and sprinkle 1 tablespoon of the deep-frying oil over them.

Carefully bring both bowls, piping hot, to the table, and quickly pour the sauce with the shrimp over the rice crusts. A hissing sound should result. Garnish the dish with green onions.

Serves 3.

NOTE: Because this dish requires almost simultaneous cooking of the shrimp and rice crusts, all ingredients should be ready to use and the cook fully aware of what to do in the final stages of preparation.

SHRIMP SHAO MAI

These little steamed snacks are eaten with savory dips.

1/4 cup white sesame seeds
1/4 pound ham skin (taken from the fresh ham)
3 green onions
4 teaspoons rice wine
3 slices fresh ginger
1 pound fresh ham, minced or ground
3 tablespoons thin soy sauce
2 tablespoons sugar
1 tablespoon cornstarch

Shrimp paste
1/4 pound fresh shrimp meat, minced
1/8 teaspoon salt
1 tablespoon egg white
1 teaspoon cornstarch
Wrappings
2 cups flour
1-1/2 teaspoons vegetable oil
2/3 cup boiling water

Pan-fry sesame seeds until they pop. Crush them into a powder with a mortar and pestle.

Place the ham skin in a pot, cover with water and add onion. Bring to a boil and simmer for 45 minutes, or until the skin can be pierced with a fingernail.

Remove the skin and onion, and mince them. Return them to the pot, add 1 teaspoon wine and simmer for 1/2 to 1 hour, or until the liquid is reduced and the mixture resembles a paste. Stir occasionally to prevent burning. Refrigerate for about 3 hours, or until the paste jells.

Put the ginger slices, one by one, in a garlic press and squeeze the juice into 1/4 cup water. Then soak the mashed ginger in the same water for 15 minutes. Discard the ginger and put the ginger water in a large bowl. Add

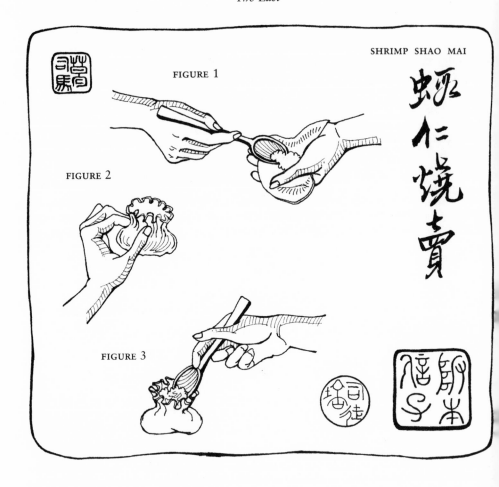

SHRIMP SHAO MAI

FIGURE 1

FIGURE 2

FIGURE 3

虾仁烧賣

sesame seed powder, ham, 3 teaspoons wine, soy sauce and sugar. Mix in one direction until all liquid is absorbed. Add 1 to 2 tablespoons water and mix again. Add the jelled paste and cornstarch, and blend until the mixture is slightly sticky. (This is the filling. It can be made up ahead of time and stored in the refrigerator.)

Thoroughly mix together the ingredients for the shrimp paste.

Now make the wrappings. Place flour in a bowl. Add oil to boiling water and slowly add the liquid to the flour, stirring until a dough forms. Knead the dough lightly, then turn it out on a floured board and continue kneading until it is smooth and shiny. Return it to the bowl, cover with a damp cloth and let it rest for 15 to 20 minutes. Dust the board with flour and shape the dough into a roll 16 inches long and 1 inch in diameter. Slice into 1/2-inch pieces. Roll into balls, then flatten with the palm of the hand. Use a rolling pin to roll into disks 3 to 4 inches in diameter, with the centers slightly thicker than the edges. Stack on an oiled plate sprinkling flour between them to keep them separated.

Place a wrapping in your left hand and put about 2 teaspoons filling in the center (Figure 1). With the fingers of the same hand, pinch the wrapping two-thirds of the way up so that the edges of the wrapper are pulled up around the filling—leaving the opening only *partially* closed (Figure 2). Through the opening place 1/4 teaspoon shrimp paste on top of the filling and press down lightly (Figure 3).

Oil the steamer tray and arrange the stuffed dumplings on it, leaving space between them. Steam vigorously for 5 minutes.

Carefully remove the steamer cover and sprinkle a little water over the dumplings so that they will not have dry white spots. Re-cover and steam vigorously for 1 to 2 minutes. When the wrappings are translucent, carefully feel the bottom—if it is solid, the dumplings are done.

Makes 32 cakes.

PHOENIX-TAILED SHRIMP NANKING STYLE

The rendered chicken fat used to deep-fry the shrimp imparts a special color and flavor to this dish.

1-1/2 cups fresh or frozen green peas	1-1/2 teaspoons rice wine
18 fresh jumbo shrimp	1/2 teaspoon salt
Batter	2 tablespoons water mixed with 1 tablespoon corn-
2 egg whites	starch
2-1/2 tablespoons water mixed with 1-1/2 table-	2 cups rendered chicken fat
spoons cornstarch	8 green onions, white part only
1/4 teaspoon salt	1/2 teaspoon crushed flower
Sauce mixture	pepper
1 cup chicken stock	

Parboil peas for 1 minute in boiling water, rinse with cold water and drain. Mix together the ingredients for the batter and combine the ingredients for the sauce mixture.

Prepare and deep-fry the shrimp according to the illustrated instructions on pp. 9b–9c.

Heat chicken fat in a wok over high heat to about 325°. Add shrimp and deep-fry until the meat turns white and the tails turn red, about 1 minute. Quickly remove the shrimp. Pour out all but 2 tablespoons fat.

Add the sauce mixture to the wok, then the onions, and stir until the sauce begins to thicken. Turn off heat, add shrimp and peas, and stir a few times to coat with the sauce. Transfer to a heated platter and garnish with crushed flower pepper.

Serves 3–4.

BRAISED SALMON

The Chinese believe there is great nutritional value and flavor in the fat found in fish scales. Thus, in the preparation of many fish dishes the fish is scaled only on one side. When steaming or braising, the unscaled side is kept on top, allowing the fat to run down into the flesh and sauce. In serving the fish, the unscaled side is placed on the bottom so that the diner can "eat just down to the scales."

1-1/2 pounds fresh salmon slice, with scales left on one side
Seasoning mixture
  2 tablespoons thin soy sauce
  2 tablespoons rice wine
  1 tablespoon sugar
  1/4 teaspoon salt
  1 cup water
1 tablespoon thick soy sauce
1/4 cup vegetable oil
2 strips (2 inches by 1/2 by 1/4 inch) pork fat

2 teaspoons minced green onion, white part only
2 teaspoons minced fresh ginger
1/2 cup sliced (2 inches by 1/2 by 1/4 inch) canned bamboo shoots
1/2 cup sliced fresh mushrooms
2 teaspoons water mixed with 1 teaspoon cornstarch
1 teaspoon minced Chinese parsley

With a sharp knife, make 2-inch slashes on both sides of the salmon slice. Wash and dry the salmon thoroughly.

Mix together the ingredients for the seasoning mixture. Smear thick soy sauce all over the salmon.

Put oil in a wok over moderate heat, add pork fat and stir-fry for 1 minute. Add the salmon slice, unscaled side down, and fry gently for 4 to 5 minutes. Turn over the slice carefully and fry the scaled side. Add green onion, ginger, bamboo shoots, mushrooms and the seasoning mixture and bring to a boil. Reduce heat and braise gently for 15 minutes, or until the sauce is reduced to about two-thirds of the original volume. Carefully remove the salmon with a wide spatula to avoid tearing the skin. Place the salmon, scaled side down, on a heated platter.

Add the cornstarch mixture to the sauce to thicken it. Pour the sauce and vegetables over the salmon and garnish with parsley.

Serves 2–3.

PREGNANT FISH

This dish with its unusual name is really a whole stuffed fish.

1-1/2 pounds whole fresh fish
  (pike or whitefish are
  good)
Filling
  1/2 pound pork meat,
    minced
  2 tablespoons bamboo
    shoots cut in 1/4-inch
    cubes
  1 tablespoon thin soy sauce
  1/2 teaspoon sugar
  1 tablespoon rice wine
  1 tablespoon vegetable oil
  1/2 teaspoon sesame oil
  2 tablespoons chopped
    preserved mustard greens
Seasoning mixture
  1 tablespoon thick soy
    sauce
  2-1/2 teaspoons sugar

1 tablespoon rice wine
1/4 teaspoon salt
3 tablespoons preserved
  mustard greens cut in
  2-by-1/2-inch sections
3 tablespoons shredded
  bamboo shoots
3 cups water
2 tablespoons slivered almonds
1 tablespoon thick soy sauce
1 cup plus 1 tablespoon vegetable oil
3 slices fresh ginger
1 tablespoon chopped green
  onion
2 tablespoons water mixed
  with 1 tablespoon corn-
  starch

At the fish market, have the fish scaled and the fins removed; make sure that it is not eviscerated and that the head and tail are left intact.

With a small, sharp knife make a 4-inch opening lengthwise just below the backbone. With kitchen shears, cut through the ribs as needed to make an opening into the body cavity and eviscerate the fish through this opening. Wash the fish well inside and out. Dry thoroughly with paper towels.

Prepare the filling and mix well.

Combine the ingredients for the seasoning mixture and stir.

Pan-fry the almonds lightly in a little oil.

Stuff the fish with the filling through the opening, using a tablespoon to push it down into every part of the cavity. Cut lightly through the skin only on both sides in an XX pattern. Smear the fish with thick soy sauce.

Heat 1 cup oil in a large, deep frying pan over high heat to about 350°. Fry the fish on the stuffed side for 3 to 4 minutes, or until it is a deep golden yellow. Carefully turn the fish, using 2 spatulas, and fry the other side. Remove from heat and drain off the oil.

Carefully slip ginger slices under the fish and sprinkle onion over it. Return the pan to heat and add the seasoning mixture. Bring to a boil and add 1 tablespoon oil. Lower the heat, cover and braise gently for about 1 hour. The belly of the fish will split.

Put the fish on a warm platter. Discard the ginger slices. Thicken the sauce in the pan with cornstarch paste, pour it over the fish and garnish with almonds.

Serves 4.

HSI HU (WEST LAKE) VINEGAR FISH

Very often the simplest treatment of fine ingredients produces the best results. In this dish, the famous delicate flavor of the grass carp from West Lake is preserved by gentle poaching and only a simple sweet-sour sauce is served over the fish.

1-1/4 pounds fresh grass carp,* cleaned and scaled, with tail removed but head left on

Seasoning mixture
1 teaspoon thick soy sauce
1/2 teaspoon minced fresh ginger
2 tablespoons rice wine
1/4 teaspoon salt
1/4 teaspoon salt

2 tablespoons sugar
3 tablespoons Chinese red vinegar
2 tablespoons water mixed with 1 tablespoon cornstarch
2 tablespoons minced water chestnuts
1/2 cup chopped trimmed watercress

Wash and dry the fish. With a sharp knife carefully cut the fish lengthwise into two equal halves. To do this, enlarge the cut made when the fish

* Chinese fish markets in this country often have live carp in tanks. These are ideal, but any very fresh fish, such as bass, pike or lake trout, will do.

HSI HU (WEST LAKE) VINEGAR FISH

西 湖 醋魚

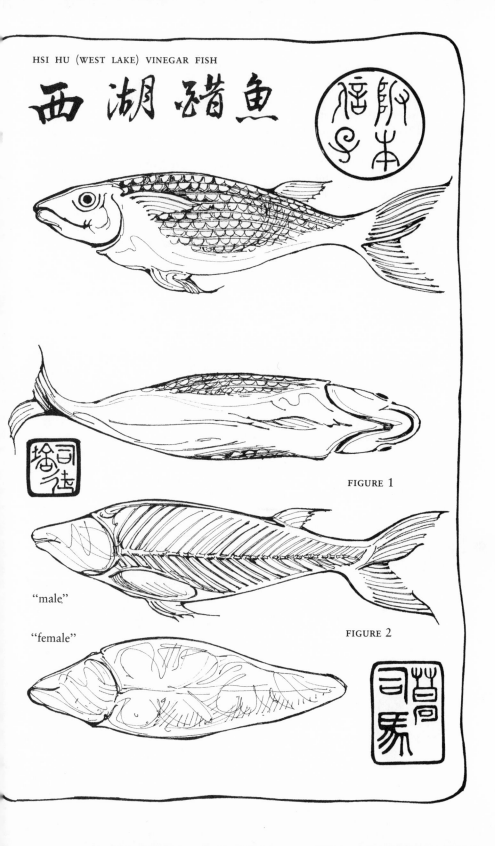

FIGURE 1

"male"

FIGURE 2

"female"

was eviscerated so it extends from jaw to tail. Press the fish open and, from the inside, cut down through the ribs along one side of the spine. With sharp kitchen shears, cut the lower part of the jaw in half in the middle and continue around the head (Figure 1).

The fish is now separated into two halves, "the male" (with the backbone) and "the female" (without it) (Figure 2). To facilitate even cooking, make little slashes about one-third deep on the inner side of each half, where the flesh is thickest, taking care not to cut through to the skin.

Bring about 2 inches water to a gentle boil in a small roasting pan. Carefully lower the fish, skin side up, into the pan, putting the halves side by side. There should be just enough hot water to barely cover the fish. (If there is too much water, the fish will be overcooked; if too little water, it will be undercooked.)

Cover the pan and return the water to a boil. Uncover and cook gently for 3 minutes. Skim off the foam. If a toothpick can pierce through the male half's chin area, the fish is properly cooked.

Remove 1-1/3 cups liquid from the pan, discard the remainder and add the seasoning mixture to the liquid. With two spatulas, carefully transfer one fish half, skin side down, to a heated platter, then put the other half, skin side up, on top. Sprinkle salt over the fish. In a pot, bring the reserved liquid to a boil. Add sugar, vinegar and cornstarch paste and stir until thickened. Pour the sauce over the fish, and garnish with water chestnuts and watercress.

Serves 3.

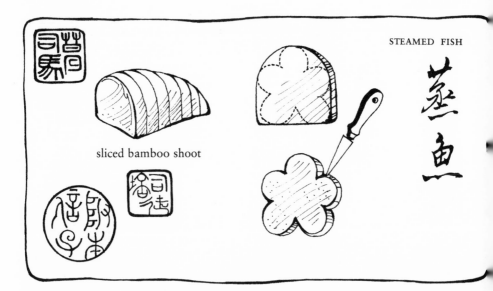

STEAMED FISH

sliced bamboo shoot

STEAMED FISH

This classic dish is a specialty of Chenkiang, known throughout China for its unequaled fish dishes.

3 large dried black
  mushrooms
1-1/2 pounds whole fresh fish
  (pike, bass, or whitefish are
  good), with head and tail
  intact and scaled on one
  side only
Seasoning mixture
  1 tablespoon rice wine
  1 teaspoon sugar
  3/4 teaspoon salt
  2 slices fresh ginger
  1 whole green onion

3 tablespoons Chinese stock
  (p. 30) or chicken stock
1/4 cup ham strips (2 inches
  by 1/4 by 1/4 inch)
6 bamboo shoot flowers (see
  illustration on oppo-
  site page)
2 tablespoons vegetable oil
Pork caul fat,* large enough
  to cover the fish
1/4 teaspoon freshly ground
  black pepper
1/4 teaspoon MSG

Soak mushrooms in hot water for 15 minutes. Rinse, squeeze out the water, remove the stems and cut the caps in half.

Make 3 deep cuts in the thickest part of the fish, near the spine, on both sides. Slice the fish in half across the middle so that one half has the head and the other the tail. Wash the pieces.

Combine the ingredients for the seasoning mixture.

Fill a deep pot two-thirds full with water and bring to a boil. Hold the fish halves by the head and tail and immerse in boiling water for 1 minute each. (This process cooks and seals the skin so that later the oil from the caul fat does not penetrate and the juices within the fish do not escape during the steaming.) Rinse halves with cold water and drain well.

Place the fish halves in a shallow, heatproof bowl, scaled sides up. Arrange the ham, mushrooms, and bamboo flowers over the fish. Heat the oil and sprinkle it over the fish. Add the seasoning mixture and cover with the caul. Cover the bowl with aluminum foil, place in a steamer and steam vigorously for 10 minutes.

Remove the foil and caul. Pick out the onion and ginger and discard.

---

* Pork caul is also known as pork omentum and is available at Chinese butcher shops. As a substitute, six large strips of ham fat, about 4 inches by 1/2 inch, can be layered on top of the fish. These can be taken from the edges of a slice of cured ham or the outer layer of a half or whole cured ham.

Pick out the bamboo shoots, mushrooms and ham and set aside. Transfer the fish to a heated platter, scaled sides down, putting the two pieces together so that the fish looks whole. Garnish with bamboo, ham and mushrooms. Mix pepper and MSG into the sauce from the steaming bowl and pour over the fish.

Serves 3–4.

HSI HU (WEST LAKE) STUFFED STEAMED FISH

heatproof platter

family-sized cans with top and bottom removed

HSI HU (WEST LAKE) STUFFED STEAMED FISH

1-1/2 to 2 pounds fresh whole
  fish (pike, white fish or
  bass are good), scaled and
  eviscerated, with head and
  tail intact
Marinade
  2 tablespoons thin soy
    sauce
  1 tablespoon rice wine
  1/4 teaspoon grated fresh
    ginger
Stuffing
  3 large dried mushrooms
  1/2 cup canned minced
    bamboo shoots
  2 tablespoons minced
    water chestnuts
  2/3 cup thinly sliced celery
  1/4 cup minced ham
  1/2 cup minced cooked
    pork butt

Seasoning mixture
  1 teaspoon thin soy sauce
  1 teaspoon rice wine
  1/4 teaspoon salt
  1/4 teaspoon sugar
  Pinch of white pepper
Sauce
  2/3 cup Chinese stock
    (p. 30) or chicken stock
  1/2 teaspoon thin soy sauce
  1 teaspoon rice wine
  Pinch of MSG
  Pinch of sugar
  3 drops sesame oil
  3 tablespoons vegetable oil
  2-1/2 tablespoons water
    mixed with 1 tablespoon
    cornstarch
  1/4 cup finely sliced lettuce
  1/4 cup shredded ham

Wash and dry the fish. With a small, sharp knife, enlarge the opening on the underside from jaw to tail. The ribs should be detached by cutting along both sides of the spine (sharp little scissors work well) without piercing the skin.

Wash the fish and cut slashes from the inside of the cavity where the flesh is thick. Mix the marinade ingredients together and smear all over the fish.

Soak mushrooms in hot water for 15 minutes. Rinse, squeeze out the water, remove the stems and shred the caps. Mix the mushrooms and the other stuffing ingredients together.

Mix together the ingredients for the seasoning mixture.

Combine the sauce ingredients.

Heat a wok over high heat. When very hot, add oil. Add the stuffing ingredients and stir-fry for 1-1/2 minutes. Add the seasoning mixture and stir-fry for about 1/2 minute. Add 1/2 tablespoon of the cornstarch mixture and stir until thickened. Remove from heat and cool.

Stuff the fish, taking care that the cavity does not bulge too much.

Place the fish on its side on a lightly oiled heatproof platter. Place the platter on top of an inverted bowl, saucer or two shallow cans (of the type for canned tuna, with the top and bottom removed) inside a large roasting pan (see illustration on p. 148). Fill the pan with 1 to 2 inches water. Cover and steam vigorously for 10 to 12 minutes. Add more water if necessary.

Meanwhile heat the sauce, add the remaining 2 tablespoons of the cornstarch paste and stir until thickened. Remove the fish from the steamer and pour the sauce over it. Garnish with lettuce and ham shreds.

Serves 4.

BRAISED CRAB, SHRIMP AND PORK LION'S HEAD

This dish is called Lion's Head because of the arrangement of the meatballs and vegetable on the serving platter—one represents the lion's head, the other its mane.

Meatballs
- 1/3 cup minced onion
- 2 tablespoons minced fresh ginger
- 3/4 pound pork butt with some fat, minced
- 1/4 pound frozen or canned crabmeat, drained well
- 1/4 pound fresh shrimp, shelled, deveined, washed and minced
- 2 tablespoons rice wine
- 1/2 teaspoon salt
- 1/2 teaspoon MSG

- 3 1/2 tablespoons cornstarch
- Vegetable oil for deep-frying plus 2 tablespoons
- 1/2 teaspoon salt
- 4 cups diagonally sliced celery cabbage
- 2 teaspoons rice wine
- Pinch of ground black pepper
- 2 teaspoons Chinese red vinegar
- 2/3 cup Chinese stock (p. 30) or chicken stock
- 5 drops sesame oil

Put onion, ginger and 2 tablespoons water in a blender and liquefy. Place all other meatball ingredients in a large bowl, add the onion-ginger juice and stir in one direction only. (The mixture will be soft and sticky.) Shape the mixture into balls about 2 1/2 inches wide.

Heat 3 inches in a heavy, deep pot or deep-fryer until it reaches 350°. Add the meatballs, two at a time, and deep-fry. Stir to keep the balls from sticking and turn them for even browning. Fry until golden-brown on all sides and a solid crust is formed. (Maintain a temperature between 350° and 360°.)

Heat 2 tablespoons oil in a wok. Add salt, celery cabbage, wine, pepper, vinegar and stock. Add meatballs and gently stir a few times. Cover, reduce heat and gently braise, for 20 to 30 minutes, or until the liquid is almost gone.

Put the meatballs in the center of a heated platter, arrange celery cabbage around them and sprinkle a little sesame oil over the dish.

Makes 5–6 meatballs, enough to serve 3–4.

NANKING PAI TS'AI HEARTS

In China, this specialty vegetable dish is prepared in a large unglazed ceramic pot. A good substitute for such a pot is a nonmetal flameproof casserole.

8 small *pai ts'ai* hearts
Marinade
  2 egg whites
  2 teaspoons cornstarch
  1/4 teaspoon salt
1/2 cup shredded chicken
  breast
Seasoning mixture
  3/4 teaspoon salt
  1/4 teaspoon thin soy sauce
  1 teaspoon rice wine
  1/4 teaspoon sugar

1 cup Chinese stock
  (p. 30) or chicken stock
Oil for deep-frying
1/2 cup shredded ham
2/3 cup drained canned straw
  mushrooms
1/2 cup sliced (2 inches by
  1/2 inch) bamboo shoots
2 teaspoons chicken fat
1/2 teaspoon freshly ground
  black pepper

Wash and dry the hearts thoroughly. With a sharp knife, trim the bottom of each heart until only the tender part remains. Leave the bottom intact so stalks do not separate.

Mix together the ingredients for the marinade. Put the chicken in it, coat well, and marinate for 10 minutes. Stir together the ingredients for the seasoning mixture.

Heat 2 to 3 inches oil in a wok over medium heat. When the oil begins to smoke, carefully slide the hearts into the oil, bottoms first. Deep-fry until the bottoms turn translucent and the leaves bright green. Carefully transfer the hearts to a large casserole, arranging them in a circle with leaves pointing outward and bottoms on the inside. Place the shredded chicken in the center on top of the bottoms of the hearts. Then put successive circles of ham, mushrooms and bamboo shoots around the chicken in the center.

Carefully pour the seasoning mixture over the dish, cover and gently braise for about 5 minutes, or until most of the liquid is reduced. Be careful not to let it burn. Sprinkle with chicken fat, pepper and salt to taste.

Serves 4.

SIMMERED PAI TS'AI

This easily prepared vegetable dish makes an excellent accompaniment to duck or pork.

6 small *pai ts'ai* hearts	1/2 teaspoon MSG
1/4 cup vegetable oil	1 tablespoon water mixed
1-1/3 cups Chinese stock	with 1/2 tablespoon corn-
(p. 30) or chicken stock	starch
1 1/2 tablespoons rendered	1/4 teaspoon finely crushed
chicken fat	flower pepper
1 teaspoon salt	

Trim and cut hearts in half lengthwise. Wash and dry thoroughly with paper towels.

Put oil in a wok and heat over moderate heat. Add the hearts and gently move them around, keeping them intact and coating all surfaces with oil. After about 1 minute, the hearts will be half cooked, with the leafy parts shiny and very green. Don't overcook or allow to brown. Remove from heat and set aside.

Pour out the oil from the wok and raise the heat. Add the stock, chicken fat, salt, MSG and the hearts. When the liquid comes to a boil, lower the heat and simmer for several minutes. The hearts should be tender but green and the liquid slightly reduced.

Remove the hearts and set aside. Thicken the liquid with the cornstarch mixture. Slice the hearts into 2-inch sections. Arrange them on a heated serving plate, pour the sauce over them and sprinkle with flower pepper.

Serves 3.

SIMMERED PAI TS'AI

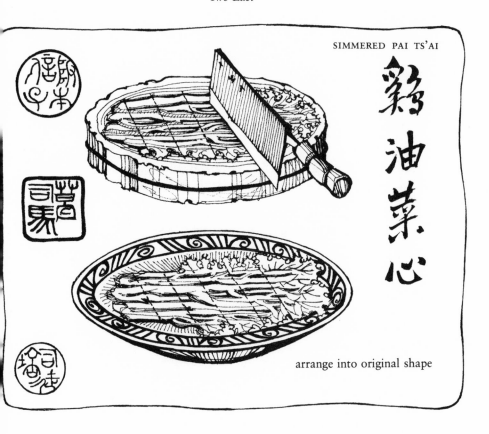

arrange into original shape

YANGCHOU NOODLES

1 pound fresh Chinese egg
noodles or dried packaged
noodles
Seasoning mixture
2 tablespoons thin soy
sauce
2-1/2 teaspoons salt
1 teaspoon sesame oil
1 teaspoon MSG
2 tablespoons rice wine
2 tablespoons vegetable oil
1/4 pound fresh shrimp,
shelled, deveined, washed
and sliced lengthwise
1/2 cup snow peas, halved
diagonally
8 water chestnuts, sliced
8 fresh mushrooms, sliced
8 cups Chinese stock (p. 30)
or chicken stock
Salt to taste

1-1/2 cups cooked chicken
breast cut into slices 2
inches by 1 by 1/4 inch
2 cooked chicken livers,
sliced into 6 pieces
1/2 cup canned abalone cut
into slices 2 inches by 1 by
1/8 inch
1 cup barbecued pork (p. 194)
or cooked pork cut into
slices 2 inches by 1 by 1/8
inch
8 canned quail eggs or 3
hard-boiled chicken eggs,
halved lengthwise
3 tablespoons slivered green
onion (cut in half lengthwise and slice diagonally
into 1/2-inch sections)

Boil 3 quarts water in a large pot. Add noodles and stir to keep them from
sticking (1 teaspoon oil may be added to help prevent sticking). Fresh
noodles require 5 to 6 minutes, dry noodles 7 to 8 minutes. Test for doneness by cutting a noodle with a fingernail—if it cuts easily, the noodles
are ready. Drain them in a colander and rinse with cold water.

Mix together the ingredients for the seasoning mixture.

Bring the stock to a boil in a large pot. Reduce heat and simmer.

Heat a wok over high heat. When very hot, add oil, then the shrimp, and
stir-fry until the shrimp turn white. Remove and set aside.

Add the seasoning mixture to the wok. Add peas, water chestnuts and
mushrooms and stir-fry. Add the hot stock, turn up the heat and bring to a
boil. Add the noodles and boil for 1 to 2 minutes. Adjust the salt seasoning
and transfer to a heated 10- to 12-cup serving bowl or soup tureen. Arrange the shrimp, chicken, chicken livers, abalone and pork on top of the
noodles in individual sections and garnish with sliced eggs (yolk side up)
and green onion.

Serves 6–8.

SUNG SAO'S NOODLE SOUP

This provincial soup is attributed to the wife of a fisherman named Sung who offered it to Emperor Ch'ien Lung as he was sightseeing in a pleasure boat on West Lake. It is said that the emperor enjoyed it so much that he ordered his imperial chefs to cook it for him, but theirs was never quite as good as the original.

4 dried black mushrooms
Coating mixture
  1 egg white
  2 tablespoons cornstarch
  1/2 tablespoon cold water
1/3 pound fish fillets cut into
  1/4-inch cubes
Seasoning mixture I
  1 tablespoon brown bean
    sauce
  1 teaspoon minced fresh
    ginger
  1-1/2 tablespoons chopped
    green onion
  1/2 teaspoon salt
Seasoning mixture II
  1-1/2 teaspoons thin soy
    sauce

2 tablespoons rice wine
1 tablespoon white vinegar
1/4 teaspoon sesame oil
1/4 teaspoon MSG
1/2 pound fresh or dried
  Chinese noodles
Vegetable oil for deep-frying
  plus 2 tablespoons
1/4 pound fresh shrimp,
  shelled, deveined, washed
  and cut into 1/2-inch pieces
1/2 cup slivered bamboo
  shoots
1 cup canned bean sprouts
4 cups Chinese stock (p. 30)
2 tablespoons water plus 1
  tablespoon cornstarch

Soak the mushrooms for 15 minutes in hot water. Rinse, squeeze out the water, remove the stems and shred the caps.

Stir together the ingredients for the coating mixture and add the fish cubes. Mix well.

Combine the ingredients for seasoning mixture I and do the same for seasoning mixture II.

Bring 3 quarts water to a vigorous boil, add noodles and cook until just done (5 to 6 minutes for fresh noodles, 7 to 8 minutes for dry noodles). Rinse and drain the noodles, divide into large soup bowls and set aside in a warm place.

Bring the stock to a boil, then lower the heat and let it simmer.

Heat about 2 inches oil in a deep, heavy pot. When the oil is about 350°, add half the fish and fry until browned. Drain and set aside, keeping it warm. Repeat this process with the rest of the fish.

Heat a wok over high heat. When very hot, add 2 tablespoons oil and seasoning mixture I. Stir several times and add shrimp and mushrooms. Stir-fry for 1/2 minute and add bamboo shoots. Stir-fry another 1/2 minute, then add bean sprouts, followed by seasoning mixture II. Stir-fry a few seconds, add the stock and bring to a boil. Add the cornstarch mixture and stir until the stock thickens. Pour the soup over the noodles in the serving bowls, putting some crispy fish pieces on top of each.

Serves 4.

JUICY STEAMED ROLLS
WITH EGG SKIN SOUP

Filling
  3/4 pound lean smoked
    ham hock with skin
  1/4 pound minced pork
    meat
  1/3 cup sesame seeds
Seasoning mixture
  2 tablespoon rice wine
  2 tablespoon sugar
  1 teaspoon ginger water
    (see Ginger root, p. 25)
    made from 2 slices fresh
    ginger
  2 tablespoon light soy
    sauce
  1 tablespoon cornstarch
  1 cup minced green onion
Rolls
  3/4 cup warm water

2-1/2 teaspoons sugar
1/2 teaspoon salt
1-1/2 teaspoons oil
1 package yeast
1-3/4 cups flour
Soup
  2 large eggs
  2 tablespoons water
  8 cups chicken stock
  2 teaspoons chopped green
    onion
Dip I
  1/3 cup Hoisin sauce
Dip II
  1/4 cup Chinese red vinegar
  1/4 teaspoon grated ginger
  1 teaspoon thin soy sauce
  Few drops of sesame oil

Wash the ham hock and make several cuts to the bone. Pan-fry sesame seeds until golden and lightly crush them. Put the ham hock with 1/2 cup water in a pressure cooker and cook under 10 pounds pressure for 1 hour, or until the fat is melted and the skin and meat falls away from the bone. If you do not have a pressure cooker, put the hock into a pot with 3 cups water. Bring the water to a boil, then lower the heat and cook for 2 to 3 hours, or until the meat is done.

When the ham hock is cooked, pour off the fat and liquid. Remove the hock, discard the bone and mince the skin and meat. Put the minced ham and skin in the pot and add the minced pork and seasoning mixture. Braise gently while stirring until the pork is cooked and most of the liquid is gone. Add green onion and continue cooking and stirring until it becomes transparent. (The mixture should be thick.) Transfer to a bowl and add the sesame seeds and cornstarch. Mix well and cool. (This is the filling.)

To make the rolls, first put warm water in a large bowl, add sugar, salt and yeast and mix to dissolve. Stir in the oil and gradually add the flour, mixing to form a dough. Knead gently in the bowl until the dough leaves the sides of the bowl—add a little warm water or flour as needed. Place the dough on lightly floured board and knead for 3 to 5 minutes, or until smooth and elastic. Place it in the bowl and cover with a damp cloth in a warm place (80–85°). Let it rise for 45 to 50 minutes, or until twice its original volume. Return the dough to a lightly floured board and shape into a long roll 1-1/2 inches in diameter. Slice it into 12 pieces and form each piece into a ball.

To fill each ball of dough, with your thumb punch a hole about 1 inch deep in the center. Put about 1 teaspoon filling in the hole. Carefully pull the edges over the filling and pinch together on top to seal.

Lightly oil two steamer trays and put hot water in the steamer. Arrange the rolls, sealed side down, about 2 inches apart on the trays. Put the trays in the steamer and cover. Keep the steamer covered for 10 minutes to make the rolls rise. Place the steamer over high heat and steam vigorously for 10 minutes.

While the rolls are steaming, prepare the soup. Combine the eggs and water and beat until foamy. Oil a 10-inch frying pan and heat over medium heat. Pour the eggs into the pan and cook slowly until a thin egg pancake is formed. Cook gently until the top is dry. Remove from the pan and slice into very thin strips. Divide into 6 portions for serving bowls. Heat the stock, season with salt and pour into the bowls. Garnish with the green onion and serve with the hot rolls and dips.

Serves 6.

STEAMED ROLLS WITH DATE PASTE, HAM AND GREEN ONION

This snack, served with an assortment of teas, is very popular in China. Each person takes a warm roll, splits it in two and fills it with ham, date paste and green onion.

1/4 pound dried Chinese
  dates
Seasoning mixture
  1 tablespoon sesame seeds
  1/4 teaspoon sesame oil
  3 tablespoons water
  2 tablespoons honey
  1 teaspoon thin soy sauce
  1 teaspoon water mixed
    with 1/2 teaspoon corn-
    starch

Rolls
  1-1/2 tablespoons sugar
  1 teaspoon salt
  1-1/2 cups lukewarm water
  2 packages dry yeast
  1 tablespoon vegetable oil
  3-1/2 cups flour
8 large green onions—use
  white part only, sliced in
  half lengthwise
1 pound best-quality ham (on
  the salty side), cut into
  slices 2 inches by 1 by 1/4
  inch

Wash dates and soak in water to cover for 1 hour. Drain, place in a pan and cover with 3 cups water. Bring to a boil and simmer the dates for about 2 hours, or until they are soft and pulpy and most of the liquid is absorbed. Cool them and discard the pits, if any. Mash the dates into a paste.

To prepare the seasoning mixture, lightly pan-fry sesame seeds in sesame oil. Add water, honey and soy sauce and heat to dissolve the honey. Add the cornstarch mixture and stir until thickened.

To make the rolls, first dissolve the sugar and salt in 1-1/2 cups lukewarm water in a large bowl. Add yeast and stir to dissolve. Add oil and then the flour, a little at a time, mixing well until a soft dough is formed. Knead lightly in a bowl until the dough begins to leave the sides of the bowl. Add more water or flour if needed.

Place the dough on a lightly floured board and knead for about 5 minutes, or until smooth and elastic. Place in an oiled bowl, cover with damp cloth and let it rise in a warm place for about 45 minutes, or until double in bulk.

Return the dough to the board, knead gently and shape into 2 long rolls. Cut each roll into 8 equal pieces and shape each piece into a ball. Put enough hot water for steaming in a multitiered metal steamer. Oil the tiers well and place on them the balls of dough about 2 inches apart. Arrange the tiers, one on top of another, and cover the steamer. Let the balls rise for about 10 minutes, or until double in bulk. Turn on the heat and steam vigorously for 10 to 12 minutes. Remove the cover and allow the rolls to cool a bit before arranging them on a heated platter. Cover to keep warm.

On another warm platter, arrange the mashed dates in the center. Place green onion sections on one side and ham slices on the other. Reheat the seasoning mixture and spoon it over the ham and date paste. Serve with the hot rolls and tea.

Serves 4–5.

CHINESE DATE CAKES

A Suchou specialty, this steamed date cake is reminiscent of English plum pudding.

1/2 pound dried Chinese dates, pitted	1/4 teaspoon salt
4 cups water	1 teaspoon vanilla
4 tablespoons lard or margarine	1/4 cup glutinous rice flour
1/2 cup canned red bean paste	1/4 cup rice flour
	3 tablespoons all-purpose flour
	1/4 cup slivered almonds

Put dates in the water and bring to a boil. Reduce heat and cook for 1 hour, or until very tender. Drain the dates, reserving the liquid (there should be about 1/4 cup, but if not, add a little water to make up the difference). Cool and mash into a fine paste or put in a blender.

Mix the date paste, lard or margarine, red bean paste, salt, and vanilla in a large bowl. Bring the liquid in which the dates have cooked to a boil and add to the date mixture. Add the glutinous rice flour, rice flour and all-purpose flour and stir vigorously until a thick dough is formed.

Oil an 8-by-8-inch cake pan and pour in the date mixture. Place the pan in a steamer and steam vigorously (add additional water if necessary) for 30 minutes, or until the cake is firm. Carefully remove and cool. Slice into small squares and garnish with almonds.

Makes about 16 little cakes.

SAVORY EGGPLANT AND BEAN CURD

This simple and nourishing dish, like the four recipes that follow it, is a good example of China's "new cuisine."

2 cups bean curd, cut in
  1-inch cubes
Seasoning mixture
  1/3 cup Chinese stock
    (p. 30) or chicken stock
  1/2 teaspoon minced fresh
    ginger
  1 tablespoon rice wine
  2-1/2 tablespoons thin soy
    sauce

4 teaspoons sugar
Vegetable oil for deep-frying
  plus 3 tablespoons
2 1/2 cups eggplant cut in
  1-inch cubes
1/2 cup sliced onion
Pinch of MSG
Pinch of white pepper
1 teaspoon sesame oil

Put bean curd in a pot, cover with boiling water, and let stand 1 minute. Drain carefully.

Mix together all seasoning-mixture ingredients *except* sugar.

Lightly oil a small frying pan. Add sugar and heat over medium heat until it melts and starts to turn golden. Remove the pan from heat immediately. Add 1 tablespoon hot water and stir to liquefy over medium heat. Add this caramel mixture to the seasoning mixture.

Heat about 3 inches oil to 340° in a deep, heavy pot or deep-fryer. Add eggplant and deep-fry for 1 minute, or until golden. Scoop out and drain.

Heat 3 tablespoons oil in a wok over high heat. Add the onion, eggplant, bean curd and seasoning mixture. Stir and bring to a boil. Lower the heat and simmer gently until only a little liquid remains. Add MSG, white pepper and sesame oil and stir a few times until the liquid is almost absorbed. Transfer to a heated platter.

Serves 3.

PORK SHREDS, BAMBOO SHOOTS AND ONION

1/2 pound pork cut from the loin
3 tablespoons vegetable oil
1 large garlic clove, peeled and crushed
3 green onions, slivered (cut in half lengthwise and slice diagonally into 1/2-inch sections)

1 cup slivered bamboo shoots
Seasoning mixture
  2-1/2 tablespoons thin soy sauce
  1 tablespoon rice wine
  1/2 tablespoon sugar
  1/4 teaspoon sesame oil
1/2 teaspoon black pepper

Using a sharp knife or cleaver, cut the pork into the thinnest possible slices, then cut the slices into the thinnest possible shreds.

Heat a wok over high heat. When very hot, add oil and then the garlic. After 5 seconds, discard the garlic. Add pork, stir-fry for 1 minute, then add onions and bamboo shoots and stir-fry for 2 minutes. Add the seasoning mixture, stir a few times and sprinkle with pepper.

Serves 2.

STIR-FRIED GINGER SHREDS AND PORK

Seasoning mixture
  1-1/2 tablespoons rice wine
  1-1/2 tablespoons thin soy sauce
  Pinch of salt
4 tablespoons vegetable oil
1/2 pound loin of pork cut in slices 2 inches by 1/8 by 1/8 inch

1 tablespoon shredded preserved ginger root in brine*
4 cups fresh bean sprouts, washed and drained
1/2 teaspoon MSG
3 drops sesame oil

Combine the ingredients for the seasoning mixture.

Heat a wok over high heat. When very hot, add 1 tablespoon oil and then

---

* May be bought in Japanese grocery stores, where it is known as *beni-shoga*, or red ginger.

the pork. Stir-fry for 1 minute, or until lightly browned. Add the seasoning mixture and stir-fry for 1/2 minute. Remove the pork and set aside.

Add to the wok 3 tablespoons oil and heat until it smokes. Add ginger and bean sprouts and stir-fry for 1/2 minute, making sure the sprouts are well coated with oil. Add the pork and MSG and stir-fry for 1/2 minute. Quickly transfer to a heated platter and sprinkle with sesame oil. Serves 3.

STIR-FRIED FRESH CUCUMBER AND JUMBO SHRIMP

Marinade
- 1 teaspoon thin soy sauce
- 1/2 teaspoon rice wine
- 1/4 teaspoon sesame oil
- 16 fresh jumbo shrimp, shelled, deveined, washed and halved lengthwise
- 2 medium-sized, thin, firm cucumbers

Seasoning mixture
- 1-1/2 teaspoons thin soy sauce
- 1/2 teaspoon rice wine
- 1/4 teaspoon sugar
- 1/8 teaspoon salt
- 2-1/2 tablespoons vegetable oil
- 1/2 teaspoon sesame oil
- 1/2 teaspoon crushed flower pepper

Mix the ingredients for the marinade. Add the shrimp and marinate for 5 minutes. Peel the cucumbers with a potato peeler leaving on thin strips of skin at 1/2-inch intervals. Halve the cucumbers lengthwise and remove the seeds. Slice the halves diagonally into pieces about 2 1/2 inches by 1/2 inch. There should be 2-1/2 to 3 cups.

Combine the ingredients for the seasoning mixture.

Heat a wok over high heat. When very hot, add vegetable oil and then the shrimp. Stir-fry the shrimp, then press them for 1 minute against the sides of the wok. Add cucumber and the seasoning mixture and stir several times. Add 2 tablespoons water. When the liquid comes to a boil, add sesame oil and stir a few times. Transfer to a heated platter and sprinkle with flower pepper.

Serves 3–4.

STIR-FRIED
STRING BEANS SHANGHAI STYLE

1 pound fresh string beans
2 teaspoons sesame seeds
Seasoning mixture
  1 tablespoon sugar
  2 tablespoons rice wine
  1/4 teaspoon white pepper

2 teaspoons thin soy sauce
1/2 teaspoon sesame oil
1/4 teaspoon MSG
2-1/2 tablespoons vegetable
  oil
1/2 teaspoon salt

Trim, wash and parboil string beans for 2 minutes in rapidly boiling water. Drain and rinse with cold water.

Heat sesame seeds in a dry frying pan over moderate heat. Remove when seeds begin to pop.

Combine the ingredients for the seasoning mixture.

Put a wok over high heat. When very hot, add oil, salt and then the string beans and stir-fry for 1 minute. Add the seasoning mixture and stir-fry for another minute. Add sesame seeds and blend well. Transfer to a heated platter.

Serves 2–3.

The
SOUTHEAST

Because of its tropical climate, its location and its early contact with foreign lands and new ideas, the province of Kuangtung in the southeastern region of China has an extremely varied cuisine. Its long coastline offers sea cucumbers, squid and a wide variety of fish. Also found are oysters, eels, shrimp, crabs and lobsters. The inland waters are filled with freshwater fish and sweet-fleshed crustaceans, and their shores abound with duck. On farms, melons of many varieties are grown, as well as prize vegetables, nuts and tropical fruits.

In the capital of Kuangchou (Canton), the Cantonese have been versatile and innovative in their cooking. Their forte seems to be in the imaginative creation of special sauces, such as black bean garlic sauce, rich and smooth oyster sauce and the finest culinary achievement of them all—lobster sauce.

The finest fish dishes are found in the capital. Steaming is the favorite method of preparation—one that requires the fish to be very fresh. Smaller fish (less than one pound) are preferred, since they require a minimum of cooking, thus preserving the natural flavors. Only a simple sauce made with a little oil, fresh ginger, soy and minced green onion is served with it—poured over the fish after the steaming. For those who enjoy a heartier dish, a large fish (tail and head intact) is prepared and steamed with a flavorful brown bean sauce enlivened with wine, ginger shreds, sesame oil and minced green onion.

The Cantonese are unexcelled in barbecuing and roasting. Different barbecued pork dishes use a variety of marinades, but the barbecuing method itself is the secret of their success. It renders the pork a beautiful reddish brown while the inside is white and juicy. A specialty of the region is roast duck, with succulent meat that has absorbed the delicious flavors of the seasonings used in preparing it.

Only by extensive experience in dining and cooking can the wide range of dishes and the variety expressed in the Cantonese cuisine be appreciated. To many experts it is the best of Chinese cooking.

SOUTHEAST RESTAURANTS

The Li K'ou Fu (Blessed Taste) Seafood Restaurant was very small when it opened in 1940. Today the restaurant is large and famous. Its chefs are experts in the local cooking style, particularly of the Cantonese district of Feng Ch'eng, an example of which is honey tender chicken. The Ta T'ung (Brotherhood) Wine House is renowned for its Cantonese dishes, such as crispy skin chicken, and delicate pastries. The Ning Ch'ang (Peace and Prosperity) Dining Hall has specialized in the dishes of Kuangchou Province for over a hundred years. The Yu Yuan (Happy Garden) Dining Hall is famous for its preparation of banquets. The Ts'ai Ken Hsiang (Fragrant Vegetable Root) bears the same name as a restaurant in Yangchou but serves only vegetarian dishes, such as braised black mushrooms in oyster sauce. The Canton Restaurant of Peking offers only Cantonese dishes. Other restaurants are the Kuangchou Market Restaurant, the Pei Yuan (Northern Garden) Wine House and the Peking Hotel Restaurant.

SPINACH SOUP

Chinese spinach is less acid in taste than the Western variety and has a lovely cresslike flavor. If unavailable, ordinary spinach is an acceptable substitute.

1-1/2 pounds Chinese spinach (leaves only)	2 large garlic cloves, peeled and lightly mashed
5 cups Chinese stock (p. 30) or chicken stock	1 teaspoon salt
1 bean curd cake cut into 1-inch cubes	1 teaspoon rice wine
2 tablespoons fresh vegetable oil	2 tablespoons water mixed with 1 tablespoon cornstarch
	1/4 cup shredded ham

Wash and drain the spinach leaves. Put the stock in a pot and bring to a boil, then lower the heat and let it simmer.

Put the bean curd cubes in a pan and pour enough boiling water over them to cover. Let stand a few minutes and drain.

Heat the oil in a wok over medium heat. Add garlic, stir-fry until lightly browned and discard it. Add salt, wine and spinach and stir-fry until well coated with oil and tender. Add the stock, bring to a boil and thicken with the cornstarch mixture. Adjust the salt seasoning, add the bean curd and shredded ham and stir.

Serves 3.

WINTER MELON SOUP

A favorite banquet soup, cooked in a whole winter melon filled with a variety of choice ingredients. The sweet flesh of the melon is scooped out and served with the rest of the soup.

1 duck	1 cup raw shrimp meat cut
1 4-pound pork butt with bone	into 1/4-inch slices
12 to 14 cups rich soup stock*	1 cup crabmeat, fresh or
Salt to taste	frozen
1 teaspoon MSG	1 cup sliced fresh mushrooms
Ground black pepper to taste	1 cup sliced canned water
1 8- to 9-pound whole winter	chestnuts
melon	1 cup sliced canned bamboo
1 cup Smithfield ham cut into	shoots
1/4-inch cubes	

A day ahead, slice the meat from the duck and pork butt and cut into 1/4-inch cubes to make 2 cups each. Reserve the bones. Put the meat in plastic wrap and refrigerate for use the next day. (Save the remainder to use in other dishes.) Add the duck bones and pork bones to the stock and simmer for several hours. Season to taste with salt, MSG and pepper to taste. Set aside.

The next day, wash, dry and cut the melon crosswise 4 inches from the stem. Remove the stem and take out the seeds and fibers from inside the melon. Place the melon, cut side up, in a large heatproof bowl in such a way that it can't tip (Figure 1). Fill a large steamer (such as a clam steamer

---

* Add duck bones and pork bones to 12 to 14 cups of chicken stock and simmer for several hours. Additional chicken stock may be added the next day to make up enough soup to fill the melon.

or a canning pot with a cover) with hot water and place the bowl with the melon on a metal ring stand in the steamer (Figure 2).

Put all the solid ingredients in the melon, then fill it two-thirds full with stock and cover with the melon cap. Cover the steamer and bring to a boil, then reduce heat a little and steam for 4 to 5 hours, adding water as needed, or until the inside of the melon tests done with a long-handled fork. (Be careful in removing the steamer cover and the cap of the melon shell.) The length of time required to steam the melon will depend on its size and quality.

When the melon is done, let it cool a bit. Remove the cap and ladle the soup into a large pan. Season to taste with additional salt and pepper. Carefully scoop out the melon meat up to 2 inches of the rind. Take care not to dip too deeply, or the skin may break. Pour the hot soup back into the melon and add the scooped-out pieces of melon.

Serves 8–10.

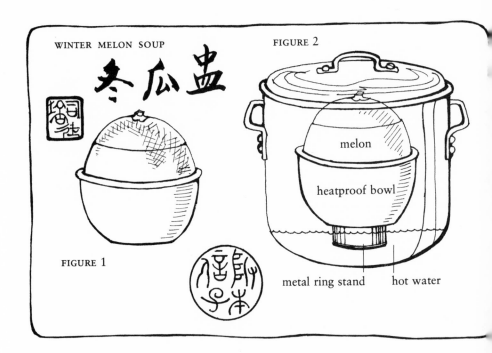

WINTER MELON SOUP

冬瓜盅

FIGURE 2

melon

heatproof bowl

FIGURE 1

metal ring stand   hot water

FISH AND BEAN CURD CHOWDER
CANTONESE STYLE

1 pound fish fillets (any firm,
thick, white-fleshed fish,
such as haddock or cod)
2 bean curd cakes, cut into
1-inch cubes
6 cups rich Chinese stock
(p. 30) or chicken stock
2 tablespoons fresh vegetable
oil
1-1/2 teaspoons salt
3/4 teaspoon grated fresh
ginger
1 cup fresh broccoli cut into
spears 2 inches by 1/2 inch
and parboiled 1 minute

3 tablespoons water mixed
with 2-1/2 tablespoons
cornstarch
2 egg whites
1 teaspoon sesame oil
1/4 teaspoon ground black
pepper
1/2 cup slivered ham
2 slivered green onions (cut
in half lengthwise and slice
diagonally into 1/2-inch
sections

Wash and dry the fish fillets, and cut them into 2-inch cubes. Put the
bean curd cubes in a pan, pour boiling water over them and let stand for a
few minutes, then drain them.

Put the stock in a pot, bring to a boil and let it simmer.

Heat the oil and salt in a wok over medium heat. Add ginger and stir-fry
for a few seconds. Add the fish cubes and stir-fry, taking care not to break
them. When the fish turns white and then golden, carefully remove from
the wok and set aside.

Add the hot stock, broccoli and bean curd and bring to a gentle boil.
Thicken with the cornstarch mixture and gently stir the egg whites into the
stock. Add sesame oil and pepper. Adjust the salt seasoning. Remove the
wok from heat and add the fish, ham and green onions. Transfer to a
heated tureen and serve.

Serves 4–6.

FISHBALL SOUP CANTONESE STYLE

4 large dried black
  mushrooms
5 cups rich Chinese stock
  (p. 30)
Seasoning mixture
  1/2 teaspoon kosher salt
  1 teaspoon rice wine
  1 teaspoon thin soy sauce
  1/4 teaspoon MSG
Dip
  1/4 cup Chinese red vinegar
  1 teaspoon thin soy sauce
Fishballs
  1 pound fresh fish fillets
  (cod, haddock, pike,
  whitefish)
  1 large egg white

1/4 cup minced canned
  water chestnuts
2/3 teaspoon kosher salt
1/8 teaspoon ground black
  pepper
1 teaspoon sesame oil
1/8 teaspoon grated fresh
  ginger
2 tablespoons rice wine
1 teaspoon MSG
5 to 6 tablespoons cornstarch
2 tablespoons fresh vegetable
  oil
1-1/2 cups *pai ts'ai* sliced
  diagonally into 1-by-1/2-
  inch pieces

Soak mushrooms in warm water for 30 minutes, squeeze dry, remove the stems and halve the caps.

Put the stock in a pot over low heat. Combine the ingredients for the seasoning mixture and mix the dip ingredients.

To make the fishballs, first mince the fillets with a cleaver or put through a food processor or meat grinder. Put the minced fish in a dishcloth, gently press out as much liquid as possible and place in a bowl. Add the other ingredients, always mixing in one direction. Sprinkle cornstarch on the fish mixture and blend well, adding more cornstarch if necessary to make it firm. Shape the mixture into balls about 1-1/2 inches in diameter.

Boil several quarts of water in a 14-inch wok and add 1 tablespoon oil. Carefully lower a third to half of the fishballs into the water and cook for about 3 minutes. (Adjust the heat so that the water doesn't boil too vigorously and cause the balls to break up.) Use a slotted spoon to drain and transfer to a platter. Repeat the process to cook the rest of the fishballs.

Wash and dry the wok. Put 1 tablespoon oil in the wok and heat over a high flame. Add mushrooms and stir-fry for 1 minute. Add the seasoning mixture and *pai ts'ai* and stir-fry for 2 minutes. Add the stock and bring to a rapid boil, then turn off the heat. Adjust the salt seasoning. Carefully transfer the fishballs to a large bowl or soup tureen and pour the stock over them. Use the dip for some of the fishballs.

Serves 4–5.

WON TON SOUP

This Cantonese soup differs from the Szech'uan version in that the *won tons* are filled with vegetables only and are deep-fried. For an all-vegetarian dish, substitute vegetable stock and add a few drops of sesame oil, soy sauce and salt to taste.

Wrappings
  3/4 cup flour
  Pinch of salt
  1/4 cup boiling water
  1 teaspoon vegetable oil
Filling
  4 large dried black
    mushrooms
  1/4 teaspoon grated fresh
    ginger
  1/4 cup canned, minced
    water chestnuts
  1/2 cup canned, minced
    bamboo shoots
  1/4 cup minced green onion

2 teaspoons cornstarch
1/3 cup Chinese stock
  (p. 30) or chicken stock
Seasoning mixture
  1/2 teaspoon MSG
  1 tablespoon thin soy sauce
  1/4 teaspoon salt
  1/2 teaspoon vegetable oil
1 egg white (for sealing *won ton*)
1 *pai ts'ai* or mustard green
  heart
6 cups soup stock
3 to 4 drops sesame oil
Salt to taste

First make the wrappings. Place flour and salt in a bowl. Add oil to boiling water and slowly add to the flour, mixing well. (Add extra hot water as needed.) When the dough leaves the sides of the bowl, turn out onto a lightly dusted board and knead gently for 3 to 4 minutes, or until it becomes elastic. Shape into a long roll about 1-1/4 inches in diameter and cut off 12 equal pieces. Shape the pieces into balls and then flatten them into disks about 3 inches in diameter and of even thickness. Stack them, lightly dusting the top of each disk with flour.

To make the filling, first soak mushrooms in warm water for 30 minutes. Drain and squeeze them dry, remove the stems and mince the caps. Add the remaining ingredients for the filling and mix well. Combine the ingredients for the seasoning mixture and add to the filling, mixing well. Bring 1/3 cup stock to a boil, add the mixture and stir until thickened. Cool.

Spoon about 1 tablespoon filling onto the middle of each wrapping, gather up the sides and pinch at the top to close, using the egg white to seal.

Wash and trim the *pai ts'ai* or mustard green heart. Slice diagonally into 2-by-1/2-inch pieces. Bring the stock to a boil, add the vegetable and turn off the heat. Add sesame oil and season with salt.

Heat about 3 inches fresh vegetable oil to about 340° in a deep, heavy pot or deep-fryer. Add the *won ton,* about four at a time, and deep-fry until golden and crispy. Drain.

Place the *won ton* in individual soup bowls and pour hot soup over them.

Serves 4–5.

CRYSTAL COLD CHICKEN

A Cantonese banquet dish especially suited for summer.

1 2-1/2- to 3-pound pullet	Dip
4 to 5 Chinese dried dates	2 tablespoons dried mus-
1/4 pound prosciutto	tard plus enough water
1/2 pound smoked ham hock	to make a paste
2 teaspoons salt	Dip
1 tablespoon rice wine	1/4 cup thin soy sauce
2 packages plain gelatin	1 teaspoon minced fresh
Seasoning mixture	ginger
2 tablespoons Chinese red	1/2 teaspoon sesame oil
vinegar	1/2 head lettuce, shredded
1 teaspoon rice wine	
1/8 teaspoon fresh grated	
ginger	

Wash the chicken and cut slashes in the thickest part of the thighs. Parboil the dates for about 15 minutes in a little water, drain, remove the pits and cut them in half. Cut the prosciutto into 2-by-1/2-inch slices. Wash and slash the ham hock to the bone. Combine the ingredients for the seasoning mixture. Make the two dips.

Boil enough water with 1 teaspoon salt to cover the chicken. Cook the chicken for 15 minutes, then turn and cook another 15 minutes. Remove and test for doneness by piercing the thickest part with a fork. If blood comes out, cook for 5 to 10 minutes more. Reserve the stock.

Immerse the chicken in cold water until it cools. Drain. Sprinkle 1 tablespoon wine and 1 teaspoon salt over the chicken. Prick the skin all over with a fork and let the chicken air-dry.

Measure out 4 cups of the reserved stock into a pot. Add the ham hock and simmer slowly for about 30 minutes.

Ladle out 1 cup stock and let it cool. Add gelatin, stirring well to dissolve. Add to the stock in the pot and bring to a boil while stirring. Add the seasoning mixture, adjust the salt, and stir well.

Cut the chicken, skin side up, into serving pieces. In a large dish about 2 inches deep, arrange the chicken into its original shape, with the skin side down. Arrange ham slices on both sides and the date halves on both top and bottom.

Pour the gelatin mixture over the entire dish to cover all or most of the chicken. Refrigerate for 3 or 4 hours, or until firmly jelled.

Unmold the chicken on a large platter covered with a bed of shredded lettuce, and serve with the dips.

Serves 4–5.

TA T'UNG CRISPY SKIN CHICKEN

A distinctive Cantonese version of fried chicken which derives its special flavor from the herbs in which the chicken is steeped.

1 3- to 3-1/2-pound chicken	Coating mixture
Bouquet garni	3 tablespoons malt sugar
1/2 teaspoon star anise	or honey
1/2 teaspoon whole cloves	1-1/2 tablespoons rice wine
1/2 teaspoon Chinese lico-	1 teaspoon Chinese vinegar
rice root	1/2 teaspoon salt
1/2 teaspoon minced fresh	2 tablespoons cornstarch
ginger	1-1/2 tablespoons salt
1/2 teaspoon flower pepper	Fresh vegetable oil for deep-
1/2 teaspoon cardamom	frying
1 piece cinnamon stick	

Tie up the ingredients for the bouquet garni in a 4-inch-square piece of cheesecloth.

To make the coating mixture, first put a double boiler over low heat and add malt sugar (or honey). When the sugar softens, add rice wine, vinegar and 1/2 teaspoon salt. Mix and then stir in the cornstarch, a tablespoon at a time. Continue stirring until the mixture becomes whitish and very sticky. Keep the mixture over low heat to prevent hardening.

Boil about 12 cups water in a pot and add the bouquet garni. Reduce the heat and simmer for 40 minutes. Add 1 1/2 tablespoons salt and let the water come to a boil. Tie heavy string around the chicken under the wings. Holding the string, immerse the chicken for 1 minute and remove. (The sudden heat should shrink the chicken.) Reduce heat, put the chicken in the pot and simmer for 30 minutes.

Remove the chicken, dry with a dishcloth and hang it over the pot containing the coating mixture. Smear the coating mixture over the chicken—recoat if necessary to cover the entire surface. Hang the chicken to dry for 2 to 4 hours. An electric fan will help dry it, or the chicken can be put in the refrigerator overnight. In cool, dry weather it can be hung outdoors. (The skin should have a firm layer of coating on it.)

Put enough oil for deep-frying in a deep, heavy pot and heat to about 360°. The Chinese method is to hold the chicken over the oil in a wire scoop and repeatedly douse it with the hot oil both inside and out until the skin is golden-brown. Alternatively, the chicken can be put in the scoop and left in the oil for 5 minutes on each side.

Remove the chicken and drain it. Cut it in two from breast to back and then into about 24 pieces.

Serves 4.

FENG CH'ENG HONEY TENDER CHICKEN

Seasoning mixture
2 teaspoons honey
1 tablespoon oyster sauce
2 tablespoons thin soy
   sauce
1 tablespoon Chinese stock
   (p. 30) or chicken stock

1 tablespoon rice wine
1-1/2 teaspoons sesame oil
1/4 teaspoon MSG
1-1/2 pounds boned chicken
   breast
1/2 head lettuce, sliced

Combine the ingredients for the seasoning mixture.

Put the chicken in boiling water in a pot over high heat, immediately reduce the heat and cook for 5 to 6 minutes. Remove the chicken and let the water come to a boil again. Put the chicken back in and cook for 5 minutes over low heat. Repeat this process at least once more, until the chicken turns white. Cool and cut the chicken into pieces about 1 by 1/2 by 1/2 inch. Arrange the pieces of chicken on a bed of lettuce. and spoon the seasoning mixture over them.

Serves 3.

WHITE CUT CHICKEN

Succulent chicken in a sauce with a real bite to it.

Seasoning mixture
1/2 teaspoon salt
1/2 teaspoon MSG
1-1/2 teaspoons thin soy
  sauce
1 teaspoon rice wine
1 3-pound frying chicken
1 tablespoon grated fresh
  ginger

3 tablespoons vegetable oil
1/2 teaspoon crushed flower
  pepper
1/2 cup Chinese stock
  (p. 30) or chicken stock
1 teaspoon water mixed with
  1/2 teaspoon cornstarch
1 tablespoon minced green
  onion

Combine the ingredients for the seasoning mixture.

Boil enough water to cover the chicken in a large pot. Put the chicken in and boil for 20 to 30 minutes. Remove and test for doneness by piercing the thickest part of the thigh—if blood appears, cook for 5 to 10 minutes more. Drain and carve into serving pieces (see illustrated instructions on p. 9). Sprinkle with grated ginger.

Put oil in a small pan over medium heat. When the oil begins to smoke, add the flower pepper and after 1/2 minute remove from heat.

Put 1/2 cup stock in a wok over high heat. When it begins to boil, add the seasoning mixture and then the cornstarch paste. Stir until thickened.

Pour the hot seasoned oil over the chicken, then pour the sauce mixture over it and garnish with green onion.

Serves 3–4.

CRISPY PAPER-WRAPPED CHICKEN

Marinated chicken is wrapped in waxed-paper packets and briefly deep-fried. At the table, each diner rips open a packet with his chopsticks to find the fragrant tidbits inside.

1 chicken breast
5 slices boiled ham
Marinade mixture
  2 tablespoons green onion
    cut into 1/2-inch sections
  1/3 teaspoon salt
  1 tablespoon rice wine
  1-1/2 teaspoons sugar
  1 teaspoon sesame oil
  1 tablespoon oyster sauce
  2 teaspoons grated fresh
    ginger

Sealing mixture
  2 egg whites from large
    eggs
  1 tablespoon cornstarch
3 tablespoons slivered almonds
4 canned water chestnuts
  sliced in fifths
1/4 cup Chinese parsley
  leaves
20 4-inch squares waxed
  paper
Vegetable oil for deep-frying

Cut the chicken breast into 20 pieces about 2 by 2 by 1/4 inch. Also cut the ham into 20 pieces the same size.

Combine the ingredients for the marinade, stir well and marinate the chicken in it for about 15 minutes.

Stir the cornstarch into the egg whites to make the sealing mixture. Layer the following ingredients one on top of another in this order on each waxed-paper square (Figure 1): 1 piece chicken, 2 almond slivers, 1 piece ham, 1 slice water chestnut and a few parsley leaves. Fold the packets as in Figures 2 to 4 and seal with the sealing mixture. With a brush apply the remaining sealing mixture all over the packets.

Heat enough oil to about 350° in a deep, heavy pot for deep-frying. Add the packets, four at a time, and deep-fry over high heat for 3 to 4 minutes. The outside of the packets should be slightly browned. Remove and drain. Serve on a heated platter.

Serves 4–5.

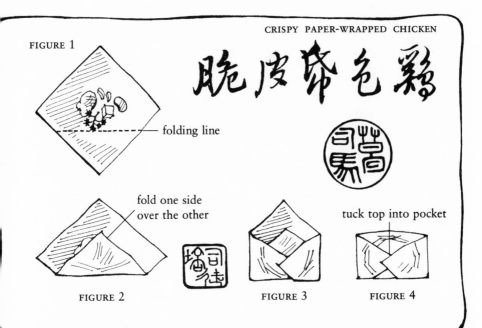

FIGURE 1

folding line

fold one side over the other

FIGURE 2

FIGURE 3

tuck top into pocket

FIGURE 4

CRISPY PAPER-WRAPPED CHICKEN

DARK SWEET AND SOUR CHICKEN

3 pounds large chicken legs
Seasoning mixture
   2 large garlic cloves, peeled
     and lightly crushed
   1/3 cup sugar
   1/2 cup oyster sauce
   Juice of 2 lemons
   1/2 teaspoon sesame oil
   1/2 teaspoon MSG

   1/2 teaspoon five-flavored
     spice
1/2 to 1 cup Chinese stock
   (p. 30) or chicken stock
2 tablespoons water mixed
   with 1 tablespoon cornstarch
2 tablespoons chopped green
   onions

Disjoint the chicken legs and lightly slash the thick parts. Wash and pat dry with paper towels.

Combine the ingredients for the seasoning mixture.

Put the chicken legs in a wok and pour the seasoning mixture over them. Heat the wok over medium heat and cover, then reduce heat and gently braise for about 40 minutes. Occasionally uncover the wok and stir to prevent burning. If necessary, add a little stock.

Remove from heat and transfer the chicken to a heated platter. Heat the stock and pour it into the wok over medium heat, stirring constantly until it begins to bubble. Thicken with the cornstarch mixture and pour it over the chicken. Garnish with green onions.

Serves 5–6.

SOY SAUCE CHICKEN

1 pound boned chicken
   breasts
2 medium-sized green peppers
2 small onions
1 garlic clove
Seasoning mixture
   1 tablespoon fermented
      black beans
   1 teaspoon grated fresh
      ginger
   1/2 teaspoon minced dried
      orange peel (soak in hot
      water for 10 minutes be-
      fore mincing)

1 small fresh chili pepper
2 teaspoons thick soy sauce
2 teaspoons rice wine
1 teaspoon sugar
1/2 teaspoon MSG
4 tablespoons vegetable oil
1/4 teaspoon salt
1/2 cup Chinese stock (p. 30)
   or chicken stock

With a sharp knife, cut the chicken into pieces about 1 1/2 inches by 1 by 1/2 inch.

Wash and cut green peppers lengthwise, remove the seeds and membrane, then cut into pieces about 1 1/2 inches by 1/4 inch. Peel and cut the onions into 1/2-inch slices. Peel and crush the garlic.

To prepare the seasoning mixture, wash, drain and chop the black beans. Remove the seeds and membrane from the chili pepper and mince it. Combine the black beans and chili pepper with the other ingredients for the seasoning mixture and stir well.

Heat 3 tablespoons oil in a wok over high heat. Add garlic, and when it begins to brown remove and discard. Add salt and chicken and stir-fry for 2 to 3 minutes. Add green pepper and onion and stir-fry for about 1 minute. Remove the chicken and vegetables from the wok and set aside.

Add 1 tablespoon oil to the wok over medium heat. Add the seasoning mixture and stir several times. Put the chicken and vegetables back into the wok, mix and add the stock. Stir a few times and transfer to a serving platter.

Serves 4.

TOMATO SAUCE CHICKEN

3 dried mushrooms
3/4 pound skinned chicken
  meat
Coating mixture
  1 egg white
  2 tablespoons cornstarch
Seasoning mixture
  2 tablespoons rice wine
  1/2 teaspoon salt
  2 tablespoons catsup
  3 tablespoons sugar
  3 tablespoons white vin-
    egar

2 teaspoon thin soy sauce
4 tablespoons vegetable oil
1 teaspoon minced fresh
  ginger
1 garlic clove, minced
1 green onion, cut in half
  lengthwise and sliced
  diagonally into 1/2-inch
  sections
1/3 cup green peas
Pinch of cayenne
1/2 cup sliced canned
  bamboo shoots

Soak mushrooms in warm water for 15 minutes. Squeeze dry, remove the stems and quarter the caps.

Cut the chicken into pieces 1 1/2 inches by 1 and 1/2 inch. Combine ingredients for the coating mixture and mix until smooth. Put the chicken pieces in the mixture and stir to coat well.

Combine the ingredients for the seasoning mixture.

Put a wok over high heat and add 3 tablespoons oil. Add the chicken and stir-fry for about 2 minutes, or until it is cooked. (Some browning may occur because of the egg white.) Remove the chicken and set aside. Reserve the bowl with the remains of the coating mixture.

Add 1 tablespoon oil to the wok, then add ginger, garlic and green onion. Stir twice and add mushrooms, peas, cayenne and bamboo shoots. Stir-fry for 1/2 minute. Mix the leftover coating mixture with the seasoning mixture and add to the wok. When the mixture boils, add the chicken. Stir a few times and transfer to a platter.

Serves 3.

CHICKEN FRITTERS
AND BARBECUED PORK STIR-FRIED
WITH CHOICE VEGETABLES

5 large dried black
  mushrooms
Marinade
  3 tablespoons rice wine
  2 teaspoons sugar
  1/4 teaspoon salt
  Pinch of MSG
  1/4 teaspoon shredded ginger
  1/2 teaspoon sesame oil
  1/2 teaspoon thin soy sauce
1 pound chicken breasts cut
  into slices 1-1/2 inches by 1
  by 1/2 inch
2 cups zucchini cut into 2-by-
  1/2-inch strips or snow
  peas halved diagonally
2/3 cup onion cut
  into 1-inch slices
1/2 cup sliced canned water
  chestnuts
1 tablespoon green onion cut
  into 1/2-inch sections
1 cup barbecued pork (p. 194)
  cut into 1/2-inch cubes

Batter
  2 large eggs
  2/3 cup water chestnut
    flour
  1/4 cup cold water
  Pinch of MSG
  Pinch of salt
Seasoning mixture
  1 teaspoon thin soy sauce
  1/4 teaspoon grated fresh
    ginger
  Pinch of MSG
  1/2 teaspoon salt
  1 tablespoon rice wine
  3/4 teaspoon sugar
  1/4 teaspoon pepper
  3/4 cup rich Chinese stock
    (p. 30) or chicken stock
  1-1/2 tablespoons water
    mixed with 1 tablespoon
    cornstarch
Vegetable oil for deep-frying
  plus 3 tablespoons

Soak mushrooms in warm water for 30 minutes, rinse dry, remove the stems and quarter the caps. Combine the ingredients for the marinade and marinate the chicken for 15 minutes.

Mix together the ingredients for the batter and combine the ingredients for the seasoning mixture.

Heat about 3 inches vegetable oil in a deep pot over medium heat to about 350°. Shake off the excess marinade from the pieces of chicken and coat them well with the batter. Add them, four to five at a time, to the oil and deep-fry, turning occasionally, for about 3 minutes or until golden and crisp. Drain on paper towels and set aside in warm place.

Put a wok over high heat. Put in 3 tablespoons oil; when it almost begins to smoke, add the mushrooms and onion. Stir-fry about 1-1/2 minutes, coating well with oil. Add zucchini, water chestnuts, the seasoning mixture and the stock. Cover and cook for another 1-1/2 minutes. Remove the cover and thicken with cornstarch mixture.

Turn off the heat and add the chicken and pork. Mix two or three times and transfer to a heated platter. Garnish with green onion.

Serves 3–4.

PINEAPPLE DUCK

Cooked chicken may be substituted for the duck, but neither the texture nor the flavor would be quite as good.

1-1/2 pounds boned cooked
  duck meat
1 large can sliced pineapple
  (in natural juice)
Marinade
  1 tablespoon rice wine
  3 to 4 drops sesame oil
  1/8 teaspoon salt
  1/8 teaspoon five-flavored
    spice
Batter
  1 large egg
  1/2 cup water chestnut
    flour
  1/2 cup cold water
  1/8 teaspoon salt

Sauce
  1/4 cup pineapple juice
    (from canned pineapple)
  1/2 cup white vinegar
  1/2 cup sugar
  1/8 teaspoon salt
  1/4 cup Chinese stock
    (p. 30) or chicken stock
  1/4 teaspoon thin soy sauce
  4 drops sesame oil
  1 large garlic clove, minced
  1/8 teaspoon grated fresh
    ginger
2 tablespoons water mixed
  with 1 tablespoon corn-
  starch
Vegetable oil for deep-frying
Pinch of cayenne

Slice duck meat into pieces 2 by 3 inches. Drain pineapple slices well. Mix together the ingredients for the marinade and marinate the pieces of duck. Stir together the ingredients for the batter and combine the ingredients for the sauce.

Heat 2 to 3 inches oil in a deep pan or wok over high heat. Shake off excess marinade from the pieces of duck and dip them in the batter, coating well. When the oil is about 350°, add the duck in batches to deep-fry. Turn from time to time until golden-brown and very crisp. Drain on paper towels.

Carefully pour out all oil except 1 tablespoon. Heat it until hot. Pour in the sauce, and let it come to a boil and thicken with the cornstarch mixture. Remove from heat.

On a heated platter, arrange alternating slices of duck and pineapple.

Pour the hot sauce over the slices and lightly sprinkle cayenne over the duck.

Serves 4–5.

CANTONESE ROAST DUCK

1 4- to 5-pound duck
Seasoning mixture
  2-1/2 cups Chinese stock
    (p. 30)
  3/4 teaspoon salt
  2 tablespoons brown bean
    sauce
  2 large garlic cloves, peeled
    and minced
  1 tablespoon rice wine
  1-1/2 tablespoons sugar
  3 green onions, minced
  2-1/2 tablespoons thin soy
    sauce
  1-1/2 teaspoons minced
    fresh ginger
  2 tablespoons dried *pai ts'ai*

  2 tablespoons minced dried
    tangerine peel (soak in
    warm water for 10
    minutes before mincing)
  1/4 teaspoon five-flavored
    spice
  4 pieces star anise
  1-1/2 teaspoons heavy soy
    sauce
  1-1/2 teaspoons honey
Coating mixture
  1/3 cup honey (or malt
    sugar if available)
  1 tablespoon heavy soy
    sauce
  1/2 cup boiling water
  1/2 teaspoon MSG

Wash the duck and sew up the posterior opening into the body cavity. Dry well and hang it (preferably outdoors in cool weather) to dry the skin thoroughly or place it upright in a bowl and refrigerate for 3 or 4 hours.

When the duck is nearly ready to cook, mix together the ingredients for the seasoning mixture in a pan, bring to a boil and simmer for about 30 minutes. Combine the ingredients for the coating mixture.

Put a hook on the top rack in the oven for suspending the duck and a pan on the bottom rack to catch the drippings. Preheat oven to 400°.

Hang the duck over a bowl and pour the coating mixture over it. Repeat the coating about six times.

Suspend the duck in the oven. Bring the seasoning mixture to a boil and pour it into the duck through the neck opening. Roast for 20 minutes, or until the skin turns golden-brown. Lower the heat to 250° and roast for about 50 minutes, or until done.

Remove the duck and pour the juice from the body cavity into a pot. Correct the salt seasoning and add MSG. Cut the duck into serving pieces (see illustrated instructions on p. 9) and arrange the pieces on a warm platter. Pour 1 cup of the sauce over the duck and serve the rest in a bowl. Serves 4.

ALMOND DUCK CANTON STYLE

1 4-pound duck
Seasoning mixture
  1-1/2 tablespoons rice wine
  1-1/2 tablespoons thin soy
    sauce
  1-1/2 tablespoons sugar
3 slices fresh ginger
3 green onions
Coating mixture
  1/2 cup water chestnut
    flour
  1/2 cup crushed blanched
    almonds
  1/2 teaspoon five-flavored
    spice

Sauce mixture
  1-1/2 cups duck juice (from
    steaming)
  2 tablespoons rice wine
  2 tablespoons thin soy
    sauce
  1 teaspoon sugar
  1 teaspoon MSG
1/2 head lettuce, sliced
1 tablespoon chopped green
  onion
2 tablespoons water mixed
  with 1 tablespoon corn-
  starch
Vegetable oil for deep-frying

Wash and dry the duck. Cut in half down the side of the spine and between the breast. Place in a large bowl for steaming. Combine the ingredients for the seasoning mixture. Add ginger slices and green onions and sprinkle the seasoning mixture over the duck. Steam vigorously for 30 to 40 minutes or until tender (legs should be easy to move). Cool. Reserve the juices.

With sharp kitchen shears and a knife, bone the duck by making incisions and pulling out the bones. If the meat falls apart, pat gently into shape again.

Combine the ingredients for the coating mixture and roll duck halves in it until well coated. Place on a platter, cover with plastic wrap and refrigerate overnight.

The next day, reheat the reserved duck juice and measure out 1-1/2 cups (add extra stock if needed to make up the amount). Combine the ingredients for the sauce mixture, place over medium heat and thicken with the cornstarch mixture. Keep the sauce heated, but do not let it burn.

Heat about 3 inches oil in a wok over high heat to about 350°. Add one half of the duck and deep-fry until crisp and golden. Turn and fry the other side, taking care not to scorch the skin. Remove and drain. Repeat the process with the other half of the duck.

Position duck halves skin side up and, with a sharp cleaver, cut into about 6 pieces. Arrange the pieces on a bed of lettuce (see Figure 4 on p. 9). Pour the hot sauce mixture over the duck and garnish with green onion.

Serves 4.

BRAISED DUCK WITH
CHESTNUTS AND CHINESE DATES

1 5-pound duck
Seasoning mixture
    4-1/2 tablespoons thin soy
      sauce
    1/2 teaspoon salt
    3 tablespoons rice wine
    2 large pieces dried tanger-
      ine peel
    3 large lumps rock sugar
      or about 2 tablespoons
      granulated
    1-1/2 teaspoons five-
      flavored spice
    2 to 3 drops sesame oil

3 slices peeled fresh ginger
    the size of a quarter
1 cup canned whole
    chestnuts in syrup
4 ounces dried Chinese dates,
    pitted
1/4 cup blanched almonds
1 teaspoon vegetable oil
2 tablespoons water mixed
    with 1 tablespoon corn-
    starch
3 tablespoons canned water-
    chestnuts, minced

Wash the duck and place in a large, heavy pot. Add enough water to just cover the duck. Combine the seasoning mixture and add it to the water in the pot. Bring the water to a boil, then reduce heat and gently boil, turning the duck from time to time, for 1-3/4 to 2 hours, or until tender (a fork should easily pierce the thickest part of the thigh and juices should run clear). The skin should be glossy and the liquid reduced to a thick, dark sauce. Turn off heat.

Meanwhile, simmer the chestnuts in syrup until the liquid is reduced by half. Mash and put them in a bowl. Wash the Chinese dates and boil in water to cover until tender and liquid is reduced. Mash them lightly and place in a separate bowl. Lightly pan-fry the almonds in oil.

Carefully drain the duck and cool on a carving board. Remove all fat on top of the sauce. Strain the sauce. If it measures less than 2 cups, add enough water to make up the difference. Heat the sauce and thicken with the cornstarch mixture.

Cut the duck into serving pieces (see illustrated instructions on p. 9) and arrange on a heated platter. Sprinkle the minced water chestnuts over the duck and place the mashed chestnuts and Chinese dates at each end of the platter. Spoon the sauce over the dish.

Serves 4.

PORK, BEAN CURD
AND PEANUTS WITH OYSTER SAUCE

1/2 pound pork tenderloin
2-1/2 cups bean curd cut into
1-inch cubes
8 fresh mushrooms cut into
1/4-inch slices
2 garlic cloves, peeled and
crushed
2 green onions—white part
only, sliced lengthwise and
cut into 1-inch sections
Seasoning mixture
2 teaspoons thin soy sauce
1-1/2 teaspoons sugar
2 teaspoons rice wine
1/4 teaspoon white pepper

Thickening mixture
1/4 cup water
1 tablespoon cornstarch
1/2 teaspoon MSG
1 teaspoon heavy soy sauce
2 teaspoons oyster sauce
1 cup Chinese stock
(p. 30) or chicken stock
2 tablespoons lightly crushed
peanuts
3 tablespoons fresh vegetable
oil
1/2 teaspoon salt

Cut the pork into slices 2 inches by 1/4 by 1/4 inch. Combine the ingredients for the seasoning mixture and stir together the ingredients for the thickening mixture.

Put 1 1/2 tablespoons oil in a wok over high heat. Add salt and garlic. After a few seconds remove and discard the garlic. Immediately add bean curd and gently stir-fry until browned, remove and set aside. Reserve the oil and clean the wok.

Combine the reserved oil with 1 1/2 tablespoons oil and put in a wok over high heat. Add the pork and stir-fry until it turns white. Add the seasoning mixture, mushrooms and the browned bean curd. Add stock, cover and simmer for 2 minutes. Remove the cover, add the thickening mixture and stir until the sauce thickens. Transfer to a heated platter and garnish with green onion and crushed peanuts.

Serves 3.

PORK AND FERMENTED BEAN CURD SAUCE

1 pound pork tenderloin
Seasoning mixture
  2 teaspoons thin soy sauce
  2 tablespoons rice wine
  1 tablespoon sugar
  1/2 teaspoon MSG
2 tablespoons vegetable oil
1/4 teaspoon salt
2 large garlic cloves, peeled
  and crushed

2 cups onion cut into
  1/2-inch slices
4 pieces fermented bean curd
1 teaspoon fermented bean
  curd juice (from the bottle)
1 cup Chinese stock (p. 30)
  or chicken stock
2 tablespoons water mixed
  with 1 tablespoon corn-
  starch

Slice the pork against the grain into slices about 1 1/2 inches by 1/4 by 1/4 inch. Combine the ingredients for the seasoning mixture.

Put oil and salt in a wok over medium heat. Add garlic and stir-fry until golden, then discard it.

Add pork and stir-fry for 1 minute. Add the onion and stir-fry for 1 to 2 minutes, or until just transparent. Add the seasoning mixture and the fermented bean curd with the juice and stir-fry a few times until well mixed.

Add stock, cover, lower the heat and gently simmer for 1 minute more. Thicken with the cornstarch mixture and transfer to a heated platter.

Serves 3.

BLACK BEAN SPARERIBS WITH GREEN PEPPER

2 pounds back spareribs
2 medium-sized green peppers
Seasoning mixture
  2-1/2 tablespoons black
    beans
  2 garlic cloves, minced
  2 teaspoons thin soy sauce
  1 tablespoon rice wine
  1-1/2 tablespoons water
  1/4 teaspoon sesame oil

Thickening mixture
  1 tablespoon cornstarch
  1/2 cup water
  2 teaspoons heavy soy sauce
  1 teaspoon sugar
  1 teaspoon MSG
2 tablespoons vegetable
  oil
3/4 teaspoon salt
1/2 cup Chinese stock (p. 30)
  or chicken stock
3 tablespoons minced green
  onion

Cut the spareribs into pieces about 2 inches in length and 1 rib in width. Wash and pat dry. Halve the green peppers lengthwise, remove the seeds and membrane and cut into 2-by-1-inch strips. Combine the ingredients for the seasoning mixture and stir together the ingredients for the thickening mixture.

Arrange the spareribs on a heatproof plate in a steamer and steam for 10 minutes. Remove and dry well.

Put oil in a wok over high heat and add salt. Stir several times and add the spareribs. Stir-fry for 1 minute, add green peppers and stir-fry for 1 minute more. Add the seasoning mixture and stir-fry for 2 minutes. Add stock, cover and braise for 2 minutes. Uncover, add the thickening mixture and stir until the sauce thickens. Transfer to a heated platter and garnish with green onion.

Serves 4.

ROAST SUCKLING PIG BANQUET

2 dozen pancakes (see recipe
    under Peking Duck Home
    Style, p. 64)
1 10-pound suckling pig
Inside coating
    1 tablespoon salt
    3/4 teaspoon cinnamon
    1/4 cup rice wine
    1/4 cup minced fresh ginger
    1/4 cup sweet bean paste
    1/4 cup sugar
    2 tablespoons sesame paste
    1/4 cup thin soy sauce
    3/4 teaspoon five-flavored
      spice

Outside coating
    1/2 cup malt sugar
    1/4 cup Chinese red vinegar
    1 cup water
2 cups slivered green onions
    (cut in half lengthwise and
    slice diagonally into
    1/2-inch sections)
2 cups Hoisin sauce
Parsley for garnish
3 tablespoons vegetable oil
1 teaspoon salt
4 cups sliced broccoli spears
1 cup Chinese stock (p. 30)
    or chicken stock
Skewered Sugar-Glazed Crab
    Apples (p. 71)

Make the pancakes ahead of time and refrigerate, wrapped well in aluminum foil.

Wash and dry the pig thoroughly. It should have an opening on the underside along the entire length of the body. Insert a long, sturdy metal rotisserie skewer lengthwise into the meaty portion of the body from the buttocks through the mouth. Insert 6 metal shish kabob skewers (about 12 inches long) at different points to keep the underside open (Figure 1). (The object is to flatten out the body so that there are only two sides to roast.) Place the pig over the sink and pour boiling water over the back three or four times to shrink the skin. Dry well.

Meanwhile, prepare an outdoor grill, using wood charcoal.

Mix together the ingredients for both the inside coating and the outside coating. Coat the pig liberally both inside and out and let it air-dry on a board (Figure 2) until the fire in the grill becomes hot but not red-hot. Place the pig about a foot above the fire, first drying one side and then the other, turning the skewer until the pig becomes red. If, during the drying, little bubbles form on the skin side, pierce them lightly with a fine needle. (If there are deep holes, oil will ooze out and prevent the skin from crisping properly. To plug up any holes, break off the sharp ends of wooden toothpicks and insert them.)

When the pig is dried, transfer it to a board, skin side up, and cool for

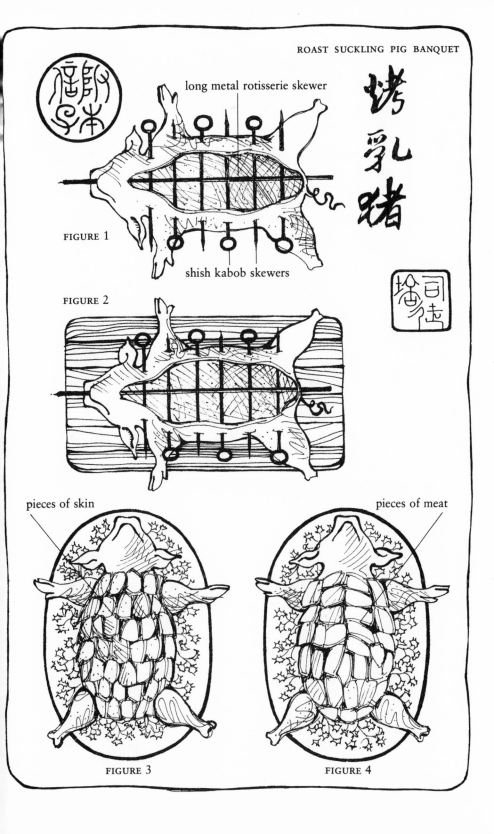

long metal rotisserie skewer

FIGURE 1

shish kabob skewers

FIGURE 2

pieces of skin

pieces of meat

FIGURE 3

FIGURE 4

about 20 minutes. Put it, skin side down, about 8 inches from the fire, making sure the fire is hot but not too intense. Manipulate the skewer for about 7 minutes, or until all the skin is cooked evenly. Remove to a board and carefully remove any toothpick plugs.

Make sure the fire is still hot and put the pig skin side down, about 6 inches above it for about 15 minutes. Manipulate for even crisping of the skin and use a pastry brush to remove oil and scorched bits of skin. (The pores must be kept open so that steam can escape freely.) The skin's color should change from red to golden and the oil that flows out should be clear. Do not allow the skin to become extensively scorched.

Return the pig to the fire (it should not be too hot). Put the pig, underside down, about 12 inches above the fire and roast until the flesh is white and firm when sliced open. (There may be a slight pink tinge due to the juices of the coating mixtures.) Varying conditions, such as the quality of the pig and the temperature of the coals, will determine the cooking time—individual judgment is necessary. When done, the skin will have pulled away from the flesh here and there and will be a crisp golden-brown; the flesh should be white and firm.

Remove the pancakes from the refrigerator and place them in a steamer for 10 to 12 minutes.

Put the green onion in two small serving bowls and the Hoisin sauce also in two bowls.

First course
Transfer the pig, skin side up, to a board. With a sharp knife, cut and lift off the skin. Slice it into pieces about 1 inch by 2 inches. The original recipe calls for reassembling the pieces of skin on top of the pig (Figure 3). Place the pig on a heated platter and garnish with parsley. Serve with pancakes, green onion and Hoisin sauce. Each diner takes a pancake and opens it up, adds a piece or two of skin, more Hoisin sauce and green onion and rolls it up.

Second course
Return the pig to the kitchen and slice into halves lengthwise. Slice each half into bite-sized pieces and reassemble into the original shape (Figure 4). Serve with the same accompaniments as for the first course.

Third course
Return the pig to the kitchen. Heat oil in a wok over high heat and add salt and broccoli. Stir-fry for 1/2 minute, add stock and cover the wok. When the broccoli is half cooked, add the leftover pork, and stir a few times. Transfer to a heated platter and serve.

Fourth course
Skewered sugar-glazed crab apples are excellent served with tea as a finale to this banquet. They should be made in the morning and refrigerated and skewered just before serving. (Small, firm Anjou or Bosc pears may be pre-

pared in the same manner, with the omission of cinnamon and red food coloring. Add whatever flavoring you like. A good addition is 2 tablespoons butter or rum.

SWEET AND SOUR PORK

2/3 pound pork tenderloin
Marinade
  1/2 teaspoon salt
  4 teaspoons rice wine
  2 tablespoons cornstarch
  2 egg yolks
Sweet-sour sauce
  2/3 cup white vinegar
  2/3 cup sugar
  1/2 teaspoon salt
  2 tablespoons catsup
  2 teaspoons thick soy sauce

1/4 cup vegetable oil
2 garlic cloves, minced
6 green onions cut in 1/2-inch sections
1 cup canned bamboo shoots cut into slices 2 inches by 1/2 inch
2 large green peppers cut into slices 2 inches by 1/2 inch
4 tablespoons water mixed with 2 tablespoons cornstarch

Cut the pork against the grain into slices 2 inches by 1/4 by 1/4 inch. Mix together the ingredients for the marinade and marinate the pork.

Put the ingredients for the sweet-sour sauce in a small pan over low heat and stir until the sugar dissolves. Mix well.

Put oil in a wok over high heat. Add pork and stir-fry until well browned. Remove and set aside. Add garlic, green onion, bamboo shoots and green pepper to the wok and stir-fry for 1/2 minute, then add the sweet-sour sauce. Add the pork and thicken with the cornstarch mixture. Stir a few times and transfer to a heated platter.

Serves 4–6.

BARBECUED PORK CANTONESE STYLE

This delicious dish requires some preliminary work in terms of equipment, but once you have fashioned the requisite hooks,* they can be used over and over again.

2 pounds lean pork tenderloin
Marinade
6 tablespoons thin soy
   sauce
2 tablespoons sugar
2 tablespoons rice wine
2 tablespoons oyster sauce
3 large slices fresh ginger
2 whole green onions,
   chopped

1 tablespoon five-flavored
   spice
1 to 2 drops red food color-
   ing
Dips
   Dry mustard moistened
      with white vinegar or
      white wine
   Thin soy sauce
   Plum sauce

Wash and dry the pork. Cut lengthwise (with the grain) into strips 6 by 2 inches.

Combine the ingredients for the marinade and marinate the pork, covered tightly with aluminum foil, for 3 to 4 hours or overnight in the refrigerator. Turn it occasionally.

Preheat the oven to 450°. Remove the pork from the marinade and drain. Impale each strip, about 1/2 inch from one end, on a barbecue hook, attaching the other hook to an oven rack (Figure 2). When all pieces are hooked, carefully slide the rack into the highest rung of the oven. Insert another rack on the lowest rung and place on it a large cookie sheet or roasting pan to catch the drippings.

Roast for 10 minutes at 450°, then reduce heat to 350° (or less, around 325°, if the pork darkens too fast) and roast for 20 to 30 minutes.

When the pork is done, the outside will be glazed a reddish brown and the inside will be white. Slice the meat thinly across the grain and arrange on a bed of lettuce. Serve with the dips.

Serves 4–5.

* With a pair of pliers, straighten four wire coat hangers. (Alternatively, you can use plain wire.) With a pair of wire clippers, cut them into 6-inch lengths. Using pliers, bend a 1-inch hook at each end, the two hooks bent in opposite directions (see Figure 1).

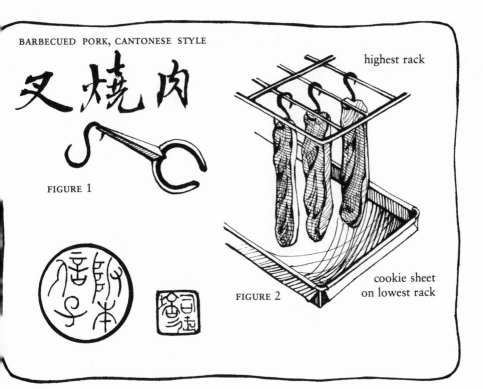

BARBECUED PORK, CANTONESE STYLE

FIGURE 1

highest rack

FIGURE 2

cookie sheet
on lowest rack

STEAMED MINCED PORK
WITH PRESERVED HOT VEGETABLE
(CHA TS'AI)

1 pound boneless pork butt
  with some fat
1/4 cup preserved turnip cut
  into 1-inch-long shreds

Seasoning mixture
1 teaspoon thin soy sauce
1/2 teaspoon MSG
1/2 teaspoon sesame oil

Cut the pork into strips, then mince with a cleaver or put through a meat grinder or food processor. Place in a shallow heatproof bowl (do not press down). Sprinkle the turnip shreds on top of the meat. Combine the ingredients for the seasoning mixture and spoon over the meat.

Place the bowl with the pork in a steamer and steam vigorously for 20 to 25 minutes, or until the pork is no longer pink.

Serves 4–5.

BRAISED PORK,
CHESTNUTS AND ALMONDS

1/4 cup blanched almonds
Vegetable oil for pan-frying
Seasoning mixture
    2-1/2 tablespoons thin soy
      sauce
    1 tablespoon rice wine
    1/2 teaspoon grated fresh
      ginger
    1/2 tablespoon sugar
    Pinch of MSG
    1/2 teaspoon five-flavored
      spice
2 tablespoons vegetable oil

1 pound pork tenderloin, cut
  into 3/4-inch cubes
1 cup stock
1 cup onion, cut into 1/2-inch
  slices
1/4 cup sliced canned water
  chestnuts
1-1/2 cups canned chestnuts
  in syrup
1 tablespoon water mixed
  with 1/2 tablespoon cornstarch

Pan-fry almonds in a little oil until golden, then drain on paper towels.
Combine the ingredients for the seasoning mixture.

Put oil in a wok over high heat. When very hot, add pork and stir-fry
until browned. Add the seasoning mixture and stock, lower the heat and
simmer gently for 1 to 2 minutes. Turn up the heat, add onion, water
chestnuts and chestnuts and stir-fry until the onion turns slightly translucent. Add the cornstarch mixture to thicken. Transfer to a heated platter
and garnish with almonds.

Serves 3–4.

SWEET AND SOUR SPARERIBS
CANTONESE STYLE

In the United States, this dish is usually modified in various ways to please the American palate. The following is the true Cantonese version.

1-1/2 pounds back spareribs
Marinade
   1 tablespoon thin soy sauce
   2 tablespoons rice wine
Batter
   1 large egg
   1/4 cup water
   1/2 cup cornstarch
Sauce
   3/4 cup white vinegar
   1/2 cup sugar
   1/4 teaspoon salt
   1 tablespoon catsup
   1 teaspoon thin soy sauce
Vegetable oil for deep-frying
   plus 2 tablespoons

1 large garlic clove, peeled and
   gently mashed
1 large green pepper, cut
   into strips 2-1/2 inches by
   1 inch
3 tablespoons slivered green
   onion (cut in half lengthwise and slice diagonally
   into 1/2-inch sections)
1/4 teaspoon freshly ground
   black pepper
2 tablespoons water mixed
   with 1 tablespoon
   cornstarch

Have the butcher cut the spareribs into pieces about 2 by 1-1/2 inches. Wash and dry with paper towels. Put the ribs in the marinade, mix and let stand for 15 minutes.

Combine the ingredients for the batter, mixing vigorously until smooth. Mix together the ingredients for the sauce.

Heat about 3 inches oil in a wok or deep-fryer over medium heat. Remove the ribs from the marinade and put them in the batter, coating them well. When the oil almost begins to smoke, add the ribs, fry for 1 minute and remove. (Do not crowd the ribs—fry in batches if necessary.) Fry the ribs a second time over high heat (the temperature should be about 360°) for about 1 minute, or until brown and crisp. Scoop them out, drain and arrange on a heated platter.

Pour out all but 2 tablespoons oil from the wok. Put the wok over medium heat and add garlic, green pepper, green onion and black pepper. Stir-fry for about 1 minute, remove the garlic and add the sauce. Bring to a boil, thicken with the cornstarch mixture and pour over the ribs.

Serves 4.

BEEF CURRY

1-1/2 pounds beef sirloin
3 cups peeled potatoes cut
 into 1/2-inch cubes
1 cup vegetable oil
2 garlic cloves, peeled and
 minced
3 cups onion cut into
 1-1/2-inch wedges

2 teaspoons thin soy sauce
1/2 teaspoon five-flavored
 spice
1 teaspoon curry powder
1 teaspoon rice wine
3 cups Chinese stock (p. 30)
2-1/2 teaspoons sugar

Cut beef into 1/2-inch cubes. Soak potato cubes in cold water for about 15 minutes and then dry them thoroughly.

Put oil in a wok over high heat. When it almost begins to smoke, add potato cubes and fry until golden on all sides. Remove and set aside. Pour out all but 3 tablespoons oil and stir-fry garlic and onion for 1 minute, then add soy sauce, five-flavored spice, curry powder, wine and beef. Stir-fry until the beef is browned.

Add potato cubes and 2-1/2 cups stock. Cover, lower the heat and simmer for 1 hour. If the sauce becomes too reduced, add more stock.

Add sugar and 1/2 cup stock and simmer for 1 hour more.
Serves 3.

OYSTER SAUCE BEEF

3/4 pound beef tenderloin
Seasoning mixture
 4 tablespoons oyster sauce
 1/4 teaspoon thin soy sauce
 3/4 teaspoon sugar
 1 teaspoon rice wine
 1/2 teaspoon sesame oil
 1/3 cup Chinese stock
  (p. 30)
 1/2 teaspoon MSG
1-1/2 tablespoons water
 mixed with 2 teaspoons
 cornstarch
1/2 teaspoon heavy soy sauce

Marinade
 1/4 teaspoon baking soda
 1 teaspoon rice wine
 1 teaspoon thin soy sauce
 1 teaspoon water mixed
  with 1/2 teaspoon corn-
  starch
 2 teaspoons cold water
2 tablespoons vegetable oil
1 garlic clove, peeled and
 crushed
3 tablespoons green onion cut
 into 1-inch sections

Slice the beef against the grain into 1-by-2-by-1/4-inch strips. Combine the ingredients for the seasoning mixture, and blend the cornstarch mixture with the heavy soy sauce.

Mix together the ingredients for the marinade and mix the beef in it (the meat should soak up all the liquid). Let stand 10 to 15 minutes.

Put a wok over high heat. When very hot, add oil and garlic and stir for a few seconds. Add beef and stir-fry for 1 minute to sear. Discard garlic and set the beef aside.

Put the seasoning mixture into the wok. Stir a few times and allow it to come to a boil. Thicken with the cornstarch-soy mixture.

Return the beef to the wok and stir. Transfer to a heated platter and garnish with green onion.

Serves 3.

STIR-FRIED BEEF TENDERLOIN WITH GREEN ONION

A quick dish that takes split-second timing to avoid overcooking the meat. Ingredients must be in readiness, in order of use, and the tender beef slices quickly stir-fried over a very hot fire just until the juices are sealed in.

1-1/2 pounds beef tenderloin	2 tablespoons vegetable oil
Seasoning mixture	1 large garlic clove, peeled
1/2 teaspoon sugar	and crushed
1 teaspoon sesame oil	2 teaspoons water mixed
1/4 teaspoon fresh ground	with 1 teaspoon cornstarch
black pepper	1-1/2 cups slivered green
1-1/2 tablespoons Chinese	onion (cut only the green
red vinegar	part in half lengthwise
1/2 teaspoon MSG	and slice diagonally into
3 tablespoons Chinese	1/2-inch sections)
stock (p. 30)	2/3 teaspoon salt

Slice meat against the grain into 2-by-1/8-by-1/8-inch strips. Combine the ingredients for the seasoning mixture.

Heat a wok over high heat, and when very hot, add oil and garlic. After a few seconds, remove and discard the garlic. Immediately put in the beef strips and stir-fry for about 1-1/2 minutes pressing them against the bottom and sides of the wok. (All surfaces of the beef should be seared.) Remove the beef and set aside to keep warm.

Add the seasoning mixture and let it come to a boil. Stir in the cornstarch mixture to thicken the sauce. Add the beef-strips, onion and salt and stir several times.

Serves 3.

BEEF AND PRESERVED MUSTARD GREENS

3/4 pound flank steak
Marinade
   1/4 teaspoon baking soda
   1 teaspoon thin soy sauce
   1/2 teaspoon cornstarch
   1 tablespoon water
2 cups preserved mustard greens
Seasoning mixture
   1-1/2 teaspoons rice wine
   1-1/2 teaspoons thin soy sauce
   1 teaspoon sugar

1/4 teaspoon ground black pepper
3 tablespoons vegetable oil
1/4 teaspoon salt
1-1/2 tablespoons water mixed with 2 teaspoons cornstarch
1-1/2 tablespoons slivered green onion (cut in half lengthwise and slice diagonally into 1/2-inch sections)
1/2 cup Chinese stock (p. 30)

Remove the membrane and cut the steak against the grain into thin slices about 1 1/2 inches by 1/2 by 1/8 inch. Combine the ingredients for the marinade and marinate the beef slices, mixing them, until all the liquid is absorbed. Rinse the mustard greens several times, dry well and slice. Stir together the ingredients for the seasoning mixture.

Add oil and salt to a wok over high heat. When very hot, add the meat slices and stir-fry for about 1 minute. The beef should be just browned. Remove the wok from heat and remove the beef, leaving as much oil in the wok as possible.

Reheat the wok until very hot and add mustard greens. Stir-fry for about 1/2 minute, then add stock and the seasoning mixture. When the liquid boils, add the beef and thicken with the cornstarch mixture. Transfer to a serving bowl and garnish with green onion.

Serves 4.

DEEP-FRIED STUFFED SHRIMP
WITH SWEET AND SOUR SAUCE

12 fresh jumbo shrimp
Batter
  1/2 cup cornstarch
  1/2 cup flour
  2 eggs
  1/2 cup water
Filling
  1/4 pound pork butt,
    minced
  3 tablespoons lightly
    crushed peanuts
  1 tablespoon minced green
    onions (white part only)
  2 tablespoons canned water
    chestnuts, minced
  2 teaspoons thin soy sauce
  1/8 teaspoon sugar
  Pinch of salt

Pinch of MSG
2 teaspoons rice wine
1-1/2 teaspoons cornstarch
Sauce
  1/2 cup white vinegar
  4 tablespoons thin soy
    sauce
  5 tablespoons sugar
  4 drops sesame oil
  1 large garlic clove, peeled
    and minced
  1-1/2 tablespoons water
    mixed with 1 tablespoon
    cornstarch
1 tablespoon sesame seeds
1/2 cup cornstarch
Vegetable oil for deep-frying
Pinch of cayenne

Clean and shell the shrimp according to the illustrated instructions (p. 9b) for preparing phoenix-tailed shrimp.

Stir together the ingredients for the batter and mix together the ingredients for the filling. Make the sauce by stirring together all its ingredients and heat it until it thickens. In a dry pan toast sesame seeds until golden (do not burn). Set aside.

Dust a board with cornstarch and lay the flattened shrimp on it. Place the filling (about 1/2 inch thick) along the entire inner length of each shrimp and press down gently. Sprinkle cornstarch on top.

Heat about 3 inches oil in a large, deep pot to about 350°. Stir the batter. Pick up each shrimp, holding both ends, with the filling side up, and dip it in the batter, coating well. Carefully slip the shrimp into the hot oil and deep-fry for about 3 minutes, pushing it down from time to time so the filling will cook. Fry in batches of four or so, adjusting the heat to maintain even temperature. When they turn golden, turn them over with a large slotted spoon, filling side down, and fry for 2 to 3 minutes. Remove and drain.

Arrange the shrimp on a preheated platter. Reheat the sauce, pour over the shrimp and sprinkle sesame seeds and cayenne over the shrimp.

Serves 3.

STIR-FRIED JUMBO SHRIMP
WITH VEGETABLES

A fresh-tasting dish traditionally made with Japanese chrysanthemum greens. However, watercress, which has a similar bite, makes a good substitute.

18 fresh jumbo shrimp
Coating mixture
  2 egg whites
  1/2 teaspoon salt
  2-1/2 tablespoons corn-
    starch
Vegetable oil for deep-frying
1-1/4 teaspoons salt
2 large garlic cloves, peeled
  and crushed
1/2 cup chopped green onion
1/4 teaspoon minced fresh
  ginger

1-1/2 pounds fresh Japanese
  chrysanthemum greens or 2
  bunches watercress cut into
  2-inch lengths
3/4 cup Chinese stock (p. 30)
1/4 teaspoon fresh ground
  black pepper
1 tablespoon water, mixed
  with 1/2 tablespoon cornstarch
4 drops sesame seed oil

Following the illustrated instructions on p. 9a, shell, clean and slice the shrimp. Mix together the ingredients for the coating mixture and put the shrimp in it for several minutes mixing them from time to time.

Heat about 1-1/2 inches oil in a wok over medium heat until hot but not smoking (about 340°). Add shrimp and fry, stirring to keep from sticking, for about 1 minute. Remove shrimp and carefully pour out all but 2 table-spoons oil.

Reheat the oil in the wok until it almost begins to smoke. Add salt, garlic and ginger and stir-fry until the garlic turns golden. Discard the garlic, add green onion and chrysanthemum greens or watercress, and stir-fry. Add stock, cover and cook for about 1 minute or until the vegetable is limp but still green. Be careful not to overcook. Return the shrimp to the wok and stir once or twice. Stir in the cornstarch mixture to thicken the sauce. Transfer to a heated platter and sprinkle with sesame oil and pepper.

Serves 3–4.

STIR-FRIED SHRIMP

16 jumbo fresh shrimp
Thickening mixture
  2 teaspoons water mixed
    with 1 teaspoon corn-
    starch
  2 tablespoons Chinese
    stock (p. 30)
  1/4 teaspoon MSG
Batter
  1 egg
  2 teaspoons water
  1/4 teaspoon MSG
  1/4 teaspoon salt
  2 tablespoons cornstarch

2 tablespoons water-
  chestnut flour
Vegetable oil for deep-frying
4 green onions, white part
  only, cut in half lengthwise
  and sliced diagonally into
  1/2-inch sections
1/3 cup canned water-
  chestnuts, sliced
1 teaspoon minced fresh
  ginger
2 tablespoons Chinese stock
  (p. 30)

Following the illustrated instructions on p. 9a, shell, clean and slice the shrimp.

Combine the ingredients for the thickening mixture.

To prepare the batter, beat the egg and water together, add MSG and salt, then mix in the cornstarch and water chestnut flour, stirring vigorously until smooth. Put the shrimp in a large bowl and pour the batter over them. Mix to coat the shrimp and refrigerate for at least 3 hours (this will make the batter less fluid).

Heat about 3 inches oil in a wok over medium heat to about 350°, or until it almost smokes. Add shrimp, stirring to prevent their sticking together. In about 1 minute (they should be crisp outside and almost but not completely cooked) scoop out and drain.

Remove all but 2 teaspoons oil from the wok. Reheat the oil until hot. Add green onion, water chestnuts and ginger and stir a few times. Add the stock, and when it comes to a boil, add the thickening mixture. Stir for about 1/2 minute until thickened. Add the shrimp, stir several times and transfer to a serving platter.

Serves 3–4.

DRAGON-BOAT SHRIMP
WITH PINEAPPLE
AND SWEET AND SOUR SAUCE

A very colorful and delicious dish celebrating the dragon-boat races held on the Pearl River in Kuangchou each year. When deep-fried, the giant shrimps—dipped in batter and rolled in chopped nuts—look like miniature dragons covered with scales. Placed between half-circles of green-dyed pineapple slices, they become "dragon boats" riding the crest of the wave.

1 large can sliced pineapple
Few drops of green food
  coloring
18 to 20 fresh jumbo shrimp
Marinade
  1/4 teaspoon salt
  1/4 teaspoon grated
    fresh ginger
  1/2 teaspoon thin soy sauce
  1 tablespoon rice wine
  1/8 teaspoon sesame oil
Batter
  1 large egg
  4 tablespoons water-
    chestnut flour
3/4 cup thinly sliced almonds

3/4 cup coarsely chopped
  cashews
Vegetable oil for deep-frying plus
  1 tablespoon
1 large garlic clove, peeled
  and crushed lightly
Pinch of salt
3/4 cup white vinegar
3/4 cup sugar
1/4 cup water
1 teaspoon thin soy sauce
2 teaspoons catsup
1 teaspoon sesame oil
2 tablespoons water mixed
  with 1 tablespoon corn-
  starch
6 water chestnuts, minced

Drain the pineapple and transfer the juice to a large bowl. Add 2 or 3 drops of green food coloring and stir well. Add pineapple slices and refrigerate overnight.

With fingernails or kitchen shears, lightly snip the shell of each shrimp at the point where it joins the tail. Carefully remove the shell, leaving the tail intact, and devein. Rinse and pat dry with paper towels.

Combine the ingredients for the marinade and marinate the shrimp. Make the batter by thoroughly mixing the egg with the water chestnut flour. Put the almonds and cashews on separate plates. Drain the pineapple slices, halve them and arrange, rounded side up (to resemble waves), on a large platter.

Heat 1 tablespoon oil in a pan over medium heat until it almost begins to smoke. Add the garlic, stir-fry until golden and discard. Add salt, vinegar, sugar and water and stir until the sugar is dissolved. Add the soy sauce, catsup and sesame oil. When the mixture comes to a boil, stir and thicken with the cornstarch mixture. Set aside.

Stir up the batter. Holding each shrimp by the tail, dip it in the batter, coating the body only. Coat with cashews and then with the almonds.

Heat about 3 inches oil in a wok or deep, heavy pot to about 350°. Fry the shrimp, three or four at a time, for about 3 minutes, or until golden-brown. Keep the temperature within the range of 340° to 350°. Drain the shrimp and arrange between the semicircles of pineapple.

Reheat the sauce and pour over the shrimp. Garnish with water chestnuts.

Serves 4–5.

OYSTER SAUCE ABALONE

1 large can abalone
Seasoning mixture
  2 tablespoons oyster sauce
  2 teaspoons rice wine
  1/2 teaspoon grated fresh
    ginger
  1 teaspoon sugar
  Pinch of MSG
  Few drops of sesame oil
3 tablespoons vegetable oil

1 garlic clove, crushed
3 cups *pai ts'ai* hearts cut
  diagonally into 2-by-1-inch
  pieces
8 water chestnuts, sliced
1/2 cup abalone juice
1 tablespoon water mixed
  with 1/2 tablespoon cornstarch

Drain the abalone and reserve the juice. Cut the abalone into slices 2 inches by 1 by 1/4 inch.

Combine the ingredients for the seasoning mixture. Stir the abalone juice into the cornstarch mixture.

Heat oil in a wok until hot but not smoking. Add garlic and stir-fry until golden. Discard the garlic. Add the *pai ts'ai* hearts and water chestnuts and stir-fry for 1 minute. Add abalone and stir-fry for about 1/2 minute. Add the seasoning mixture and stir a few times. Add the abalone juice mixed with cornstarch and stir. When the sauce thickens, remove from heat.

Serves 3–4.

SHRIMP WITH LOBSTER SAUCE

A dish which typifies Cantonese ingenuity in sauce making and in the combination of ingredients used. There is no lobster in this dish but the sauce is similar to that used in lobster Cantonese.

1 pound fresh jumbo shrimp
1-1/2 tablespoons fermented
   salted black beans
1/4 pound boneless pork
Marinade
   1/2 teaspoon fresh ginger
    (peeled and grated)
   1/4 teaspoon sugar
   1/2 teaspoon light soy sauce
   1/2 teaspoon rice wine
Seasoning mixture
   1 teaspoon sugar
   1/4 teaspoon Chinese
    molasses
   2 teaspoons oyster sauce
   1/2 teaspoon ground black
    pepper

1 teaspoon rice wine
1/2 teaspoon MSG
1/2 teaspoon sesame oil
2/3 cup Chinese stock
   (p. 30)
2 tablespoons water mixed
   with 1 tablespoon cornstarch
3 large eggs
4 tablespoons vegetable oil
2 large garlic cloves, minced
1/4 teaspoon salt
2 tablespoons minced canned
   water chestnuts
2 tablespoons green onion cut
   into 1-inch sections

Shell, clean and halve the shrimp (see illustrated instructions on p. 9a). Wash and pat dry with paper towels. Rinse the black beans, drain and mash.

Mince the pork with a cleaver or put through a meat grinder or food processor and place in a bowl. Mix together the ingredients for the marinade and marinate the pork.

Stir together the ingredients for the seasoning mixture. Break the eggs into a bowl.

Heat 2 tablespoons oil in a wok over high heat. When hot, add garlic, black beans and salt and stir-fry for about 1/2 minute, or until the mixture becomes aromatic.

Add the pork and stir-fry for about 2 minutes, or until browned. Remove the pork and set aside. Heat 2 tablespoons oil in the wok. Add shrimp and stir-fry, alternately pressing them against the sides of the wok, for about 1 minute, or until they turn white. Remove and set aside.

Return the pork to the wok. Quickly add stock, and when it comes to a boil, stir in the seasoning mixture. Add water chestnuts and the cornstarch mixture and stir to thicken the sauce. Make a large depression in the center of the wok by pushing aside the solid ingredients, then quickly beat the eggs and pour them into it. Allow them to set a bit, then gently stir until they become thick and creamy. Mix them into the surrounding sauce.

Remove the wok from heat. Add the shrimp, mix and transfer to a heated platter. Garnish with green onions.

Serves 4–5.

LOBSTER CANTONESE

2 salted and preserved duck
  eggs
Marinade
  1/2 teaspoon grated fresh
    ginger
  1/4 teaspoon sugar
  1/2 teaspoon light soy
    sauce
  1/2 teaspoon rice wine
  1/4 pound pork butt, minced
Seasoning mixture
  1-1/4 teaspoons sugar
  1/4 teaspoon Chinese
    molasses
  2-1/2 teaspoons oyster
    sauce
  1/4 teaspoon ground black
    pepper
  1-1/2 teaspoons rice wine

1/2 teaspoon MSG
1/2 teaspoon sesame oil
3 large eggs
1 1-1/2- to 2-pound live lobster
4 tablespoons vegetable oil
1/4 teaspoon salt
2 large garlic cloves, minced
1-1/2 tablespoons salted black
  beans, soaked and washed
1 cup rich Chinese stock
  (p. 30)
2-1/2 tablespoons water
  mixed with 1-1/2 table-
  spoons cornstarch
3 tablespoons minced water
  chestnuts
2 tablespoons chopped green
  onions

Wash the duck eggs and gently boil for 12 to 15 minutes. Shell them under cold running water and slice lengthwise into halves. Mix together the ingredients for the marinade and marinate the pork. Stir together the ingredients for the seasoning mixture. Crack the eggs into a bowl.

Leaving the pegs in the claws, rinse the lobster thoroughly under running water. With a sharp cleaver, cut off the tail. Cut off the claws, then cut in two, leaving the pincers whole. Cut the underside of the body lengthwise in half, then across into four pieces. Cut the underside of the tail lengthwise in half, then across into six pieces. Remove pegs.

Heat 2 tablespoons oil in a wok over medium heat. Add salt, garlic and black beans and stir-fry for about 1/2 minute, or until the mixture becomes aromatic. Add the pork and stir-fry for about 2 minutes, or until well browned. Add 2 more tablespoons oil and turn up the heat. Add the lobster pieces and stir-fry for about 2 minutes. Add stock and the seasoning mixture, cover and simmer for about 3 minutes. Thicken the sauce with the cornstarch mixture. Make a depression in the center by pushing the solid ingredients to the sides, then beat the eggs and pour into it. Let the eggs set, then gently scramble to form large, soft curds. Turn off the heat and quickly mix the curds into the sauce.

Transfer to a heated platter and garnish with water chestnuts, green onion and half a duck egg on each corner.

Serves 4.

STIR-FRIED LOBSTER TAILS

3 large fresh or frozen rock
  lobster tails
Seasoning mixture
  1 cup tomato catsup
  1-1/2 cups Chinese stock
    (p. 30)
  2 teaspoons sweet rice wine
  1/2 teaspoon salt
  2 teaspoons sugar
  1-1/2 teaspoons white
    vinegar
  1/4 teaspoon MSG
5 tablespoons vegetable oil
1/8 teaspoon salt

1 garlic clove, peeled and
  crushed
2 slices fresh ginger
1-1/2 cups green peppers cut
  into 1-by-3-inch strips)
1/4 cup preserved turnip cut
  into pieces 1-1/2 inches by
  1/2 by 1/4 inch
5 tablespoons water mixed
  with 2 1/2 tablespoons
  cornstarch
3 green onions, (cut into
  1-inch sections)

Cut lobster tails in half lengthwise and then across into three sections. Combine the ingredients for the seasoning mixture.

Put a wok over high heat. When very hot, add 3 tablespoons oil. Add garlic, ginger, and the lobster pieces and stir-fry. Occasionally press them with a spatula against the bottom of the wok, until the meat turns white and the shells red. Remove and arrange them, shell side up, on a heated serving platter and keep warm.

Leave 1 tablespoon oil in the wok and pour the rest over the lobster pieces to coat each shell.

Add 2 tablespoons oil to the wok. Add salt and stir. When the oil becomes hot, add green pepper and turnip. Stir-fry for about 1/2 minute and add the seasoning mixture. Let the sauce heat up, stirring once or twice, then thicken with the cornstarch mixture. Pour the sauce over the lobster and garnish with green onion.

Serves 4.

QUICK STIR-FRIED FISH WITH VEGETABLES

4 to 5 large, choice dried black mushrooms

Coating mixture
  2 tablespoons cornstarch
  2 tablespoons water chestnut flour

Seasoning mixture
  3/4 teaspoon MSG
  3/4 teaspoon rice wine
  1/2 teaspoon sesame oil
  1/4 teaspoon ground black pepper

1 pound fish fillet (cod, haddock or flounder)

Vegetable oil for deep-frying plus 3 tablespoons for stir-frying

3 cups *pai ts'ai* hearts* sliced diagonally into 2-by-1-inch slices

4 tablespoons chopped green onion (white part only)

1 teaspoon fresh minced ginger

1 large garlic clove, minced

1/2 teaspoon salt

1/2 teaspoon sugar

1 cup Chinese stock (p. 30)

2 tablespoons water mixed with 1 tablespoon cornstarch

Soak mushrooms in warm water for 30 minutes, dry, remove the stems and quarter the caps. Mix together the cornstarch and the water chestnut flour for the coating mixture and stir together the ingredients for the seasoning mixture.

Wash, dry, and slice fish fillets into 2-by-1-inch pieces and roll in the coating mixture.

Heat about 2-1/2 inches oil in a wok or deep-fryer to about 350°. Deep-fry the fish slices for about 1/2 minute on each side. Remove and drain.

* 3 cups celery cabbage, 4 cups fresh bean sprouts or 3 cups broccoli (parboiled 1 minute) can be substituted.

Remove the oil, put the wok over high heat and add 3 tablespoons oil. When it is about to smoke, add mushrooms, *pai ts'ai,* green onion, ginger and garlic. Stir-fry for 1 to 2 minutes.

Add salt, sugar and stock. Stir a few times, add the fish and seasoning mixture, stirring gently so as not to break the fish. Add the cornstarch mixture and stir to thicken. Quickly transfer to a heated platter.

Serves 4.

SWEET AND SOUR CRISP-SKINNED FISH

This is a Cantonese version of the sweet-sour fish served in Peking.

1 1-1/4-pound whole fresh-water fish, such as pike or whitefish
4 to 5 large dried black mushrooms
3/4 teaspoon salt
1-1/2 tablespoons sugar
1/2 tablespoon water
Seasoning mixture
   1 tablespoon thin soy sauce
   1/2 cup Chinese stock (p. 30)
   1-1/2 tablespoons rice wine
   1/2 cup sugar
   1/2 cup white vinegar
1/2 cup water mixed with 1/3 cup cornstarch

1/2 cup flour
Vegetable oil for deep-frying plus 2 tablespoons for stir-frying
1 large garlic clove, crushed
1/4 teaspoon fresh minced ginger
3/4 cup canned bamboo shoots cut in 2-by-1/2-inch pieces
1 red sweet pepper, cut into 2-by-1/2-inch slices
1 green sweet pepper, cut into 2-by-1/2-inch slices
2 tablespoons chopped green onion

At the fish market, have the fish cleaned and scaled, split lengthwise into halves but with the back connected and the head and tail left on. At home, slash the flesh on the inner side if it is over 1 inch thick. Wash, pat dry with paper towels and place on a platter. Sprinkle 1/4 teaspoon salt over the fish.

Soak mushrooms in warm water for 30 minutes, squeeze dry, remove the stems and quarter the caps.

To caramelize sugar, lightly oil a small pan, add sugar and heat until it begins to liquefy. Remove quickly to avoid burning. Cool a bit, carefully add 1/2 tablespoon water and stir to dissolve.

Combine the ingredients for the seasoning mixture and add the caramelized sugar. Stir up the cornstarch mixture and reserve 2 tablespoons (for thickening the sauce). Pour the rest of the mixture over the fish, coating all surfaces, then coat well with flour.

Heat 3 inches oil to about 350° in a deep-fryer over high heat. Lower the fish, head first, into the pan. Deep-fry until golden-brown, turn, and fry the other side (total frying time will be about 8 minutes). Turn off the heat. Remove the fish and drain on paper towels.

Put 2 tablespoons oil in a wok over high heat. When it is about to smoke, add the garlic, stir-fry until golden and discard. Add 1/2 teaspoon salt, ginger, bamboo shoots, mushrooms and peppers and stir-fry for about 1 minute.

Add the seasoning mixture and let it come to a boil. Thicken with the reserved cornstarch mixture and pour over the fish. Garnish with green onion.

Serves 4.

CLEAR STEAMED FISH

1 1- to 1-1/4-pound fresh
   whole fish (whitefish or
   pike is excellent)
4 dried mushrooms
2 green onions
Seasoning mixture I
   1 tablespoon thin soy sauce
   1/4 teaspoon ground black
      pepper
   1 teaspoon vegetable oil
   1/2 teaspoon cornstarch

Seasoning mixture II
   2 teaspoons thin soy sauce
   Pinch of MSG
   1 teaspoon rice wine
   1 teaspoon minced fresh
      ginger
1/4 teaspoon salt
1/2 teaspoon MSG
1/2 teaspoon sesame oil
1/2 cup pork butt cut into
   shreds 1-1/2 inches by 1/8
   by 1/8 inch
2 tablespoons vegetable oil

Have the fish dealer scale and eviscerate the fish, leaving on the head and tail. Wash and dry. Soak the mushrooms in warm water for 15 minutes, squeeze dry, remove the stems and slice the caps thinly. Slice green onions crosswise into 1-inch sections. Mix together the ingredients for seasoning mixture I and do the same for seasoning mixture II.

Sprinkle salt, MSG and sesame oil on the inside of the fish. Put half of the green onion on a steaming plate and put the fish on top. Arrange the pork and mushrooms on top of the fish and pour seasoning mixture I over them. Put in the steamer (with the water boiling vigorously) for 15 to 18 minutes. Remove the plate and set aside.

Put oil in a wok over high heat. When it smokes, add seasoning mixture II, stir several times and then pour it over the fish. Garnish with the rest of the green onion.

Serves 4.

BROWN BEAN STEAMED FISH

1 pound fresh fish fillets
(pike, whitefish, cod)
Seasoning mixture
   1-1/2 tablespoons brown
     bean paste, mashed well
   1 teaspoon minced
     ginger
   2 teaspoons minced green
     onion

1/2 teaspoon MSG
1/4 teaspoon vegetable oil
1 tablespoon green onion cut
   into 1/2-inch sections
2 tablespoons chopped
   Chinese parsley leaves
2 tablespoons vegetable oil
1/2 teaspoon sesame oil
1 large garlic clove, chopped

Wash fish well and dry. Combine the ingredients for the seasoning mixture and mix well.

Put the fish fillets on a lightly oiled steaming plate and rub the seasoning mixture all over the top of the fish, using up all the mixture. Put the plate in a steamer (with water boiling vigorously) and steam for about 8 minutes, or until the fish is just done. Transfer to a serving dish, discarding any juice on the platter. Sprinkle with green onion and parsley.

Put vegetable oil and sesame oil in a pan over medium heat. When the oil just begins to smoke, add garlic. After a few seconds, pour the oil over the fish and serve.

Serves 3–4.

STEAMED FISH WITH HAM, BAMBOO SHOOTS AND MUSHROOMS

1-1/4-pound whole freshwater
    fish, such as pike or bass
3 dried mushrooms
Seasoning mixture
    2 tablespoons rice wine
    1/2 teaspoon salt
    2-1/2 tablespoons thin soy
      sauce
    1/4 teaspoon white pepper
6 slices (1-1/2 inches by 3/4
    by 1/4 inch) ham

6 slices (1-1/2 inches by 3/4
    by 1/4 inch) canned
    bamboo shoots
2 green onions, cut into
    1-inch sections
6 1/4-inch slices fresh ginger
Salt to taste
1/2 teaspoon sesame oil
1/4 teaspoon MSG

At the fish market, have the fish scaled and eviscerated, leaving the head and tail on. Soak mushrooms in warm water for 15 minutes, squeeze dry, remove the stems and halve the caps. Combine the ingredients for the seasoning mixture.

Wash the fish and dry with paper towels. Enlarge the belly opening so that the fish can be spread open flat, skin side up. Without cutting all the way through, make three deep slashes (perpendicular to the spine) on each side of the spine. Place the fish, skin side up, on a platter for steaming. Insert one mushroom slice, one ham slice and one bamboo-shoot slice in each of the six cuts in the fish's back. Arrange onion and ginger between the cuts and pour the seasoning mixture over the fish.

Place the fish in the steamer (with the water boiling vigorously) and steam for 15 to 18 minutes. Remove the platter from the steamer. Pour off the juice from the platter into a small pan, correct the salt seasoning, add sesame oil and MSG. Heat the sauce and pour it over the fish.

Serves 4–5.

STEAMED FISHBALLS

2/3 pound fresh fish fillet
(flounder, haddock, cod)
Dip I
2 teaspoons salt
1 teaspoon ground black
pepper
Dip II
3 tablespoons black vinegar
1/2 teaspoon sugar
1 teaspoon thin soy sauce
1 teaspoon shredded fresh
ginger
1/4 teaspoon sesame oil

1 large egg white, lightly
beaten
2 teaspoons Chinese red vinegar
1 teaspoon salt
1/4 teaspoon MSG
Pinch of ground black pepper
1/8 teaspoon grated fresh
ginger
Cold water as needed
1-1/2 tablespoons cornstarch
1 tablespoon minced Chinese
parsley

Remove the skin and any bones from the fish fillets and wash and dry them. Cut in strips, then mince with a cleaver or put through a meat grinder or food processor. Place in a bowl.

Prepare the dips by mixing the ingredients.

Add to the fish the egg white, vinegar, salt, MSG, black pepper and ginger. Stir well and mix in a little water and cornstarch. The mixture should be soft and just hold together. Form into balls about 1 1/2 inches in diameter.

Oil a pie plate. Place the fishballs on it about 1/2 inch apart and steam vigorously for 10 minutes. Cool a bit, sprinkle with parsley and serve with the dips.

Serves 4.

FRIED STUFFED LOBSTER

3 fresh or frozen large rock
  lobster tails
3 tablespoons cornstarch
3 tablespoons water chestnut
  flour
Stuffing mixture
  3 dried black mushrooms
  (soak for 10 minutes,
  squeeze dry, remove the
  stems and chop the caps)
  1/2 cup minced ham
  1 tablespoon minced
  Chinese parsley
  1 tablespoon minced green
  onion
  3 tablespoons minced
  shrimp
  1/2 teaspoon MSG
  1 tablespoon rice wine

1/2 teaspoon salt
1/4 teaspoon white pepper
1 tablespoon water mixed
  with 1 tablespoon corn-
  starch
Seasoning mixture
  5 tablespoons rice wine
  1 tablespoon sugar
  2 tablespoons white vinegar
  8 tablespoons catsup
  1/2 cup Chinese stock
  (p. 30)
1 egg, beaten with 1 tablespoon water
1/3 cup vegetable oil
Watercress, washed and
  trimmed

Wash and dry the lobster tails. With kitchen shears, cut through both sides of the membrane on the underside and remove it completely. Keeping the shell intact, make a deep cut lengthwise down the center of the underside and then crosswise in three places.

Mix the cornstarch and water chestnut flour together. Combine the ingredients for the stuffing mixture and stir together the ingredients for the seasoning mixture.

Place the lobster tails, shell side down, on a board. Put the stuffing between the cuts and press some firmly on the surface, using up all the stuffing. Brush the egg over the stuffing and then sprinkle with the flour mixture.

Heat oil in a wok over medium heat. When it is almost smoking, add the lobster tails, shell side down. Cover and cook for 4 minutes. Add the seasoning mixture, cover and cook for another 4 minutes. Transfer to a heated serving platter, pour the sauce over them and garnish with watercress.

Serves 3.

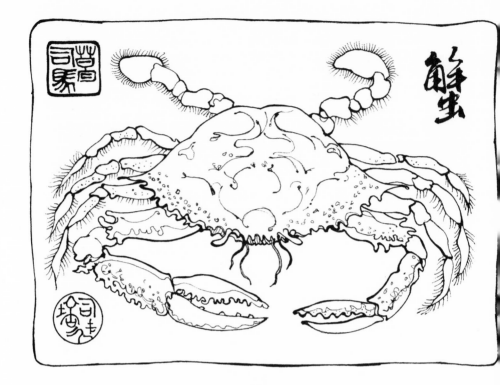

CRAB CURRY

A fresh hot curry powder should be used for this dish. The green pepper should be crisp and the sauce have a hint of sweetness.

2 cups crabmeat, canned or
   frozen
4 tablespoons vegetable oil
1/2 teaspoon salt
2 garlic cloves, minced
2 cups green pepper cut in
   1-1/2-by-1/2-by-1/2-inch
   pieces

2-1/2 cups tomato juice
2 teaspoons sugar
2 teaspoons rice wine
1 teaspoon curry powder
5 tablespoons water mixed with
   2 tablespoons cornstarch
3 tablespoons green onion cut
   into 1-1/2-inch sections

Pick over the crab, discarding any cartilage, and drain well.

Put oil in a wok over high heat. When hot, add 1/4 teaspoon salt and the garlic. Stir a few seconds, then add the crabmeat. Stir-fry for 1 minute, add green pepper and stir-fry for another minute. Add tomato juice, sugar, salt, rice wine and curry powder. Stir, cover and cook for about 5 minutes. Uncover and thicken the sauce with the cornstarch mixture. Garnish with green onion.

Serves 2–3.

CRAB CAKES

1/2 pound frozen crabmeat or fresh or canned shrimp
1/2 cup minced fresh fat pork
1 teaspoon minced green onion, white part only
1/3 cup minced canned water chestnuts
1/4 teaspoon grated fresh ginger
1 egg white from a large egg
2 tablespoons Chinese red vinegar
1 tablespoon sugar
1-1/4 teaspoons salt

1/2 teaspoon MSG
2 teaspoons rice wine
1-1/2 to 2 tablespoons corn-starch
Dip
    4 tablespoons Chinese red vinegar
    1 teaspoon shredded fresh ginger
    1/2 teaspoon sugar
    1/4 teaspoon sesame oil
    Pinch of salt
Vegetable oil for deep-frying
1/2 head lettuce, sliced

Squeeze out all liquid from the crabmeat.

Put the pork, green onion, water chestnut and ginger in a bowl. Add egg white, vinegar, sugar, salt, MSG and wine and sprinkle cornstarch on top. Mix well and form into patties about 2-1/2 inches in diameter and 1/3 inch thick. (Add up to 1/2 tablespoon cornstarch if the mixture does not hold together well.)

Heat about 2 inches oil in a wok or deep, heavy fry pan to about 350°, or until it just begins to smoke. Carefully add the patties, in batches of four or five, and deep-fry for 1 to 2 minutes on each side. Test one for doneness. Drain on paper towels. Arrange on a bed of lettuce, and serve with the dip.

Serves 3.

CRAB, BROCCOLI AND FRESH MUSHROOMS

1 large bunch fresh broccoli
1/2 pound fresh mushrooms
1 cup frozen crabmeat
Mixture I
   1/2 cup rich Chinese stock
     (p. 30)
   1 teaspoon rice wine
   1/4 teaspoon salt
Mixture II
   1/2 cup rich Chinese stock
   2 teaspoons rice wine
   1/2 teaspoon salt
   1/4 teaspoon MSG

Mixture III
   1/2 cup rich Chinese stock
   2 teaspoons rice wine
   1/2 teaspoon salt
   1/4 teaspoon MSG
6 tablespoons vegetable oil
2 tablespoons water mixed
   with 1 tablespoon cornstarch
1 egg white
1/2 teaspoon sesame oil
1/4 teaspoon white pepper

Trim and wash the broccoli. Cut into spears about 2 1/2 inches by 1/2 inch and parboil for about 1 minute. Rinse and drain. Trim and wash the mushrooms. Slice into 1/8-inch sections and parboil for 1/2 minute, rinse and drain. Squeeze the juice out of the crabmeat. Combine the ingredients for each of the three mixtures.

Heat 2 tablespoons oil in a wok over high heat. Add broccoli and mushrooms and stir-fry for 1/2 minute, add mixture I and cook for 1 minute. Transfer the vegetables to a bowl, draining off excess liquid.

Wash and dry the wok and heat 2 tablespoons oil over high heat. When it almost begins to smoke, add the vegetables again, stir twice and add mixture II. When the liquid comes to a boil, thicken with 1 tablespoon of the cornstarch mixture. Transfer to a heated serving platter.

Wash and dry the wok again and put it over high heat. Add 2 tablespoons oil and then the crabmeat. Stir-fry for 1 minute and add mixture III. When the liquid begins to boil, thicken with the remaining 1 tablespoon of the cornstarch mixture. Add the egg white and when it begins to turn white, stir gently once or twice.

Pour the crab mixture over the vegetables on the serving plate and sprinkle with sesame oil and white pepper.

Serves 4.

STRING BEANS
AND FERMENTED BEAN CURD

1-1/2 pounds fresh string
  beans
Seasoning mixture
  1 teaspoon thin soy sauce
  1/2 teaspoon MSG
  2 teaspoons sugar
  1/2 teaspoon grated fresh
    ginger
  3 cakes fermented bean
    curd

2 teaspoons rice wine
3/4 cup Chinese stock
  (p. 30)
1-1/2 tablespoons corn-
  starch
3 tablespoons vegetable oil
1 large garlic clove, peeled and
  lightly crushed
1/3 teaspoon salt

String the beans, cut off the ends, then cut in half diagonally. Put in boiling water for about 2 minutes, drain in a colander, and immediately run cold water over them to retain color and crispness. Combine the ingredients for the seasoning mixture.

Put oil in a wok over high heat. When it is about to smoke, add garlic and salt and stir-fry, stirring twice. Add beans and stir-fry for 1 minute. Add the seasoning mixture to the string beans and stir-fry for about 1 minute.

Serves 6.

OYSTER SAUCE BAMBOO SHOOTS

1 pound canned whole
  bamboo shoots
Seasoning mixture
  2 teaspoons rice wine
  1 cup Chinese stock (p. 30)
  1/4 teaspoon MSG
  3/4 teaspoon sugar
  1/2 teaspoon salt
  1/8 teaspoon freshly
    ground black pepper

Thickening mixture
  1-1/2 tablespoons water
  2 teaspoons water chestnut
    flour
Vegetable oil for deep-frying
3 tablespoons oyster sauce
1/4 teaspoon sesame oil

Wash bamboo shoots and slice into pieces about 1 by 1/4 inch. Combine the ingredients for the seasoning mixture and blend the water chestnut flour with water to make the thickening mixture.

Put about 2 inches oil in a wok over high heat. Add the bamboo shoots for about 1/2 minute and scoop them out.

Carefully pour out all but 2 tablespoons oil in the wok and put the wok over high heat. Add bamboo shoots and then the oyster sauce. Stir several times and add the seasoning mixture. Let it come to a boil, then add the thickening mixture and stir until the sauce thickens. Add sesame oil, stir and transfer to a heated platter.

Serves 4.

STIR-FRIED CHOICE VEGETABLES

1/2 cup (packed) dried
  bamboo shoots
1/2 cup canned spring
  bamboo shoots
5 dried black mushrooms
Seasoning mixture
  1/2 cup rich Chinese stock
    (p. 30)
  1 teaspoon thin soy sauce

1/2 teaspoon sesame oil
1/2 teaspoon salt
1/4 teaspoon MSG
3 tablespoons vegetable oil
3/4 cup *pai ts'ai* hearts* cut
  into 1-1/2-inch slices
1 tablespoon water mixed
  with 1-1/2 teaspoons cornstarch

Soak dried bamboo shoots in cool water for 30 minutes, trim and cut into slivers. Soak mushrooms in warm water for 15 minutes, drain, squeeze dry, remove the stems and slice thinly. Cut spring bamboo shoots lengthwise into 1/4-inch slices. Stir together the ingredients for the seasoning mixture.

Put oil in a wok over high heat. When it is about to smoke, add the dried bamboo shoots and mushrooms and stir-fry for about 1 minute. Add the spring bamboo shoots and *pai ts'ai* and cook for another minute, then reduce the heat to medium. Add the seasoning mixture and simmer for about 3 minutes. The liquid should be reduced to about a third or half. Thicken with the cornstarch mixture and transfer to a serving platter.

Serves 3.

* Celery cabbage (white parts) may be substituted.

BRAISED BLACK MUSHROOMS IN OYSTER SAUCE

12 to 14 large, finest-quality dried black mushrooms
Seasoning mixture
  1-1/2 cups rich Chinese stock (p. 30) or chicken stock
  1/2 teaspoon sugar
  5 tablespoons oyster sauce
  1/2 teaspoon MSG
  1-1/2 teaspoons Hoisin sauce or catsup
  3 tablespoons cornstarch
  1/4 teaspoon sesame oil

2 cups rich Chinese stock or chicken stock
3 tablespoons vegetable oil
1/2 teaspoon salt
1 large garlic clove, peeled and crushed
1/4 cup minced canned water chestnuts
1 tablespoon slivered green onion (cut in half lengthwise and slice diagonally into 1/2-inch sections)

Soak mushrooms in warm water for 1 hour, drain well and remove the stems, using kitchen shears to snip them off as close to the caps as possible. Combine the ingredients for the seasoning mixture.

Bring stock to a boil, then turn off the heat.

Put oil and salt in a wok over medium heat. Add the garlic, stir-fry until golden and discard. Turn up the heat, and when hot, add mushrooms and stir-fry for 2 minutes.

Add stock, lower the heat and simmer until the liquid is almost gone. (Stir from time to time to prevent burning.)

Add the seasoning mixture and stir until the sauce is thickened. Transfer to a heated platter and garnish with water chestnut and green onion.

Serves 4.

The
SOUTHWEST

T he Southwestern style of cooking is characteristically spicy, fiery and generous in the use of oil. The cooking methods are generally the same as those used by other styles of Chinese cooking, but one notices more braising, deep-frying and often several cooking methods employed in creating a dish.

The regional preference for hot seasonings, especially in the provinces of Szech'uan and Hunan, may well be due to a proximity to Burma, India and Pakistan, where the primary seasonings are curry, chili peppers, garlic, highly seasoned condiments and salted foods. All of these are commonly used in Southwestern Chinese cooking, except for curry, which is rarely used because its distinctive flavor overshadows other ingredients. On the other hand, chili peppers, properly used, will not only produce a hot taste but will help bring out the individual flavors of the ingredients. Herein lie the subtleties of Chinese cooking. Seasonings are used to either blend or enhance the flavors of the main ingredients, never to mask or overpower them. Throughout Chinese cookery this approach is upheld, whether it be in the preparation of the court dishes of Peking or the robust dishes of the South.

Chili peppers in their many forms (whole, crushed, powdered, in oil, or in condiments) are used in over half of the Southwestern regional dishes. In contrast to the peppery dishes, the banquet dishes are often surprisingly bland. This is explained by the fact that as Northerners migrated to the Southwest to escape political oppression, they brought with them the subtle dishes of the northern provinces and from the court in Peking. These dishes were the ones most often served at banquets.

Szech'uan and Hunan, known as the rice bowls of China, have rarely experienced famine. They produce a wide range of quality grains, vegetables, meats and poultry. In these southern regions rice is eaten at every meal. They also have a plentiful supply of delicacies, such as cloud ears (tree fungus), which are as highly prized in China as the truffle in France, grass mushrooms, and Szech'uan pepper (fagara pepper, known in Chinese as flower pepper.) Fresh bamboo shoots are widely used in the Southwest; their crunchiness brings to a dish the textural interest that is one of the characteristics of Southwestern cooking. Bean curd is another popular ingredient in the region. And the crucial test of a chef is his ability to produce bean curd which is permeated with both a spicy and hot flavor, rather than simply a flavorful sauce.

SOUTHWEST RESTAURANTS

Southwestern cooking is represented by restaurants from three cities, Chungking and Ch'engtu in Szech'uan Province, and Peking. The Szech'uan Dining Hall and Omei Dining Hall (named after Mount Omei in Szech'uan) of Peking are famous for their Szech'uan dishes. The Ch'i Chen Ko (Pavilion of Rarities) offers Hunan dishes and is especially known for tung an chicken. The Ma Kai is highly regarded for its Hunan dishes.

The Min Tsu Lu (People's Road) Dining Hall, formerly called the Empress Restaurant, is the largest restaurant in Chungking. Dry-fried dishes are their specialty. The Hsing Lin Hsien (Arriving Star Pavilion), a Moslem restaurant, is located near the Confucius Temple and caters to temple visitors. Spicy cold beef is one of its specialties. The Yung Ts'un (Poppy Village) Dining Hall specializes in fast-cooked dishes that are simple and have a home-cooked flavor. The Yi Chih Shih (Leisure time) Dining Hall, formerly of Ch'engtu, specializes in serving banquets and is an elegant place to dine. Last but not least is Lu's Chao Shou Stand, which specializes in a meat-filled pastry called Chao Shou.

Ch'engtu is represented by a variety of eating places. The Hsing Hua Ts'un (Apricot Blossom Village) is located in a colorful market area for the buying and selling of horses, mules and accessory items for animals. The Ch'engtu Dining Hall, though only established in 1958, has become a favorite eating place. The T'ung Ching (Copper Well) Street Noodle Shop began some fifty years ago with handcarts selling noodles in the streets. Its specialty is hot and spicy flavored noodles. The Lai T'ang Yuan (Lai's Sweet Dumpling) Shop was founded by Lai Yuan Hsin, who started out as a street peddler of sweet dumplings in 1894. His shop still features the delicious dumplings so much relished in Ch'engtu. The Ch'ing Yang Kung (Gray Lamb Palace) originated pearl balls and is reputed to serve the best version of this delicacy. The Chih Te (Cultivation of Virtue) Snack Shop has for a hundred years specialized in a rice powder beef dish. The Ch'en

Ma P'o Bean Curd Shop is named after a bean curd dish originated in the 1860s by the wife of a chef named Ch'en. This shop is now operated by a direct descendent of the original Ch'ens. Other restaurants which have contributed dishes are the Yu Lung (Jade Dragon) Dining Hall, the Fu Yung (Poppy) Dining Hall, the Ching Ch'eng Yuan (Garden of Achievement), the Shih Shih (Mealtime) Dining Hall and the Kang Yo (Health and Happiness) Southern Style Restaurant.

WON TON SOUP SZECH'UAN STYLE

Filling
1/2 pound pork butt
6 slices fresh ginger cut 1/4 inch thick
1/2 cup water
1 teaspoon thin soy sauce
1/4 teaspoon ground black pepper
Pinch of cayenne
1/2 teaspoon salt
1 teaspoon sesame oil
2 tablespoons slivered green onion (cut in half lengthwise and slice diagonally into 1/2-inch sections)

Dip I (optional)
1/4 cup thin soy sauce
1/4 teaspoon Szech'uan bean paste
Few drops of sesame oil
Dip II (optional)
1/2 cup Hoisin sauce
1/2 teaspoon sesame paste or peanut butter
2 tablespoons minced green onion
3 dozen prepared won ton skins (p. 33)
10 cups Chinese stock (p. 30) or chicken stock

In a blender, meat grinder or food processor, mince pork until it is almost a paste. In a garlic press, crush ginger slices, one at a time, reserving the juice in 1/2 cup water. Place the pork paste in a well-chilled bowl. Add the soy sauce, black pepper, cayenne, salt and sesame oil and stir in one direction throughout the mixing. Stirring, gradually add the ginger water 1 tablespoon at a time. Refrigerate the filling until ready to use.

Fill the won ton skins by placing 1 teaspoon filling in the center of each skin. Fold in half at the center line (Figure 1). Using a little water to moisten the bottom corners (A and B), bring them together (Figure 2).

In a pot, bring the stock to a boil, lower the heat and let it barely simmer. In another pot, bring 10 cups water to a boil over high heat. Carefully add the won tons, about five at a time. When they float to the top, add 1/2 cup cold water. When the water comes to a boil again, the won tons are done. Remove with a slotted spoon to a large bowl or tureen.

Bring the stock to a rapid boil, add salt to taste and pour over the won tons. Garnish with the green onion and serve with the dips if desired.

Serves 6.

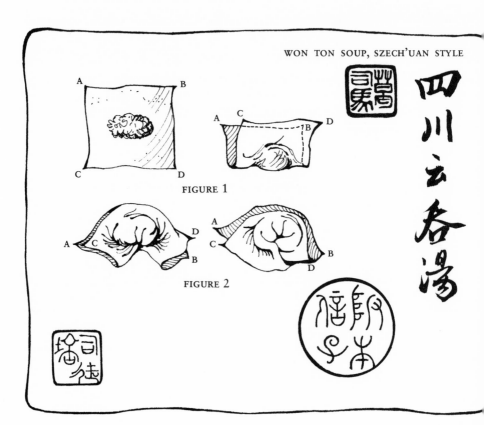

WON TON SOUP, SZECH'UAN STYLE

FIGURE 1

FIGURE 2

PICKLED VEGETABLE AND MEAT SOUP

1/2 cup preserved turnip
1/2 pound pork butt
Marinade
   2 teaspoons rice wine
   2 teaspoons cornstarch
   1/2 teaspoon (or to taste)
      hot pepper oil or 3/4 tea-
      spoon Szech'uan hot
      bean paste

6 cups Chinese stock (p. 30)
   or chicken stock
1/2 cup shredded canned
   bamboo shoots
Seasoning mixture
   1-1/2 teaspoons salt
   1 tablespoon rice wine
   1 teaspoon thin soy sauce
   Pinch of MSG

Wash the turnip, drain and cut into thin slices 2 inches by 1/4 inch. Cut the pork into shreds 2 inches long. Combine the ingredients for the marinade and place the pork in the mixture.

Put the stock in a pan and bring to a boil. Add the pork and bring to a boil again. Lower the heat to medium and add the bamboo shoots, turnip and seasoning mixture. As soon as the soup comes to a boil, remove from heat and transfer to a heated bowl or tureen.

Serves 5–6.

CLEAR PAI TS'AI SOUP

This is always a good soup to start off a Szech'uan dinner, which usually includes many rich and hot dishes. The *pai ts'ai* should be cooked so that they retain their green color and are tender but not soggy.

1 pound *pai ts'ai* hearts
Pinch of black pepper
1 teaspoon rice wine

3/4 teaspoon salt
6 cups Chinese stock (p. 30)
   or chicken stock

Trim each *pai ts'ai* heart so that it is about 5 inches long. Cut through each heart lengthwise and wash thoroughly.

Put 6 to 7 cups water in a large pot and bring to a boil. Add the *pai ts'ai* hearts and boil, uncovered, for about 2 minutes. Remove and rinse in cold

water until thoroughly cooled. Arrange the hearts in a steaming bowl and dust with pepper. Add 1/2 teaspoon wine, 1/4 teaspoon salt and 1/2 cup stock. Put the bowl in a steamer and steam for 4 minutes, then remove the bowl. Pour 3/4 cup stock over the hearts and place in a large soup tureen or bowl. Put the remaining stock in a pot. Add 1/2 teaspoon wine and 1/2 teaspoon salt, bring to a boil and pour it over the hearts.
Serves 4.

HOT AND SOUR SOUP
SZECH'UAN STYLE

Found in many areas of China, and most likely originating in Szech'uan Province, this is one of the most delicious yet easily prepared soups in the Chinese cook's repertory. Its tartness tends to be constant from kitchen to kitchen while the hotness may vary. The recipe given below will produce a mild version; if a more spicy result is desired, use Szech'uan hot bean paste in place of the white pepper.

3 dried mushrooms
Seasoning mixture
  Pinch of MSG
  3/4 teaspoon salt
  3/4 teaspoon thin soy sauce
  1 tablespoon rice wine
  1 tablespoon Chinese red
    vinegar
  1/2 teaspoon white pepper
    or 3/4 teaspoon Szech'uan
    hot bean paste
4 cups Chinese stock
  (p. 30) or chicken stock

3/4 cup chicken breast cut
  into shreds 2 inches long
2 tablespoons canned
  bamboo shoots cut into
  shreds 2 inches long
1 teaspoon water mixed
  with 1/2 teaspoon corn-
  starch
1/2 cup cubed bean curd
1 large egg, beaten

Soak the mushrooms in warm water for 15 minutes. Drain, dry well, remove the stems and quarter the caps. Combine the ingredients for the seasoning mixture.

Bring the stock to a boil in a large pot. Add the chicken and cook for about 1 minute over medium heat. Add the mushrooms and bamboo shoots. After 2 minutes, add the seasoning mixture and stir a bit. Add the cornstarch mixture and stir until the sauce is thickened. Add the bean curd and the egg. Stir several times and transfer the soup to a serving bowl.
Serves 3.

BRAISED BEAR'S PAW

A Chinese delicacy for over two thousand years, bear's paw is still available in southwest China and the best bear's-paw dishes are found there. Beef tongue is a good substitute.

1 3- to 3-1/2-pound fresh beef tongue
1 tablespoon small dried shrimp
30 green onions
Seasoning mixture
   1/4 cup thin soy sauce
   1/4 cup rice wine
   2 tablespoons sugar
   1/2 teaspoon MSG
2 fresh chili peppers
1/2 cup vegetable oil

2 large slices fresh ginger
10 to 12 cups Chinese stock (p. 30) or chicken stock
1/4 teaspoon salt
1 tablespoon minced fresh ginger
1/4 teaspoon white pepper
1/2 cup chicken cut into strips 1-1/2 inches by 1/4 inch
1/2 cup pork cut into strips 1-1/2 inches by 1/4 inch

Wash the tongue and pat dry with paper towels. Cut off the front third of the tongue and slash through the skin lengthwise (Figure 1). Slice the rest of the tongue into halves lengthwise (Figure 2).

Soak the dried shrimp in hot water for 5 to 10 minutes.

Cut off the white part of the green onions and slice the green part into 3-inch sections.

Combine the ingredients for the seasoning mixture.

Trim the chili peppers, slice lengthwise and remove all membrane and seeds.

Heat a wok over medium heat and add 1/4 cup oil. When it is about to smoke add ginger slices, the green part of the green onions and stir-fry for about 5 minutes. Add the tongue and just enough stock to cover—about 8 cups. Bring to a boil, reduce heat, cover and cook slowly for about 4 hours, or until tender. Turn occasionally so that the tongue cooks evenly and doesn't get burned. Add additional stock as needed.

When the tongue is done, transfer to a platter, and with a sharp knife, trim off the skin covering it. Strain the liquid into a bowl and add extra stock if needed to make 4 cups.

Clean the wok and reheat. Add the remaining 1/4 cup oil, the salt, chili peppers, minced ginger, white pepper, shrimp, chicken and pork and stir-fry for 1 to 2 minutes. Add the seasoning mixture and stir a few times. Add the tongue and the 4 cups stock and bring to a boil. Lower the heat a little to maintain a steady, gentle boil for about 1-1/2 hours, or until the

红 烧 熊 掌

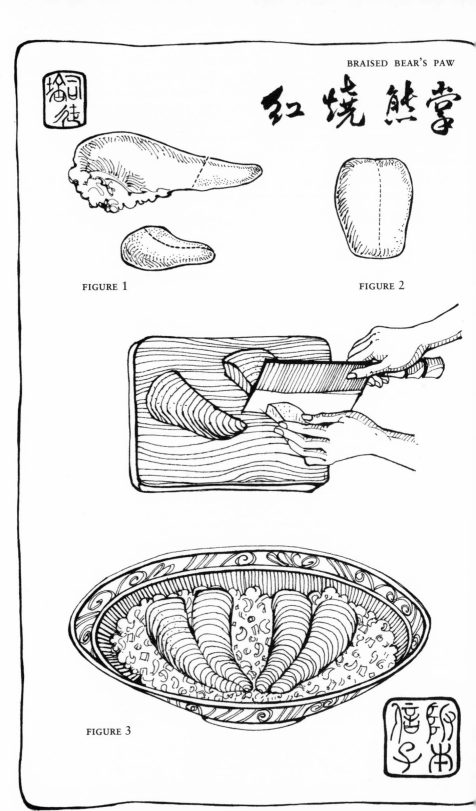

FIGURE 1

FIGURE 2

FIGURE 3

liquid is reduced to half. Add the white part of the green onions for the last 15 minutes of cooking.

Remove the tongue and cool. Trim off the gristle and slice the tongue against the grain into slices about 1/8 inch thick. Arrange the slices (Figure 3) on a platter and spoon the contents of the wok over them. Serves 4–5.

DRY-FRIED BEEF WITH CELERY

1 pound flank steak
2 cups thinly sliced celery, cut
diagonally
Seasoning mixture
  1 teaspoon grated fresh
  ginger
  1 teaspoon Szech'uan hot
  bean paste

2 teaspoons thin soy sauce
Pinch of MSG
3 tablespoons vegetable oil
1/2 teaspoon salt
1/2 teaspoon crushed flower
pepper
1/4 teaspoon sesame oil

Remove the membrane from both sides of the flank steak and slice the meat against the grain into shreds 2 inches long. Carefully pat the beef dry with paper towels. Remove any excess moisture from celery by blotting with paper towels. Combine the ingredients for the seasoning mixture.

Place a wok over high heat. When it becomes very hot, add oil. Add salt and then the beef. Stir-fry until the beef turns color, occasionally using a spatula to press the beef against the pan to aid cooking.

Add the seasoning mixture, and then the celery. Stir several times, just enough to heat the celery.

Transfer to a heated platter and sprinkle with flower pepper and sesame oil.
Serves 2–3.

DRY-FRIED BEEF SHREDS

This dish, garnished with crushed flower pepper, is a very spicy one.

1 pound flank steak
1 medium green pepper
Seasoning mixture I
  1 tablespoon black bean
    chili sauce
  1 tablespoon grated fresh
    ginger
  2 teaspoons rice wine
Seasoning mixture II
  2 teaspoons sweet rice wine
  1 teaspoon thin soy sauce

1/4 teaspoon MSG
1 tablespoon vegetable oil
1/8 teaspoon salt
2 tablespoons slivered green
  onion (cut in half lengthwise and slice diagonally
  into 1/2-inch sections)
1/2 teaspoon crushed flower
  pepper
Few drops of sesame oil

Remove the membrane from both sides of the flank steak and slice the beef against the grain into shreds 2 inches long. Pat the beef dry with paper towels. Slice the green pepper into 2-by-1/4-inch pieces and blot them dry with paper towels. Combine the ingredients for seasoning mixture I and do the same for mixture II.

Place a wok over high heat. When very hot, add oil. Add salt and beef and stir-fry until well browned. Add green pepper and stir-fry for about 1 minute. Add seasoning mixture I and stir several times, then add seasoning mixture II and stir-fry for about 1/2 minute.

Transfer to a heated platter, sprinkle with crushed flower pepper and sesame oil and garnish with green onions.

Serves 2.

LITTLE MEAT SANDWICHES WITH SAUCE

1/2 pound lean boned loin of pork
1/2 pound chicken breast
1/2 pound ham
Marinade
  1 large garlic clove, minced
  1 teaspoon grated fresh ginger
  2 green onions, minced
  1/4 cup rice wine
  2 tablespoons thin soy sauce
Sauce
  1/2 teaspoon Szech'uan hot bean paste
  2 teaspoons sweet bean sauce or Hoisin sauce
  2 tablespoons catsup
  2 tablespoons sugar

1/2 teaspoon salt
2 tablespoons white vinegar
1-1/2 cups Chinese stock (p. 30) or chicken stock
1 teaspoon thin soy sauce
2 egg whites
1/4 cup cornstarch
1-1/2 cups canned bamboo shoots cut into thin slices 2 by 1-1/2 inches by 1/8 inch
Vegetable oil for pan-frying
1/2 head lettuce, thinly sliced
2 tablespoons water mixed with 1 tablespoon cornstarch
2 tablespoons minced green onion

Cut the pork loin in half and immerse in a pot of boiling water. Turn the heat down and simmer for 5 to 10 minutes. Remove and cool. With a sharp knife, cut it into slices about 2 by 1-1/2 inches by 1/8 inch. Cut the chicken and ham into slices the same size as the pork. Mix together the ingredients for the marinade and marinate the chicken for 5 to 10 minutes. Remove and drain on paper towels.

Combine the ingredients for the sauce.

Mix the cornstarch and egg whites until smooth to make a binder for keeping together the various layers of the little sandwiches (each of these will be the size of the slices of meat and bamboo shoots). Arrange the pork slices side by side on a board and coat the top of each with the binder. Put a slice of bamboo shoot on top of each slice of pork and coat with the binder; then add a slice of ham, coating again with the binder, and finally top with a slice of chicken.

Heat enough oil in a large skillet to generously coat the bottom and sides. Place the sandwiches in the skillet with the pork side down. Reduce the heat to very low and fry gently for 2 to 3 minutes. There should be no noticeable shrinking or burning. When the pork turns golden, carefully turn each sandwich over to the chicken side. Add additional oil if needed and gently fry for 1 to 2 minutes.

Make a bed of lettuce on a serving platter and put the sandwiches on top.

Heat the sauce in a pan until it almost comes to a boil. Add the cornstarch mixture and stir until thickened. Pour over the sandwiches and lettuce and garnish with green onion.

Makes about 20 sandwiches.

FISH-FLAVORED PORK SHREDS

Despite its name, this dish contains no fish.

1 pound pork loin	1 tablespoon water
1/4 teaspoon salt	1 teaspoon rice wine
1 teaspoon cornstarch	3 tablespoons vegetable oil
Seasoning mixture	4 cups fresh bean sprouts, or
2 teaspoons water mixed	3 cups canned, drained
with 1 teaspoon corn-	1 large garlic clove, minced
starch	1/4 teaspoon grated fresh
3/4 teaspoon sugar	ginger
1-1/2 tablespoons thin soy	1/4 cup sliced water chestnuts
sauce	
1-1/2 tablespoons white	
vinegar	

Slice the pork into shreds about 2 inches long. Mix together the salt and cornstarch and dust the pork lightly. Combine the ingredients for the seasoning mixture.

Place a wok over high heat. When very hot, add oil. Add pork and stir-fry for about 2 minutes, or until it turns white. Add bean sprouts, garlic, ginger and water chestnuts. Stir-fry for about 1 minute. Add the seasoning mixture and stir-fry for 2 minutes more.

Serves 2–3.

SIZZLING RICE WITH PORK

6 dried mushrooms
1 pound pork loin with some
  fat
Marinade
  1 teaspoon cornstarch
  1 tablespoon rice wine
  1/2 teaspoon salt
  1 teaspoon water
Seasoning mixture
  1/2 teaspoon Szech'uan hot
    bean paste
  3/4 cup Chinese stock
    (p. 30) or chicken stock
  1-1/4 teaspoons sugar
  1 teaspoon Chinese red
    vinegar
  2-1/2 teaspoons thin soy
    sauce

Vegetable oil for deep-frying
  plus 2 tablespoons
1 teaspoon grated fresh
  ginger
1 large garlic clove, minced
1/2 cup canned sliced
  bamboo shoots, cut into
  pieces 1-1/2 inches by 1/4
  by 1/4 inch
4 cups rice crusts (p. 29) in
  1-by-2-inch chunks
1/4 cup slivered green onion
  (cut in half lengthwise and
  slice diagonally with
  1/2-inch sections)

Soak dried mushrooms in hot water for 15 minutes. Rinse, squeeze dry, remove the stems and shred the caps.

Slice the pork across the grain into strips 1-1/2 inches by 1/4 by 1/4 inch. Mix together the ingredients for the marinade and marinate the pork for 10 minutes. Combine the ingredients for the seasoning mixture.

Although the timing is tricky, the rice crust and the pork, which are pre-pared separately, must be cooked as simultaneously as possible so that both are ready for serving at the same time.

Heat about 3 inches oil in a deep, heavy pan or deep-fryer. While it is heating, place a wok over high heat, and when it becomes very hot, add oil. Add the pork strips and stir-fry for 2 minutes. Add ginger, garlic, bamboo shoots and mushrooms and stir-fry for about 1 minute. Add the seasoning mixture and stir-fry another minute. Transfer to a very hot bowl.

When the deep-frying oil is about 360°, add the chunks of rice crust. When they turn whitish and rise to the surface of the oil, scoop them out and place them in another very hot bowl. Pour 1 tablespoon deep-frying oil over them.

Quickly bring both bowls to the table and pour the pork portion over the rice crust. There should be a hissing sound and a sudden fragrance. Garnish with green onion.

Serves 4.

TWICE-COOKED PORK

This famous dish, consisting of highly seasoned pork, is known throughout China as characteristically Szech'uanese.

1-1/2 pounds pork loin, trimmed and boned	1/2 teaspoon sweet bean sauce or Hoisin sauce
Seasoning mixture	1 tablespoon dark soy sauce
1 large garlic clove, minced	3 tablespoons vegetable oil
3/4 teaspoon Szech'uan hot bean paste	1/2 head lettuce, thinly sliced

Put the pork in a large pot, cover with water and bring to a boil. Lower the heat and simmer for 20 minutes. Remove, cool and pat dry with paper towels. Slice into pieces 1-1/2 by 1-1/2 inches by 1/8 inch.

Combine the ingredients for the seasoning mixture.

Place a wok over high heat. When it becomes very hot, add oil. Add the pork and stir-fry for about 2 minutes, or until it is cooked. Add the seasoning mixture, stir-fry for 1/2 minute, cover and cook for 2 minutes over very low heat. Serve on a bed of lettuce.

Serves 3–4.

PEARL BALLS

Pearl balls are well-seasoned pork meatballs, rolled in glutinous rice and steamed. The glutinous rice kernels give them a glossy pearl-like appearance, thus the name.

1 cup glutinous rice	Seasoning mixture
1-1/2 cups minced pork	3/4 teaspoon salt
1/2 cup minced shrimp	2 tablespoons thin soy sauce
1/2 cup minced water chestnuts	1 tablespoon rice wine
1/4 cup minced green onion (white part only)	1 teaspoon sugar
	2 tablespoons cornstarch
	2 teaspoons crushed flower pepper

Soak rice in 2 cups water for 30 minutes. Carefully rinse and drain the rice without breaking the kernels. Let stand for 15 minutes.

Put pork, shrimp, water chestnuts and green onion in a large bowl. Combine the ingredients for the seasoning mixture and add to the pork-shrimp mixture. Mix well.

Layer the rice over a large cookie sheet. Form little balls 1 1/2 inches in diameter with the pork-shrimp mixture. Roll the balls over the rice kernels until each is well coated.

Spread wet cheesecloth over a steamer tray. Arrange the balls on a tray on top of the cheesecloth so that they don't touch each other. Place the tray in a steamer and steam for 1 hour. Remove and serve.

Makes about 24 balls.

PALACE PORK PIECES

1 pound boneless pork loin
Marinade
  1 tablespoon rice wine
  1/2 teaspoon salt
  2 teaspoons sugar
  1 tablespoon Chinese red
    vinegar
  1 tablespoon thin soy sauce
  3 tablespoons water mixed
    with 2 tablespoons corn-
    starch
  1/4 cup Chinese stock
    (p. 30) or chicken stock

  Pinch of MSG
Vegetable oil for deep-frying
  plus 3 tablespoons
1/2 teaspoon salt
6 dried chili peppers*
1 large garlic clove, minced
3 green onions, sliced lengthwise in half and cut into
  2-inch sections
10 kernels flower pepper,
  crushed
1 teaspoon grated fresh
  ginger

Wash the pork and pat dry with paper towels. Cut into 1-inch squares 1/3 inch thick.

Combine the ingredients for the marinade in a large bowl. Put the pork in the marinade and mix to coat it well. Let stand for a few minutes.

In a deep heavy pot or deep-fryer, heat 3 inches oil to 350°. Shake the excess marinade from the pork and carefully put it in the oil. Deep-fry for 2 minutes and immediately scoop out. Reserve the marinade for later use.

Place a wok over high heat. When it becomes very hot, add 3 tablespoons

---

* The degree of hotness of the dish will depend on how hot the dried chili peppers are. Reduce the amount specified and supplement it with sliced green peppers as desired.

oil and salt. Then add the chili peppers, stir-frying until they turn dark red and being careful not to burn them. Add the garlic, green onions, flower pepper, ginger, pork and the remaining marinade and stir-fry for about 10 seconds.

Transfer to a heated platter.

Serves 3.

HUNAN SPARERIBS

2 pounds spareribs, cut into pieces 1 rib wide and 2 inches long
2 tablespoons water mixed with 1-1/2 tablespoons cornstarch
Seasoning mixture
    1 teaspoon Chinese red vinegar
    1/2 teaspoon sugar
    1/4 teaspoon salt
    1 teaspoon rice wine
    3/4 cup Chinese stock (p. 30) or chicken stock

Vegetable oil for deep-frying
1 teaspoon salt
2 large garlic cloves, peeled and crushed
2 1/4-inch-thick large slices fresh ginger
1 teaspoon black bean chili sauce
2 large green or red sweet peppers, cut into slices 2 inches by 1 inch
4 green onions, cut into 2-inch sections

Wash the spareribs and dry them. Put them in a large bowl and coat them well with the cornstarch mixture, leaving them in the bowl for 15 minutes. Combine the ingredients for the seasoning mixture.

Heat 2 to 3 inches oil in a deep, heavy pot to about 350°, or until it begins to smoke. Deep-fry the ribs in batches, turning them as necessary to keep them from burning or sticking. As soon as they turn a deep golden color, remove and drain.

Heat 1 tablespoon fresh oil in a wok over medium heat. When the oil is about to smoke, add salt, garlic, ginger and black bean chili sauce and stir-fry for about 10 seconds. Discard the garlic and ginger. Turn up the heat, add peppers and green onions and stir-fry for about 15 seconds. Add ribs and stir-fry for another 15 seconds or so. Add the seasoning mixture, cover and simmer for about 3 minutes or until most of the liquid is gone. Transfer to a heated platter.

Serves 3.

SMOKED PORK WITH
BLACK BEAN CHILI SAUCE

It might be said that three regions come together in this dish. The smoked meat is typical of Hunan; the black bean is commonly used in Kwangtung; and chili sauce is often found in Szech'uan cooking.

1 pound smoked pork loin
chops*
Marinade
  1 tablespoon barbecue
  smoke sauce
  2 teaspoons sesame oil
  1/4 teaspoon Chinese red
  vinegar
  1/8 teaspoon MSG
4 tablespoons vegetable oil
1 large garlic clove, peeled
  and crushed
1/4 teaspoon kosher salt

1/2 to 1 teaspoon black bean
  chili sauce (use with discre-
  tion—this is very hot)
1 cup sliced (1/2 inch) onions
3 cups celery sliced diagonally into pieces about 2
  inches by 1/4 inch
1/2 cup stock (made with the
  pork bones)
2 tablespoons water mixed
  with 1 tablespoon corn-
  starch
1 teaspoon sesame oil

Bone the chops. Put the bones in a pot, add water to cover, bring to a boil, then simmer for 30 minutes. Skim off the scum and reserve the stock. Slice the pork into slices 2 inches by 1/4 by 1/4 inch. Combine the ingredients for the marinade and marinate the pork for about 20 minutes.

Heat oil in a wok over high heat. Add garlic and salt. Stir-fry until the garlic turns golden, then discard it. When the oil is about to smoke, add black bean sauce, stir once, add the pork and continue stir-frying for about 2 minutes. Add onion, then the celery, and stir-fry for about 2 minutes. Add the stock, and when it comes to a boil, add the cornstarch mixture and stir until the sauce is thickened. Remove from heat. Sprinkle with sesame oil, stir a few times and transfer to a heated platter.

Serves 3.

---

* Generally available at the packaged-meat counter in supermarkets.

SPICY PORK AND BEAN CURD
SZECH'UAN STYLE

6 dried mushrooms
Seasoning mixture
  1/2 teaspoon sesame oil
  1/2 teaspoon salt
  1 teaspoon grated fresh
    ginger
  1 large garlic clove, minced
  1-1/2 teaspoons sugar
  1 teaspoon Szech'uan hot
    bean paste
  3/4 teaspoon white vinegar
  1 teaspoon thin soy sauce
  2 teaspoons rice wine
  1/2 teaspoon MSG
3 tablespoons vegetable oil
1/2 teaspoon salt

3/4 cup pork butt cut into
  strips 1-1/2 inches by 1/4
  by 1/4 inch
2 cups bean curd cut into
  1/2-inch cubes
1/4 cup Chinese stock (p. 30)
  or chicken stock
2 tablespoons water mixed
  with 1-1/2 tablespoons
  cornstarch
1/4 cup lightly crushed peanuts
1/4 cup slivered green onions
  (cut in half lengthwise and
  slice diagonally into
  1/2-inch sections)

Soak the mushrooms in warm water for 15 minutes. Drain, remove the stems and quarter the caps. Combine the ingredients for the seasoning mixture.

Place a wok over high heat. When it becomes very hot, add oil, salt and pork. Stir-fry for about 1 minute. Add the bean curd and mushrooms and stir-fry another minute. Add stock, let it come to a boil, then add the seasoning mixture and stir-fry for about 1/2 minute. Add the cornstarch mixture and stir until the sauce thickens. Transfer to a heated platter and sprinkle with peanuts and green onion.

Serves 3.

PRECIOUS HAM

Seasoning mixture
2 teaspoons rice wine
2 teaspoons thin soy sauce
1/2 teaspoon sesame oil
1/2 teaspoon sugar
1/2 teaspoon salt
Pinch of white pepper
1/2 teaspoon Szech'uan hot
  bean paste
1 tablespoon stock
Vegetable oil for deep-frying
2 ounces (1/4 package) rice
  vermicelli

1/2 pound Yunnan or Smithfield ham,* cut into shreds
  2 inches long
2-1/2 to 3 cups snow peas
  sliced diagonally into 4
  pieces
2 green onions, sliced in half
  lengthwise and cut into
  2-inch sections
1/2 cup Chinese stock
  (p. 30)
1/2 teaspoon sesame oil

Combine the ingredients for the seasoning mixture.

Heat 1-1/2 inches oil in a wok until it begins to smoke. Add the vermi-celli, about a quarter at a time. It will puff up immediately. Quickly turn it to let the other side puff up also. Remove at once to prevent browning.

Wipe the wok clean of all oil. Add 3 tablespoons fresh oil and heat it until it almost smokes. Add ham and stir-fry for 1/2 minute. Add snow peas, green onion and the seasoning mixture. Stir a few times, add stock and cook until the liquid is almost gone.

Sprinkle with sesame oil, add the vermicelli and lightly toss twice. Transfer to a heated serving platter.

Serves 3.

---

* If using ordinary ham, increase the amount to 2/3 pound.

MUSHROOMS STUFFED WITH CHICKEN, PORK AND HAM

15 best-quality dried black mushrooms*
Sealing mixture
  1 egg white
  1 tablespoon cornstarch
Seasoning mixture
  2 tablespoons Chinese stock (p. 30) or chicken stock
  1-1/2 tablespoons cornstarch
  1 garlic clove, minced
  1 tablespoon Chinese red vinegar
  1 tablespoon thin soy sauce
  1/2 teaspoon sesame oil
  1/2 teaspoon salt
  1 tablespoon rice wine
  1/2 teaspoon sugar
Filling
  1/4 pound chicken breast, finely chopped

1 teaspoon cold water
2 egg whites
1/4 pound ham, finely chopped
1/4 pound boneless pork butt, minced
6 water chestnuts, finely chopped
2 tablespoons rice wine
1 teaspoon salt
1/2 teaspoon finely ground flower pepper
1/4 teaspoon white pepper
1/4 teaspoon ground black pepper
1/2 teaspoon thin soy sauce
1/2 teaspoon MSG
2 tablespoons cornstarch
1 cup Chinese stock (p. 30) or chicken stock
1/2 cup shredded lettuce

Soak mushrooms in hot water for 25 minutes. Rinse, squeeze dry and remove the stems.

Blend the egg white and the cornstarch for the sealing mixture. Combine the ingredients for the seasoning mixture.

To make the filling, first put the chicken in a large bowl, add 1 teaspoon cold water and egg whites and stir in one direction for about 3 minutes. Add ham and pork and stir. The mixture should be thick and sticky. Add the water chestnuts, wine, salt, flower pepper, white pepper, black pepper, soy sauce, MSG and cornstarch. Mix well.

Coat the underside of the mushroom caps with the sealing mixture. Put a layer of filling about 1/2 inch thick on each cap. With a spoon, press and mold the filling in place.

---

* Pick out thick, large mushrooms that are whole with no pieces broken off.

Place the stuffed mushrooms, filling side up, on a heatproof plate. Put the plate in a steamer and steam vigorously for 6 minutes. Remove the mushrooms and reserve the juice for later use. Put the mushrooms back on the plate with the filling side down. Add stock, cover the plate with foil and seal the edges tightly. Punch several small holes on top with a toothpick and steam for 7 minutes. Cool a bit and transfer the mushrooms to a heated platter, reserving the stock.

Pour the reserved juice and stock in a pan and bring to a boil. Add the seasoning mixture, add more salt if necessary and stir until the sauce thickens. Pour the sauce over the mushrooms and garnish with lettuce. Serve 4–5.

COLD MIXED BEEF

Served on a bed of sliced lettuce or watercress, this Moslem beef dish is particularly good in summer.

1-1/2 pounds sirloin or rump of beef	2 tablespoons sugar
Seasoning mixture	Juice from 2 large garlic cloves
1/4 cup Chinese red vinegar	Pinch of MSG
2 tablespoons sesame oil	1/2 teaspoon finely ground flower pepper
3-1/2 tablespoons thin soy sauce	1/2 head lettuce, thinly sliced, or 2 bunches watercress, trimmed*
1/2 teaspoon Szech'uan hot bean paste	

Cut the meat into two or three chunks so it will cook through more readily. Combine the ingredients for the seasoning mixture.

Put the meat in a pot with enough water to cover. Bring to a boil and then simmer for about 30 minutes, or until tender. Remove, drain and cool. With a very sharp knife, cut the meat against the grain into 2-by-1-inch slices that are as thin as possible.

Make a bed of lettuce on a serving platter and neatly arrange the meat slices on the lettuce. Spoon the seasoning mixture over the meat. Serves 2–3.

---

* If watercress is used, parboil for 1 minute in boiling water, place in a colander, rinse with cold water and drain thoroughly.

LAMP SHADOW BEEF

This dish is so named because ideally the beef should be cut so thin that you can see shadows through a slice held up to a lamp. However, don't be discouraged if your cutting is not that expert. What counts is not the thinness but the taste of the meat, which should be hot and spicy. The amount of pepper specified below produces a very hot dish. Use less if you prefer a milder taste.

1 pound sirloin of beef	1/2 teaspoon crushed
1/2 tablespoon salt	flower pepper
Seasoning mixture	1/2 teaspoon cayenne
1 tablespoon rice wine	3 tablespoons oil
1/2 teaspoon sugar	1 tablespoon grated fresh
Pinch of MSG	ginger
1/8 teaspoon five-flavored	1/2 head lettuce, thinly sliced
spice	

Slice the beef across the grain as thinly as possible. (The slicing will be easier if the beef is partially frozen.) Put the slices in a pan, sprinkle with salt and let stand for 1 hour. Scrape all moisture and salt off the beef, then heat it in a preheated 200° oven for 3 minutes.

Combine the ingredients for the seasoning mixture.

Place a wok over high heat. When it becomes very hot, add oil. Add the beef slices and stir-fry for about 2 minutes. Push the beef to one side, turn the heat to low and remove all but 1 tablespoon oil from the wok. Add ginger, stir-fry for several seconds and then add the seasoning mixture. Stir-fry for about 1/2 minute, or until the beef has absorbed the juices. Cool a bit to bring out the flavor of the beef and serve on a bed of lettuce.

Serves 2 (as an appetizer, serves 6).

HOT SWEET AND SOUR MEATBALLS

1 pound lean ground beef
Seasoning mixture
  1 tablespoon thin soy
    sauce
  1 tablespoon rice wine
  2 teaspoons cornstarch
  1 teaspoon sugar
  1/4 teaspoon salt
6 dried mushrooms
1 tablespoon white sesame
  seeds
Thickening mixture
  1 large garlic clove, minced
  3 tablespoons water, mixed
    with 2 tablespoons corn-
    starch
  2 tablespoons water

6 tablespoons vegetable oil
1/2 cup canned bamboo
  shoots cut into slices 2
  inches by 1 by 1/2 inch
1/3 cup thinly sliced canned
  water chestnuts
1/2 cup Chinese stock (p. 30)
  or chicken stock
1/2 cup plus 1 tablespoon
  white vinegar
1/2 cup sugar
3/4 teaspoon Szech'uan hot
  bean paste
1-1/4 tablespoons thick soy
  sauce

Place the beef in a large bowl. Combine the ingredients for the seasoning mixture and add to the beef, mixing well. Form meatballs 1 inch in diameter.

Soak mushrooms in warm water for 15 minutes. Drain, squeeze dry, remove the stems and quarter the caps.

In a dry pan, lightly toast sesame seeds until they begin to pop, being careful not to burn them. Mix together the ingredients for the thickening mixture.

Place a wok over high heat. When it is very hot, add oil. Add the meatballs and gently stir-fry for about 4 minutes, or until they are cooked through. Take care to avoid breaking up the meatballs and turn frequently to prevent sticking and burning. Transfer to a heated serving bowl.

Remove all but 2 tablespoons oil from the wok. Put the wok over high heat and add mushrooms, bamboo shoots and water chestnuts. Stir-fry 2 to 3 minutes. Add stock. When it comes to a boil, add 1/2 cup vinegar. When the boiling resumes, add sugar. Stir until the sugar dissolves, then add 1 tablespoon vinegar, bean paste and soy sauce and mix well. Slowly add the thickening mixture to the sauce and stir until thickened. Pour over the meatballs and garnish with sesame seeds.

Serves 2–3.

STEAMED MEAT CAKE

This ancient and elegant Szech'uan dish is a steamed cake consisting of a delicate egg wrapping with a spicy meat filling served on a bed of stir-fried *pai ts'ai* hearts and topped with a mild sweet and sour sauce. The presentation of the cake in the form of a *wan-tze* design—representing ten thousand things or bountiful blessings—which has its origins in the early Buddhism of China and India, indicates that it is part of the fare eaten by Chinese Buddhists. Since Buddhists are largely vegetarians, the original filling was probably made of one of the many excellent mock meats consisting of soy bean products and vegetables.

3 tablespoons uncooked glutinous rice
5 tablespoons water
Wrapping
  2 large eggs, well beaten
  1/4 teaspoon vegetable oil
  1-1/2 tablespoons water
  Pinch of sugar
  Pinch of MSG
Vegetable oil for pan-frying plus 2 tablespoons
Filling
  1/2 pound pork meat, minced
  2 jumbo shrimp, minced
  2 tablespoons minced water chestnuts
  1/4 teaspoon grated fresh ginger
  1 tablespoon minced green onion

Seasoning mixture
  2 teaspoons cornstarch
  1/4 teaspoon freshly ground black pepper
  1/2 teaspoon crushed flower pepper
  1 teaspoon thin soy sauce
  1/2 teaspoon salt
Thickening mixture
  1 teaspoon sugar
  1 teaspoon thin soy sauce
  1-1/2 teaspoons Chinese red vinegar
  1 tablespoon water mixed with 2 teaspoons cornstarch
Pinch of salt
1 pound *pai ts'ai* hearts or celery cabbage
1-1/4 cups Chinese stock (p. 30) or chicken stock

Mix the rice with water in a small heatproof bowl. Place the bowl in a steamer and steam for about 30 minutes, or until the rice is cooked and soft. Dry completely in a cool place, then roast it in the same bowl in a 350° oven for 10 minutes.

To prepare the wrapping, combine all ingredients and beat well. Oil a 10-inch skillet or griddle and place over medium heat. When it becomes hot, spread egg mixture evenly over the bottom by tipping the pan. When

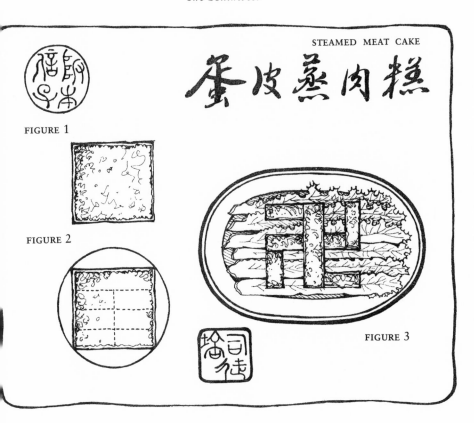

STEAMED MEAT CAKE

蛋皮蒸肉糕

FIGURE 1

FIGURE 2

FIGURE 3

large bubbles appear, carefully turn and lightly brown the other side. Place on a well-oiled board and cut into a 6-inch-square piece. Mince the trimmings and set aside.

In separate bowls, mix together the ingredients for the filling and for the seasoning and thickening mixtures.

Wash and trim the *pai ts'ai* hearts. If celery cabbage is used, remove the outer third of the stalks, wash and cut lengthwise through the cabbage twice so that there will be four sections.

Add the minced trimmings of the egg mixture, the rice and the seasoning mixture to the bowl containing the filling mixture and blend well. Spread the filling evenly over the wrapping to make a flat cake (Figure 1).

Place the cake on an oiled heatproof plate. Put the plate in a steamer and steam for 20 to 30 minutes. Pour the stock over the cake and steam for 10 minutes. Remove the steamer cover and let the plate cool. Reserve the stock. Take out the plate and, with a sharp knife, carefully slice the cake into 7 pieces (Figure 2).

Place a wok over high heat. When it becomes hot, add oil. Add the hearts, turn the heat down to medium and fry for about 1 minute. Add about 1/3 cup of the reserved stock and braise the hearts until they are translucent and slightly limp. Arrange them on a heated serving platter. With a spatula, carefully remove the meat-cake strips and arrange them on top of the hearts in the form of the *wan-tze* design (Figure 3).

Measure the reserved stock and add additional stock to make 1 1/4 cups. Put in a wok and bring to a boil. Add the thickening mixture and boil, stirring, until the sauce thickens. Pour the sauce over the cake and vegetables and serve.

Serves 3.

RICE POWDER BEEF

2 pounds flank steak
Marinade
  3-1/2 tablespoons thin soy
    sauce
  1/4 cup vegetable oil
  1 tablespoon rice wine
  1 teaspoon black bean chili
    sauce
  3 tablespoons coarsely
    chopped fresh ginger

2 tablespoons water
Coating mixture
  1/2 cup uncooked white
    rice
  1 teaspoon flower pepper
  1-1/4 teaspoons kosher salt
  1-1/2 teaspoons sesame oil
  1 tablespoon slivered green
    onion

Remove the membrane from the steak and slice the beef against the grain into 2-by 1/8-inch shreds. Mix together all the marinade ingredients except ginger and water. Squeeze the ginger in a garlic press and add the ginger juice to the water. Mix with the marinade. Place the beef in the marinade and marinate for 15 minutes.

Toast the rice in a dry frying pan until lightly browned. Toast the flower pepper in a dry pan until fragrant, then grind fine in a mortar. Mix the flower pepper with kosher salt. Place the rice and flower-pepper salt in a blender and grind until the texture resembles that of Cream of Rice.

Place the coating mixture on a plate and roll the beef strips in it.

Carefully arrange the beef in one layer on an oiled steamer tray (more than one tray may be necessary). Place the tray in a steamer and steam vigorously for 15 minutes.

Transfer the beef to a heated platter, sprinkle with sesame oil and toss once or twice. Garnish with green onion.

Serves 3–4.

DUCK WITH SNOW PEAS
IN HOT SAUCE

With a hot sauce and smoky flavor, this is another typical Hunan dish.

1-1/4 pounds cooked duck
  meat
3/4 pound snow peas
Seasoning mixture
  1 tablespoon thin soy
    sauce
  2 tablespoons rice wine
  1/2 teaspoon sesame oil
  3/4 teaspoon Szech'uan
    bean paste
  1/2 teaspoon salt
  1 teaspoon barbecue smoke
    sauce (available in most
    supermarkets)

3 tablespoons vegetable oil
1/2 teaspoon salt
1 large garlic clove, peeled
  and crushed
1/2 cup Chinese stock (p. 30)
  or chicken stock
1/4 teaspoon fresh ground
  black pepper
2 tablespoons slivered green
  onion (cut in half lengthwise and slice diagonally
  into 1/2-inch sections)

Cut the duck meat into slices 2 inches by 1 by 1/4 inch. String the snow peas and cut in half diagonally. Combine the ingredients for the seasoning mixture.

Place a wok over high heat. When it becomes very hot, add oil. Add garlic and salt, stir once and add the seasoning mixture. Stir twice and add the duck meat. Stir-fry for about 1/2 minute and add the snow peas. Stir-fry for several seconds, add the stock and braise until the liquid is reduced by half.

Transfer to a heated platter, sprinkle with pepper and garnish with green onion.

Serves 3.

FRAGRANT CRISPY DUCK

This dish might be called Ch'engtu's answer to Peking duck. It has the same characteristics of a crisp flavorful skin and tender meat, but its spicy flavor is pure Szech'uan and it is much easier to prepare. It is important to keep the salt and spice mixture on the duck's skin, to let the duck dry well before frying and to have the frying oil hot enough to crisp the skin.

Spice coating
2 tablespoons crushed
   flower pepper
2 tablespoons kosher salt
1/2 teaspoon five-flavored
   spice
1 4-1/2-pound duck
2 tablespoons rice wine
2 tablespoons thin soy sauce

2 tablespoons cornstarch
2 tablespoons water chestnut
   flour
Vegetable oil for deep-frying
12 green onion sections,
   white part only
Hoisin sauce
Pancakes (p. 64)

To make the spice coating, heat the flower pepper in a dry frying pan over low heat for 1 minute, stirring to prevent scorching. Add salt and heat for another minute. Remove from heat and mix in the five-flavored spice.

Wash the duck and dry it well. Cut off the wing tips and ends of the leg bones. Sprinkle the spice coating all over the duck. Prop the duck in a pot or bowl so that any juices running out of the duck will not wet the skin (Figure 1). Refrigerate for several hours or overnight.

Put the duck in a steaming bowl and sprinkle with rice wine, taking care not to remove the spice coating. Put the bowl in a steamer and steam for 2 hours. Remove the duck from the steamer, tie a string around it so the whole body is securely supported, and hang in a cool place (preferably out of doors in cool weather) until it dries; place a pan and newspaper under it to catch the drippings (Figure 2). If the duck is hung indoors, an electric fan will help to dry it. It should take about 20 minutes to dry the duck.

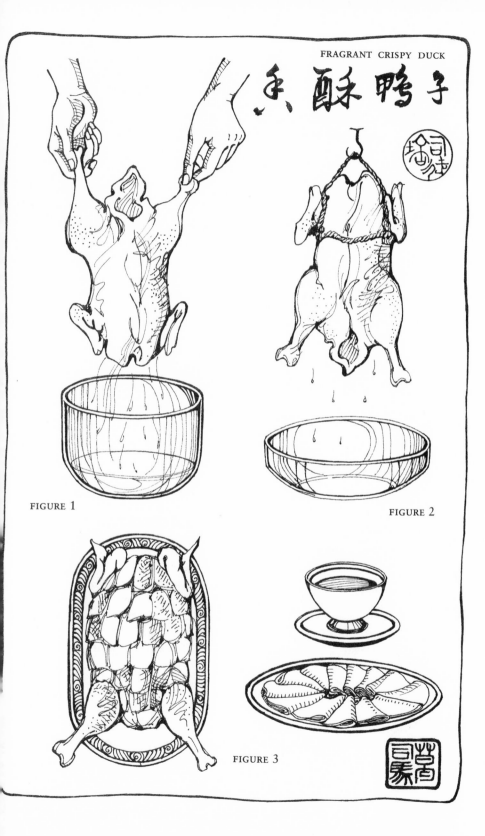

FRAGRANT CRISPY DUCK

香酥鴨子

FIGURE 1

FIGURE 2

FIGURE 3

Place the duck on a board and cut it in half along the breast and backbone. Pat soy sauce all over the skin, again being careful not to disturb the spices on the skin. Let stand 10 minutes.

Mix the cornstarch and water chestnut flour together and sprinkle the mixture all over the duck.

Heat enough oil for deep-frying to about 350° in a deep, heavy pot or deep-fryer. Put in half of the duck, skin side down, and fry for about 3 minutes, or until the skin is golden-brown and crisp. Then fry the other half. Drain on paper towels.

When the duck has cooled a bit, remove the skin and cut it into bite-sized pieces. Do the same with the meat. Arrange both skin and meat on a platter and serve with pancakes, green onion and Hoisin sauce. Each diner fills a pancake with meat and skin, adds green onion and Hoisin sauce and folds the pancake over to enjoy a delectable morsel. (See Figure 3)

Serves 4–6.

PON PON CHICKEN

This dish originated in the Lo Shan area of Szech'uan where peanuts are the principal crop and the chickens fattened on them are especially flavorful. The name *Pon Pon* refers to the noise made during the tenderizing process in which a stick is used to pound the meat.

Sauce
- 1-1/2 teaspoons sugar
- 3 tablespoons thin soy sauce
- 1/4 teaspoon MSG
- 2 tablespoons finely chopped green onion
- 2 teaspoons sesame oil
- 1 tablespoon sesame paste
- 2 teaspoons Chinese red vinegar
- 1 teaspoon hot pepper oil or Szech'uan hot bean paste

Garnish I
- 1 tablespoon grated fresh ginger
- 2 teaspoons minced garlic

Garnish II
- 1 tablespoon sesame seeds
- 1/2 teaspoon crushed flower pepper
- 3 pounds chicken thighs
- 3 tablespoons sesame oil
- 1/2 head lettuce, thinly sliced

Combine the ingredients for the sauce. Mix together the ingredients of garnish I. For garnish II, lightly heat sesame seeds in a dry pan until they begin to pop, then mix them with the flower pepper.

In a large pot, bring to a boil enough water to cover the chicken thighs. Add them and simmer for 15 minutes. Prick with a fork the heaviest part of a thigh, and if blood runs out, simmer for 10 to 15 minutes more. Turn off the heat, put the chicken thighs in a colander and rinse with cold water. Soak them in cold water for 20 minutes. Remove and let the skin dry completely. Rub sesame oil all over the chicken thighs and place them on a board. Gently pound each piece with a wooden mallet for a few minutes (the meat should be slightly mashed).

Cut the meat from the bones into bite-sized pieces about 1-1/2 inches by 1/2 inch and put it on a platter covered with a bed of lettuce. Sprinkle the chicken with garnish I, then spoon the sauce over the chicken and sprinkle with garnish II.

Serves 4–5.

CHICKEN WITH GREEN PEPPERS

In this Hunan-style dish the green peppers sweeten the taste of the sauce, which tends to be slightly hot and sour.

1-1/2 pounds boneless
  chicken meat
Marinade
  2-1/2 tablespoons thin soy
    sauce
  1/2 tablespoon sugar
  1/2 tablespoon rice wine
  2 tablespoons cornstarch
  1 tablespoon water
3 large green peppers
2 green onions
Seasoning mixture
  1 large garlic clove, peeled
    and slivered

2-1/2 tablespoons thin soy
  sauce
1/2 teaspoon salt
1-1/2 tablespoons white
  vinegar
1-1/2 tablespoons corn-
  starch
1/2 teaspoon Szech'uan hot
  bean paste
Vegetable oil for deep-frying
  plus 2 tablespoons
Few drops of sesame oil

Cut the chicken into bite-sized pieces. Mix together the ingredients for the marinade and marinate the chicken for 5 minutes. Wash and cut the peppers into 1-1/2-by-1/2-inch pieces. Cut the green onions in half lengthwise and slice diagonally into 1/2-inch sections. Combine the ingredients for the seasoning mixture.

Heat 2 inches oil to about 350° in a deep pot or deep-fryer. Add the chicken pieces one by one and deep-fry for about 1 minute. Remove and drain on paper towels.

Place a wok over high heat. When it becomes very hot, add oil. Add green peppers and green onions and stir-fry for about 1/2 minute. Add the chicken and the seasoning mixture and stir-fry for about 1 minute. Transfer to a heated platter and sprinkle with sesame oil.

Serves 4.

TUNG AN CHICKEN

Seasoning mixture
1/4 teaspoon salt
2 tablespoons thin soy
  sauce
1 teaspoon sugar
1 tablespoon rice wine
3 green onions
2 fresh chili peppers
2 pounds chicken breasts
2 slices fresh ginger
1/4 cup vegetable oil

1 teaspoon crushed flower
  pepper
2 tablespoons finely slivered
  fresh ginger
1 cup Chinese stock (p. 30)
  or chicken stock
1 tablespoon white vinegar
1 tablespoon water mixed
  with 2 teaspoons corn-
  starch
Few drops of sesame oil

Combine the ingredients for the seasoning mixture. Finely sliver 2 green onions. Remove the membrane and seeds from the chili peppers and cut them into fine slivers.

Put the chicken breasts in a pot, add enough water to cover and bring to a boil. Skim off the foam and add 1 green onion and ginger slices. Lower the heat and simmer for 10 minutes.

Remove the chicken and allow to cool. With a sharp knife, cut the meat into 2-by-1-inch slices, and lightly flatten them with the side of a cleaver.

Place a wok over high heat, and when it is very hot, add oil. Add flower pepper and stir until it browns and becomes fragrant. Add ginger slivers, green onion slivers and chili peppers. Stir-fry a few seconds, add the chicken and the seasoning mixture and stir-fry for about 1/2 minute. Add stock and simmer for 3 minutes. Add vinegar, then the cornstarch mixture and stir until thickened.

Transfer to a heated platter and sprinkle with sesame oil.

Serves 3–4.

CHICKEN OF MANY FLAVORS

This popular dish among the Szech'uanese incorporates many flavors (sour, salt, fragrant, sweet and hot), hence its name.

3 bunches watercress
5 tablespoons slivered green onion, white part only (cut in half lengthwise and slice diagonally into 1/2-inch sections)
Sauce
2 tablespoons sesame seeds

1 tablespoon sesame oil
2 whole dried chili peppers
1/4 cup vegetable oil
1/4 cup thin soy sauce
1-1/2 tablespoons sugar
2 tablespoons white vinegar
2 pounds chicken legs

Wash, trim and parboil the watercress for 1 minute. Put in a colander, rinse in cold running water and squeeze out all liquid. Cut into pieces about 2 inches long and arrange on a serving platter. Sprinkle the green onion slivers over the watercress.

To make the sauce, first pan-fry sesame seeds in a little oil until they turn golden and begin to pop, then grind them into a paste with mortar and pestle. Add sesame oil and mix well. Fry the chili peppers in oil over low heat until they turn dark. Discard them. Add the pepper-flavored oil, soy sauce, sugar and vinegar to the sesame paste and mix well.

Put the chicken legs in a large pot with enough water to cover and bring to a boil over high heat. Reduce heat and simmer for 25 minutes, or until done. Take out the legs and let them cool, then remove the bones and cut the meat into bite-sized pieces.

To serve, place the chicken pieces on top of the green onion and watercress, pour the sauce over them and toss to mix all ingredients.

Serves 4.

YUNNAN STEAM POT CHICKEN

This famous Yunnan dish is cooked in a specially designed glazed ceramic pot with an internal funnel which allows minute yet continuous amounts of steam to slowly cook the ingredients. The pot is necessary to the dish, and may be available or possible to order from Chinese grocers in large cities. No other cooking vessel will do.

1 3-pound fresh chicken*
Seasoning mixture
  1 teaspoon sugar
  2/3 teaspoon salt
  1/3 cup rice wine
  Pinch of cayenne
1/4 pound prosciutto ham,
  cut into slices 2 inches by 1
  by 1/4 inch

1-1/2 cups sliced bamboo
  shoots, cut the same size as
  the ham
1 large slice fresh ginger
1/4 teaspoon MSG
Salt to taste

Wash the chicken, dry it well and cut into pieces about 2 inches square. Stir together the ingredients for the seasoning mixture.

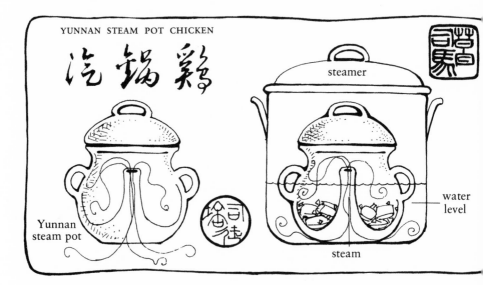

YUNNAN STEAM POT CHICKEN

steamer

Yunnan steam pot

water level

steam

* Pork butt or loin or cuts of beef such as chuck may be substituted using the appropriate cooking time.

Place all ingredients except the MSG in the special ceramic pot and cover. Place the pot in a steamer without a steamer stand, add water and bring to a rapid boil. Lower the heat and add more hot water to the steamer until the water level is halfway up the ceramic pot (see Illustration). Cover the steamer and steam for 1 hour.

Remove the steamer cover and cool. Carefully remove the ceramic pot and take off the cover. Add MSG and salt and serve in individual bowls with the juices.

Serves 3–4.

TANGERINE-PEEL CHICKEN

4 pieces (each about the size of a quarter) dried tangerine peel
Seasoning mixture
  1-1/2 teaspoons sugar
  1 tablespoon Chinese vinegar
  1 tablespoon rice wine
  1 tablespoon thin soy sauce
1-1/2 pounds boned chicken meat
Marinade
  1 teaspoon grated fresh ginger

3 green onions, minced
1 tablespoon thin soy sauce
1 tablespoon rice wine
3 tablespoons vegetable oil
1/2 teaspoon Szech'uan hot bean paste
1/2 teaspoon salt
1/2 teaspoon crushed flower pepper
1/2 teaspoon sesame oil
1 tablespoon green onion cut into 1/2-inch sections

Soak the tangerine peel in warm water for 20 minutes. Blot dry with paper towels and mince.

Combine the ingredients for the seasoning mixture.

Cut the chicken meat into 1/2-inch cubes and place them in a large bowl. Mix together the ingredients for the marinade and marinate the chicken for 20 to 30 minutes.

Place a wok over high heat. When it becomes very hot, add oil. Add the chicken and stir-fry for 2 to 3 minutes, or until it turns golden. Transfer to a heated platter.

Remove half of the oil in the wok. Add the Szech'uan hot bean paste, salt, flower pepper and tangerine peel, and stir-fry for a few seconds. Add the chicken and then the seasoning mixture and stir-fry a few times. Transfer to a heated serving platter, sprinkle with sesame oil and garnish with green onion.

Serves 3.

BROKEN RICE AND PEANUTS

Actually, there's no rice in this dish. The "broken rice" refers to the small, uneven pieces of chicken coated with batter.

1 pound boneless chicken
  breasts
Coating mixture
  2 egg whites
  2 tablespoons cornstarch
  1/2 teaspoon salt
Seasoning mixture
  2 teaspoons sugar
  2-1/2 teaspoons Chinese
    red vinegar
  2 teaspoons thin soy sauce

1 teaspoon water mixed
  with 1 teaspoon corn-
  starch
1/4 cup Chinese stock
  (p. 30) or chicken stock
2 small green peppers
2 small onions
Vegetable oil for deep-frying
  plus 2 tablespoons
1/3 cup lightly crushed peanuts

Wash the chicken breasts and pat dry with paper towels. With a sharp knife, cut them into small pieces about the size of peas.

Beat together the ingredients for the coating mixture until it is smooth and foamy. Add the chicken and mix well. Stir together the ingredients for the seasoning mixture.

Slice the onions and green peppers into matchstick-sized shreds.

Heat 2 inches oil in a deep, heavy pot or deep-fryer to 350°. Add the coated pieces of chicken. When they float to the surface, scoop them out and drain on paper towels.

Place a wok over high heat. When it is very hot, add oil. Add green peppers and onions and stir-fry for 1 minute. Add the chicken pieces and then the seasoning mixture. Stir-fry for 1/2 minute. Add the peanuts and stir until the sauce is thickened.

Serves 2–3.

SWEET AND SOUR FISH
CH'ENGTU STYLE

This Szech'uan dish is different from similar recipes because the crisp fried fish is whole and the sauce is enhanced by fresh lemon rind and hot bean paste.

3 large dried mushrooms
1 large green pepper
Marinade
    1/4 cup rice wine
    1/4 cup thin soy sauce
Coating
    7 tablespoons cornstarch
    5 tablespoons water
Seasoning mixture
    2 tablespoons sugar
    2 tablespoons white vin-
      egar
    5 tablespoons Chinese stock
      (p. 30) or chicken stock
    1 teaspoon grated fresh
      lemon rind

1/2 teaspoon Szech'uan hot
    bean paste
1 1-1/4-pound whole fresh
    fish (bass or pike is good),
    with the head and tail left
    on
Vegetable oil for deep-frying
    plus 3 tablespoons
1 tablespoon minced green
    onion
1 large garlic clove, minced
1/4 cup canned sliced
    bamboo shoots, cut in 2-
    by-1-inch pieces
1 tablespoon water mixed
    with 1/2 tablespoon corn-
    starch

Soak mushrooms in hot water for 15 minutes. Rinse, squeeze out excess water, remove the stems and cut the caps into thin slices.

Cut the green pepper into 2-by-1-inch chunks.

Separately, combine the ingredients for the marinade, the coating mixture and the seasoning mixture.

Wash the fish and pat dry with paper towels. Make several slashes on each side of the fish where it is thickest. Marinate the fish in the marinade for 10 minutes, then blot off the excess with paper towels. Smear the fish all over with the coating mixture.

Heat about 3-inches oil to about 350° in a 14-inch wok or a small roasting pan. Carefully lower the dish into the oil and fry for 3 to 4 minutes, then fry the other side for about 4 minutes. The fish should become a deep golden color. Remove from the pan and place on a heated platter.

Place a wok over high heat. When it becomes very hot, add oil. Add green onion, garlic, bamboo shoots, mushrooms, and green pepper. Stir-fry

1 minute, then add the seasoning mixture and stir-fry for 1/2 minute. Add the cornstarch mixture and stir until the sauce thickens. Pour the sauce over the fish.
Serves 3.

FRIED FISH WITH BEAN CURD

2 cups eggplant cut in pieces
2 inches by 1/2 by 1/2 inch
2-1/2 teaspoons salt
2 cups bean curd cut into
pieces the same size as the
eggplant
Seasoning mixture
1 teaspoon grated fresh
ginger
1 garlic clove, minced
1 tablespoon thin soy sauce
1 teaspoon sweet bean
paste or Hoisin sauce
2 tablespoons rice wine
1 pound fish fillets
Coating mixture
1/4 cup water chestnut
flour

1/4 cup cornstarch
4 dried mushrooms
Vegetable oil for deep-frying
1 cup onion cut into
2-by-1/2-inch pieces
1-1/2 cups Chinese stock
(p. 30) or chicken stock
3/4 teaspoon Szech'uan bean
sauce
1-1/2 tablespoons water
mixed with 2 teaspoons
cornstarch
2 green onions, cut in half
lengthwise and sliced
diagonally into 1/2-inch
sections

Put the eggplant in a bowl and add salt to enough water to cover the eggplant. Soak the eggplant for 20 minutes. Drain, rinse and gently squeeze out excess water. Dry on paper towels.

Put the bean curd in a pan and add boiling water to cover. After 1 minute, drain off the water.

Combine the ingredients for the seasoning mixture.

Wash and dry the fish fillets. Sprinkle with 1/2 teaspoon salt and cut into 1-by-1/2-inch pieces. Stir together the ingredients for the coating mixture and dredge the pieces of fish with it.

Soak the mushrooms in hot water for 15 minutes. Rinse, squeeze out excess water, remove the stems and slice the caps.

Heat about 2 inches vegetable oil in a wok to about 350°. Add the fish in three batches and fry for 1 to 2 minutes, or until the outside is crisp and golden. Remove and drain. Transfer to a heated serving platter.

Pour out all but 3 tablespoons oil from the wok. Reheat the oil until it smokes. Add the eggplant, mushrooms, and onion. Stir-fry for 1 minute and add the seasoning mixture while continuing to stir. Add the stock and then the bean curd. Simmer until the liquid is reduced by half, then stir in the Szech'uan bean paste and thicken with the cornstarch mixture.

Pour the contents of pan over the fish and garnish with green onions. Serves 4.

CHUNGKING FAMILY-STYLE FISH FRITTERS AND VEGETABLES

1 pound fish fillets
3 cups fresh bean sprouts or
  2 cups canned
Marinade
  1/4 cup thin soy sauce
  1/4 cup rice wine
  1/2 teaspoon salt
Seasoning mixture
  1-1/2 teaspoons white vin-
    egar
  1-1/2 teaspoons sugar
  3/4 teaspoon salt
  1/4 teaspoon white pepper
  3/4 teaspoon grated fresh
    ginger

Pinch of MSG
2 teaspoons thin soy
  sauce
6 tablespoons Chinese stock
  (p. 30) or chicken stock
1-1/2 teaspoons cornstarch
1/2 cup cornstarch
1/2 cup flour
Vegetable oil for deep-frying
  plus 3 tablespoons
1 cup thinly sliced celery
1/2 teaspoon Szech'uan hot
  bean paste
Few drops of sesame oil

Wash, dry and slice the fish fillets into 1-by-1-1/2-inch pieces. Wash and drain the bean sprouts well in a colander.

Mix together the marinade ingredients. Combine the ingredients for the seasoning mixture. Mix cornstarch and flour together.

Marinate the pieces of fish in the marinade for 10 minutes, turning them over once or twice. Wipe off the excess marinade and roll each piece of fish in the cornstarch-flour mixture.

Heat 3 inches oil to about 350° in a deep, heavy pot or deep-fryer. Add the fish and fry for 1 to 2 minutes, or until it turns golden. Drain on paper towels.

Put 3 tablespoons oil in a wok over high heat. Add celery and briskly stir-fry for 1/2 minute. Add bean sprouts and stir-fry another 1/2 minute. Add the seasoning mixture and stir-fry until the sauce is slightly thickened.

Turn off the heat and gradually stir in the hot bean paste. Add the fish and carefully mix with the vegetables.

Transfer to a heated platter and sprinkle with sesame oil.

Serves 3.

BEAN SAUCE FRIED FISH

1 garlic clove, minced
1 pound whitefish fillets
Cornstarch
Seasoning mixture
    4 teaspoons thin soy
      sauce
    4 teaspoons rice wine
    1/4 teaspoon MSG
    1 teaspoon sugar
Vegetable oil for deep-frying
    plus 2 tablespoons
2 tablespoons brown bean
    sauce

1 teaspoon minced fresh
    ginger
3 tablespoons minced green
    onion
1/4 cup Chinese stock (p. 30)
    or chicken stock
2 teaspoons white vinegar
4 teaspoons water mixed
    with 2 teaspoons corn-
    starch

Wash the fillets, pat dry with paper towels and cut into 1-by-2-inch slices. Coat the slices lightly with cornstarch.

Combine the ingredients for the seasoning mixture.

Heat 3 inches oil to about 350° in a deep-fryer or deep, heavy pot. Add about one-fourth of the fish slices at a time. Keep them separated and fry until they turn golden. Drain on paper towels.

Heat 2 tablespoons oil in a wok over high heat. When the oil almost begins to smoke, add the bean sauce, garlic, ginger, green onion and seasoning mixture. Stir once or twice and add the fish. Add the stock and stir a few times until it comes to a boil.

Turn off the heat, add vinegar and stir. Add the cornstarch mixture and stir until the sauce thickens. Transfer to a heated serving platter.

Serves 4.

HUNAN SWEET AND SOUR FRIED FISH

This method of cooking fish was one of the favorites of the first president of the Republic of China, Dr. Sun Yat Sen, and was taught to the author by an ex-aide of his. Those who like their food on the hot side should add 3/4 teaspoon of Szech'uan bean paste to the sauce.

1 1-1/2-pound whole fresh-water fish (bass, pike or brook trout is good), with the head and tail left on
4 tablespoons thin soy sauce
5 dried mushrooms
4 canned water chestnuts
1 knob fresh ginger the size of a large olive

4 tablespoons cornstarch
Vegetable oil for deep-frying
1 tablespoon heavy soy sauce
1-1/2 tablespoons white vinegar
2 tablespoons sugar
3 tablespoons Chinese stock (p. 30) or chicken stock

Wash the fish and make several deep slashes on each side of the fish where it is thickest. Cut the fish into two pieces, one with the head and the other with the tail. Smear the fish with 2 tablespoons thin soy sauce and let stand for 10 minutes.

Soak mushrooms in warm water for 15 minutes. Drain, squeeze dry, remove the stems and quarter the caps. Slice the water chestnuts into 1/5-inch disks. Peel and grate the ginger.

Coat the fish all over with cornstarch. Put 1 to 1-1/2 inches oil in a wok over high heat and fry the fish on each side for about 4 minutes, or until browned and cooked through.

Mix together the heavy soy sauce, vinegar, sugar, 2 tablespoons thin soy sauce and the stock.

Pour out all but 1-1/2 tablespoons of the oil used to fry the fish. Moving the fish in the pan to one side, reduce the heat to medium and add ginger, mushrooms and water chestnuts. Stir-fry for a few seconds, then add the sauce mixture, cover and cook for 2 minutes. Garnish with green onion sections.

Serves 4.

BRAISED FISH
WITH HOT BEAN SAUCE

1-1/4 pounds whole fresh fish
(sea bass, pike, scrod, or
red snapper is good), with
the head and tail left on
3 dried black mushrooms
2 green onions
Seasoning mixture
  1 teaspoon grated fresh
    ginger
  1 large garlic clove, minced
  3/4 teaspoon Szech'uan hot
    bean paste
  2 teaspoons thin soy sauce

2 tablespoons rice wine
1 teaspoon sugar
Vegetable oil for deep-frying
  plus 3 tablespoons
1/2 teaspoon salt
2 cups green pepper cut into
  2-by-1-inch slices
1-3/4 cups Chinese stock
  (p. 30) or chicken stock
2 teaspoons white vinegar
3 tablespoons water mixed
  with 2 tablespoons cornstarch

Wash the fish thoroughly and dry with paper towels. Make several slashes on the sides where the flesh is thickest.

Soak mushrooms in hot water for 15 minutes. Rinse, squeeze dry, remove the stems and slice the caps. Cut the green onions in half lengthwise and slice diagonally into 1/2-inch sections. Combine the ingredients for the seasoning mixture.

Heat about 3 inches oil to about 350° in a long, deep pan (such as a small roasting pan). Carefully lower the fish into the oil. When the skin hardens and becomes lightly browned, turn the fish over to brown the other side. Remove and drain on brown paper.

Heat 3 tablespoons oil in a wok over high heat. When the oil is about to smoke, add salt and stir, then add the mushrooms and green pepper. Stir-fry for several seconds, add the seasoning mixture and then the stock. When the sauce comes to a boil, lower the fish into the sauce. Reduce heat and simmer for about 8 minutes, frequently spooning the sauce over the fish during the cooking. Transfer the fish to a heated platter.

Add vinegar to the sauce and turn up the heat. Add the cornstarch mixture and stir until the sauce is thickened. Pour it over the fish and garnish with green onion.

Serves 3.

MA P'O BEAN CURD

This traditional hot dish is one of the best-known Szech'uan recipes. It is cooked with very little liquid over low heat, so that the bean curd absorbs the flavor of all the other ingredients.

3 cakes bean curd
1 large garlic clove
2 green onions
2/3 cup Chinese stock (p. 30) or chicken stock
3 tablespoons vegetable oil
1/3 pound ground beef
1/2 teaspoon salt
1 teaspoon Szech'uan hot bean paste

Pinch of cayenne
3/4 teaspoon sesame oil
1/2 teaspoon MSG
1/4 teaspoon crushed flower pepper
1 tablespoon water mixed with 1/2 tablespoon cornstarch

Cut the bean curd into 1/4-inch cubes. Place them in a pan and cover with boiling water for about 1/2 minute to make them firm. Drain them in a colander.

Peel and mince the garlic. Cut the green onions in half lengthwise and slice diagonally into 1/2-inch sections.

Heat the stock almost to the boiling point.

Put oil in a wok over medium heat. When the oil begins to smoke, add the beef and stir-fry vigorously until browned. Add salt and stir. Turn down the heat and add hot bean paste and cayenne. Stir until well mixed.

Add the hot stock and bean curd and simmer, stirring, for about 4 minutes. Add garlic and green onion, then the sesame oil and MSG. Add the cornstarch mixture and stir until thickened. There should be little liquid left, since most will have been absorbed by the bean curd.

Transfer to a serving bowl and sprinkle with flower pepper.

Serves 2.

COUNTRY-STYLE BEAN CURD

Although not as hot or spicy as the preceding recipe from Szech'uan, this is the Hunan counterpart of that dish.

4 cakes bean curd
1/4 pound pork butt
3 dried mushrooms
2 green onions
Seasoning mixture
    1/2 teaspoon black bean
    hot chili sauce (use 3/4
    teaspoon if you like fiery
    dishes)
    1/2 teaspoon sugar
    Pinch of MSG
    1-1/2 tablespoons thin soy
    sauce

1 large garlic clove, minced
1/4 teaspoon white pepper
Few drops of sesame oil
1 teaspoon sesame seeds
Vegetable oil for deep-frying
    plus 2 tablespoons
1/4 cup canned sliced
    bamboo shoots
1/2 cup Chinese stock
    (p. 30) or chicken stock
1 tablespoon water mixed
    with 1/2 tablespoon corn-
    starch

Cut the bean curd into 1/4-inch cubes. Mince the pork. Soak the dried mushrooms in hot water for 15 minutes. Rinse, squeeze out excess water, remove the stems and cut the caps into thin slices. Cut the green onions in half lengthwise and slice diagonally into 1/2-inch sections. Combine the ingredients for the seasoning mixture. Lightly brown the sesame seeds in a dry frying pan.

Heat 2 inches oil in a deep pot or deep-fryer to 350°. Carefully add the bean-curd cubes and deep-fry for 2 minutes, or until they turn golden-brown. Remove from heat and drain.

Place a wok over high heat. When it becomes very hot, add oil. Add pork, bamboo shoots, mushrooms and green onions and stir-fry for about 1-1/2 minutes. Add the bean curd, the seasoning mixture and the stock. Stir-fry gently, so as not to crush the bean curd, for about 2 minutes. Add the cornstarch mixture slowly and stir until the sauce is thickened.

Transfer to a heated platter and garnish with sesame seeds.
Serves 3.

RED OIL DUMPLINGS

Red Oil Dip
  1/4 cup vegetable oil
  1/2 teaspoon cayenne
  Pinch of salt
Garlic paste
  5 large garlic cloves
  Dash of white vinegar
  2 drops sesame oil
  Salt
Red soy dip
  2 1-inch pieces cinnamon
    bark
  3 star anise
  1/4 cup brown sugar
  1/4 cup thin soy sauce
  1 teaspoon sesame oil
Chinese red vinegar dip
  1/4 cup Chinese red vinegar
  1/2 teaspoon thin soy sauce
  1/4 teaspoon sugar
  4 drops sesame oil

2 cups finely sliced celery
  cabbage
Salt
3/4 cup minced pork butt
1/4 cup minced green onion,
  white part only
Seasoning mixture
  1/2 teaspoon salt
  1-1/2 tablespoons thin soy
    sauce
  1/2 teaspoon grated fresh
    ginger
  1/2 teaspoon crushed
    flower pepper
  1 teaspoon rice wine
  1/2 teaspoon sesame oil
Wrappings
  2 cups flour
  1 teaspoon vegetable oil
  3/4 cup warm water
  1 tablespoon vegetable oil

To make the red oil dip, heat vegetable oil in a pan, add cayenne and salt and mix until they are dissolved.

To make the garlic paste dip, peel and crush the garlic cloves, add vinegar and sesame oil to form a soft paste and add salt to taste.

To make the red soy dip, place in a pan all ingredients except the oil, simmer slowly for 5 minutes, stirring to prevent burning, and add the oil.

To make the Chinese red vinegar dip, mix all ingredients together.

Sprinkle a little salt over the celery cabbage and let stand for 5 minutes. Wrap in a dishtowel, press, and squeeze out as much liquid as possible.

Place the pork, celery cabbage and green onion in a bowl. Combine the ingredients for the seasoning mixture, add to the pork mixture and mix well. This is the filling.

Put flour in a bowl and add to it a mixture of oil and warm water. Mix to form a dough; when it leaves the sides of the bowl, place it on a lightly floured board and gently knead until it becomes smooth and elastic. If the dough is too sticky to handle, add a little flour; if too dry, add a little water. Cover the dough with a moist towel and leave it on the board for 15 minutes.

Work the dough into a long roll about 1 inch in diameter and slice it into 20 pieces. Lightly flour a board and roll each piece into a disk about 3 inches in diameter. Put 1 rounded teaspoon filling in the center of each disk and lightly dampen the edges with water. Fold the disk over and pinch the edges together to make a half-circle.

Bring 3 quarts water to a boil in a large pot. Add 1 tablespoon oil. Carefully add the dumplings, about eight at a time. Lower the heat to maintain a constant gentle boil so that the dumplings will remain intact. After a few minutes, when the dumplings rise to the surface, add 1 cup cold water. When the water comes to a boil again, the dumplings are done. Remove with a slotted spoon and drain well. Arrange on a platter lined with a few celery cabbage leaves and serve with the various dips.

Makes 20 dumplings.

LAI'S T'ANG YUAN

These little boiled dumplings (*t'ang yuan*) date back to the 1890s. They are named for the peddler who made and sold them on the streets of Ch'engtu.

Filling
1 cup dried Chinese dates
2 tablespoons sugar
1/4 teaspoon vegetable oil
1/4 teaspoon lemon juice
1 tablespoon cornstarch
1/4 cup almonds

2 tablespoons white sesame
  seeds
Wrappings
2 cups flour
1/4 teaspoon salt
3/4 cup warm water
2 teaspoons vegetable oil

Soak the dates overnight in cold water. Drain, remove the pits and chop coarsely. Put the dates, sugar, oil, lemon juice and cornstarch into a blender and grind for a few seconds until the texture is like that of granola. Empty the mixture into a bowl. Lightly toast the sesame seeds in a dry pan. Pan-fry the almonds and chop coarsely. Add the almonds and sesame seeds to the date mixture and mix well. Shape the mixture into firm balls about 1 inch in diameter and set aside.

Mix flour and salt in a large bowl. In another bowl, add 1 teaspoon oil to warm water and stir, then add this mixture to the flour. Stir until a light dough is formed. Add a little flour if the dough is too soft, a little warm water if too dry. Place on a lightly floured board and knead gently until it becomes smooth and elastic. Place in a bowl, cover with a damp cloth and put in a draft-free place for 20 minutes.

Place the dough on a floured board and form into a long roll about 1 inch in diameter. Cut into 20 slices and form into balls, then roll into disks about 3 inches in diameter. Brush some oil lightly on top of each disk and stack them.

Lightly moisten each disk about 1/2 inch from the edge with a little water. Put 2 teaspoons of the filling in the center and pinch together a half inch from the edge to seal securely.

Boil about 3 quarts water in a large pot and add 1 teaspoon vegetable oil. Carefully drop the dumplings, in batches of four or five, into the boiling water. When they rise to the surface, they are ready. Remove and drain.

Makes 20 dumplings.

COPPER WELL STREET
PLAIN NOODLES

This pungent dish gets its name from a Szech'uan noodle shop which first sold noodles from handcarts on Copper Well (T'ung Ching) Street.

Sauce mixture	1/4 teaspoon crushed
3 tablespoons minced green onions	flower pepper
	5 tablespoons vegetable oil
2-1/2 tablespoons thin soy sauce	1/8 teaspoon cayenne
	1-1/2 teaspoons brown sugar
1/4 teaspoon sesame oil	2 teaspoons crushed sesame seeds
3/4 teaspoon MSG	
2 teaspoons minced garlic	1 pound fresh Chinese egg noodles or dried noodles
2-1/2 teaspoons Chinese red vinegar	

In a large bowl, combine the ingredients for the sauce mixture. Heat 3 tablespoons oil, remove from heat and add cayenne. Add to the sauce mixture and mix well. Heat brown sugar in 3 teaspoons oil until it dissolves and add to the sauce. Pan-fry sesame seeds in 3 teaspoons oil until they turn golden. Add this also to the sauce.

Cook the noodles in 3 quarts boiling water for about 10 minutes, or

until they become soft enough to be easily cut with a fingernail. Drain and rinse thoroughly. While the noodles are still hot, pour the sauce over them and toss. Serve in individual bowls.
Serves 4–5.

NOODLES WITH HOT MEAT SAUCE

Seasoning mixture
  4 tablespoons sweet bean
    paste or Hoisin sauce
  1 teaspoon thin soy sauce
  3/4 teaspoon Szech'uan hot
    bean paste
  4 tablespons Chinese stock
    (p. 30) or chicken stock
  1/4 teaspoon sesame oil

1-1/2 cups canned bean
  sprouts
1 small, firm cucumber
3 eggs
3 tablespoons vegetable oil
1/2 pound Chinese noodles
2 green onions, minced
1 teaspoon grated fresh
  ginger
1/2 pound pork butt, minced

Combine the ingredients for the seasoning mixture. Put the bean sprouts in a colander, rinse and drain well. Peel the cucumber, remove the seeds and cut into 2-inch shreds. Beat the eggs and scramble them in 1 tablespoon oil.

Boil water in a large pot and cook the noodles for about 10 minutes, or until they become soft enough to be easily cut with a fingernail. Rinse with hot water and drain well. Keep warm.

Place a wok over high heat. When it becomes very hot, add oil. Add green onion and ginger, and then the pork. Stir-fry for about 2 minutes, or until the pork is cooked. Add the seasoning mixture and stir-fry for about 1 minute.

Divide the noodles into individual bowls. Top with some scrambled egg, bean sprouts and cucumber and spoon the sauce over them.
Serves 3.

STUFFED EGGPLANT WITH
HOT SWEET AND SOUR SAUCE

1 2- to 2-1/4-pound eggplant
Salt
Seasoning mixture
    4 teaspoons thin soy sauce
    1/2 teaspoon salt
    4 teaspoons rice wine
    2-1/2 tablespoons Chinese
      red vinegar
    2 tablespoons sugar
    1 cup Chinese stock (p. 30)
      or chicken stock
    3/4 teaspoon Szech'uan hot
      bean paste
    2-1/2 tablespons water
      mixed with 1-1/2 table-
      spoons cornstarch
    3 tablespoons peanuts
    1/4 teaspoon vegetable oil
Stuffing
    1/2 pound large shrimp
    1/4 pound cooked pork
      butt

    1/4 pound ham
    1/4 cup minced bamboo
      shoots
    1 tablespoon thin soy sauce
    1/2 teaspoon salt
    1 tablespoon rice wine
    1-1/2 tablespoons water
      mixed with 1 table-
      spoon cornstarch
    1/4 teaspoon sesame oil
Batter
    5 egg whites
    1 cup cornstarch
    2 tablespoons water
Vegetable oil for deep-frying
1 teaspoon grated fresh
    ginger
1 large garlic clove, minced
1-1/2 tablespoons green onion
    cut into 1/2-inch sections

Peel the eggplant and cut lengthwise into sticks about 3 by 1-1/2 by 1-1/2 inches (Figure 1). Sprinkle lightly with salt and let stand for 10 minutes. Wash off the salt and gently squeeze out excess liquid. Dry thoroughly with paper towels.

Combine the ingredients for the seasoning mixture.

Lightly pan-fry peanuts in 1/4 teaspoon oil until they become fragrant. Drain well and crush them coarsely.

Shell, devein and wash the shrimp. Cook in boiling water for only 1/2 minute. Quickly drain and rinse with cold water. Dry and mince.

Mince the pork and ham. Put the shrimp, pork, ham and all the remaining ingredients for the stuffing in a bowl and mix well.

With a sharp knife, cut, beginning at one end, the eggplant sticks to the depth of about 1 inch lengthwise down the center up to about 1/2 inch at the other end (Figure 2). Gently work the sides of the cut apart to form a

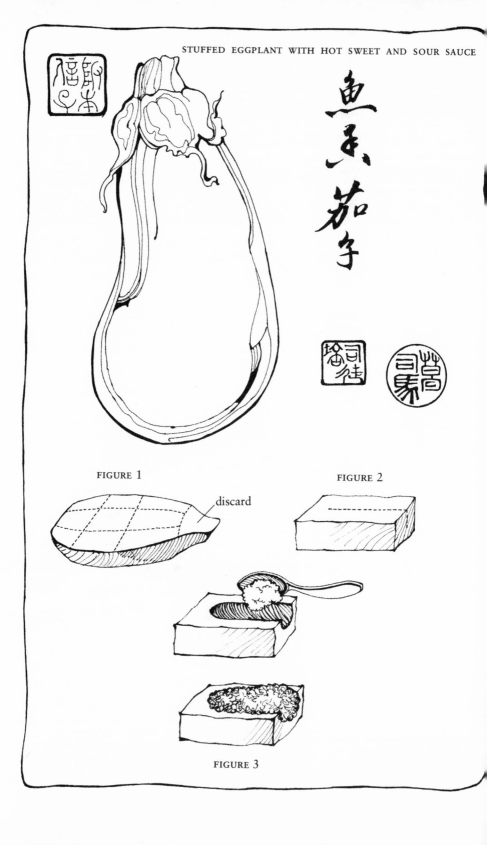

FIGURE 1

FIGURE 2

discard

FIGURE 3

pocket for the stuffing. Put 1 to 2 tablespoons of the stuffing into each pocket and press down gently to form a firm mound (Figure 3).

To make the batter, first beat the egg whites until they become foamy. Continue beating while adding cornstarch a little at a time. Add water and mix well.

Heat about 4 inches oil in a large, heavy pot or deep-fryer to 350°. Dip the stuffed eggplant sticks one at a time into the batter, keeping the filling side up and coating the sticks thoroughly. Carefully lower them, filling side up, into the hot oil in batches of three or four. Deep-fry until the edges turn golden. Remove with a slotted spoon and drain on paper towels.

Remove the food particles from the oil in the pot. Dip the eggplant sticks in the batter again and deep-fry a second time at 350° for about 2 minutes, or until they turn golden-brown. Drain on paper towels and transfer to a heated platter.

Place a wok over medium heat, and when it becomes hot, add 3 tablespoons of the oil used for deep-frying the eggplant. Add ginger and garlic and stir-fry for a few seconds. Add the seasoning mixture and stir until the sauce thickens. Pour the sauce over the stuffed eggplant and garnish with peanuts and green onion.

Serves 4–5.

EGGPLANT SZECH'UAN STYLE

1 1- to 1-1/2-pound eggplant
3 green onions, minced
1 large garlic clove, minced
1/2 teaspoon grated fresh
  ginger
Seasoning mixture I
  1/2 teaspoon Szech'uan hot
    bean paste
  2 tablespoons thin soy
    sauce
  2 tablespoons rice wine
Pinch of MSG

1 tablespoon sugar
1 cup Chinese stock (p. 30)
  or chicken stock
3 tablespoons vegetable oil
1/4 pound pork butt, minced
Seasoning mixture II
  1 tablespoon white vinegar
  1/4 teaspoon sesame oil
3 tablespoons water mixed
    with 2 tablespoons corn-
    starch

Trim the ends of the eggplant and cut it into eighths lengthwise. Cut each section into 1/4-inch slices and cut the slices into 2-inch lengths. Lightly sprinkle with salt and let stand for 20 minutes. Scrape off the salt and dry with paper towels.

Mix together the green onion, garlic and ginger. Combine the ingredients for seasoning mixture I, and do the same for seasoning mixture II.

Place a wok over medium heat. When it is very hot, add oil. Add the eggplant and stir for 2 to 3 minutes, or until lightly browned. Remove and set aside. Put the pork in the wok, add the garlic-ginger-onion mixture and stir-fry for 1 minute. Add the stock and the eggplant. Cover and simmer for 2 minutes. Add seasoning mixture II and the cornstarch mixture. Stir until the sauce has thickened and transfer to a heated platter. Serves 3–4.

DRY-FRIED VEGETABLES WITH SESAME SEEDS

This simple, quick dish can be served as an entrée by itself or it can accompany a meat dish.

4 cups fresh bean sprouts or
  3 cups canned
Seasoning mixture
  1 teaspoon grated fresh
    ginger
  2 tablespoons rice wine
  2 tablespoons thin soy
    sauce
  1/4 cup canned shreds of
    Szech'uan hot turnips or
    1/2 teaspoon Szech'uan
    hot bean paste
  1/2 teaspoon salt

2 tablespoons sesame seeds
4 tablespoons vegetable oil
2 cups canned bamboo
  shoots cut into 2-by-1/4-
  inch strips
1 large green pepper, cut into
  2-by-1/4-inch strips
1 medium onion, sliced
1/2 teaspoon sesame oil
1/2 teaspoon freshly ground
  pepper
1 tablespoon green onion cut
  into 1/2-inch sections

Wash and drain the bean sprouts in a colander. Combine the ingredients for the seasoning mixture. Lightly toast the sesame seeds in a dry pan.

Put oil in a wok over high heat. When it becomes hot, add the bean sprouts, bamboo shoots, green pepper and onion and stir-fry for about 2 minutes. Add the seasoning sauce and stir-fry for about 1 minute, then add sesame oil and stir a few times. Transfer to a heated platter, sprinkle with black pepper and garnish with green onion and sesame seeds. Serves 3–4.

CLOUDS AND MUSHROOMS

5 dried cloud ears
5 large dried black
  mushrooms
Vegetable oil for deep-frying
  plus 3 tablespoons
2 ounces (1/4 package) rice
  vermicelli
3/4 teaspoon salt
1 large garlic clove, peeled
  and crushed
2 cups fresh mushrooms
  sliced into thirds
1/2 cup canned golden
  mushrooms

1 cup shredded ham (cut in
  2-inch-by-1/8-by-1/8-inch
  pieces)
1/2 cup drained crabmeat
3/4 teaspoon Szech'uan bean
  paste
1/2 cup rich chicken stock or
  Chinese stock (p. 30)
1/2 cup slivered green onion
  (cut in half lengthwise and
  slice diagonally into
  1/2-inch sections)
1 teaspoon sesame oil

Soak cloud ears in warm water for 30 minutes. Rinse several times and drain. Cut into pieces to make about 4 tablespoons. Soak dried mushrooms in warm water for 15 minutes. Drain, squeeze dry, remove the stems and sliver the caps.

Heat 2 inches oil to about 350° in a wok. Test the temperature by dropping one strand of vermicelli in hot oil—if it puffs up instantly and turns white, the oil is ready.

Add the vermicelli, one handful at a time, to the hot oil. It should expand instantly into a white, puffy mass. With a wire scoop, quickly pick it up and turn it over to let the other side puff up also. Transfer to a heated serving platter. (Regulate the heat so the vermicelli does not brown. It should remain as white and puffy as possible.)

Carefully remove the oil from the wok. Add 3 tablespoons fresh oil and salt, and reheat the wok. When the oil is about to smoke, add garlic and stir-fry for about 1/2 minute. Add cloud ears and the three kinds of mushrooms (dried, canned and fresh). Stir-fry for a few minutes, or until all ingredients are well coated with oil and partially cooked.

Add ham, crabmeat and Szech'uan bean paste. Stir-fry for about 1/2 minute. Add stock and simmer until the liquid is reduced by half. Turn off the heat. Add green onion and sprinkle with sesame oil. Pour over the vermicelli and toss all ingredients together a few times.

Serves 3.

SZECH'UAN PICKLED VEGETABLES

These delicious, refreshing hot pickled vegetables are usually served first at dinner.

1 medium-sized celery cab- bage or regular cabbage	2 tablespoons salt
4 medium-sized turnips	1-1/2 teaspoons flower
1 bunch radishes	pepper
2 large slices fresh ginger	1/2 cup white wine
2 dried chili peppers	1/2 cup white vinegar
	8 to 10 cups water

Wash, trim and dry the vegetables. Discard the outer cabbage leaves; separate the inner leaves and slice them in half. Halve the turnips and cut off the radish tops.

Wash a 1- to 1-1/2-gallon ceramic crock with a cover. Pour boiling water up to the top, let stand for 10 minutes and pour it out.

Line the bottom of the crock with cabbage leaves, add a layer of turnips and then a layer of radishes on top. Fill only two-thirds of the crock. Add the remaining ingredients.

Bring 8 to 10 cups water to a boil and add just enough to the crock to cover the vegetables. Cover the crock and wipe it dry.

Use heavy masking tape to seal the crock. Put it in a cool place for 6 days, by which time the pickles will be ready to use.

Serve as a relish to accompany other dishes. Remove a portion of cabbage, turnip and radish, lightly rinse in cold water, squeeze dry, and slice thinly.

Keep the crock covered (it need not be retaped) and refrigerated during warm weather. The pickles should be eaten within a few days, since they will become too pungent if kept too long.

Index

About the Author

NOBUKO SAKAMOTO is of Japanese descent and spent her early years in Seattle, Washington, prior to World War II. The outbreak of war and the subsequent internment of Japanese-Americans brought an identity crisis which led to intensive study of the language, cultural history, philosophy and art of both Japan and China.

The practical application of these studies was the translation of several sets of cookbooks published by the government of the People's Republic of China. In an effort to preserve their authenticity, these recipes were faithfully translated and tested. Over a twenty-year period, her family as well as her friends in various parts of the United States have sampled the same dishes enjoyed in the People's Republic of China. The reopening of Sino-American relations in 1972 reinforced her feeling that this treasury of Chinese dishes should be introduced to the West.

The author lives in Mendon, New York, on a farm with her two children and psychologist husband, who shares her interests.